# SNIPER

*To my mother Ann, my father Augustine,*
*and to Specialist Francisco Martinez*

*—Gina*

*To Steven Langmack, Chris Willoughby,*
*and Shawn Benjamin*

*—Matt*

# SNIPER

## American Single-Shot Warriors
## in Iraq and Afghanistan

Gina Cavallaro

Matt Larsen

LYONS PRESS
Guilford, Connecticut
An imprint of Globe Pequot Press

Lyons Press is an imprint of Globe Pequot Press.

Text design: Sheryl Kober
Layout artist: Kevin Mak
Project editor: Kristen Mellitt

Library of Congress Cataloging-in-Publication Data is available on
file.

ISBN 978-1-59921-855-7

Printed in the United States of America

10 9 8 7 6 5 4

# CONTENTS

# FOREWORD

In 2003, in response to the quick rise in the enemy's use of improvised explosive devices in the war on terror and the emergence of
more deadly complex attacks, we stood up the Improvised Explosive Device Task Force and redirected the efforts of the Rapid
Equipping Force to support counter-IED, countermortar, and countersniper operations.

For this new organization, we recruited and hired experienced
former Special Forces noncommissioned officers and teamed them
up with active-duty soldiers to form the nucleus of the Improvised
Explosive Device Task Force.

Then Col. Joe Votel, former commander of the Seventy-fifth
Ranger Regiment, was chosen to lead that effort.

The task force's mission was simple: assess the needs of the
troops downrange in Iraq and Afghanistan and find out more about
the threats they faced, not only from improvised explosive devices
but indirect fires and snipers as well.

It was also tasked with looking beyond the horizon at emerg-
ing asymmetrical threats so we could bring the information to the
drawing board and develop—and quickly employ—countermeasures, tactics, techniques, and procedures.

The Improvised Explosive Device Task Force members started
by interviewing wounded soldiers at Walter Reed Army Medical
Center in Washington to get fresh ideas from the warriors recently
back from battle on what they thought was needed in terms of
equipment and training.

At the same time, we dispatched members of the task force to
Iraq and Afghanistan and embedded them with units on the ground
to collect the lessons learned directly from the troops in combat.

All of this information was assimilated and pushed through
the Army Center for Lessons Learned, then transmitted to the units
getting ready to deploy.

As the work of the Improvised Explosive Device Task Force evolved, so did both the complexity of the operational environment and our understanding of it. In response, we built an organization called the Asymmetric Warfare Group and made the members of the Improvised Explosive Device Task Force a part of it.

The Asymmetric Warfare Group, first commanded by Col. Robert Shaw and Command Sgt. Maj. Greg Birch, though focused on the improvised explosive device threat, was also charged with looking past the current problem set to anticipate the next asymmetrical challenge downrange so we could develop training as well as an effective way to advise brigades, battalions, and below on what to look for.

The task force was looking at the pointy end, but just as importantly, it was digging into the network left of "Bang!" to get ahead of it—the people who planted the bombs, made the bombs, and paid for the bombs.

Sometime in early 2004, we started seeing snipers arrive on the battlefield. There were reports of sniper activity from the commanders downrange, and the enemy snipers who weren't successful, the ones we caught, started to yield intelligence on what types of weapons they had and where they had gotten them.

We also wanted to know if that sniper was an untrained guy who just got lucky or a guy with a pretty nice rifle and a pretty nice scope, whether he was positioned professionally when he took a shot, who trained him, and where he was getting his money.

We learned that quite a few of the improvised explosive devices were coming from Hezbollah and a lot of the training of the snipers was coming from Iranian forces.

But to begin countersniper measures, you have to understand how a sniper team operates, how it sets up, and what tactics it uses.

The best people to talk to about that were our own professional snipers, and we had several former Special Forces snipers on our Improvised Explosive Device Task Force and in the Asymmetric Warfare Group.

Between their expertise and knowledge and the operational needs statements we were getting from the field, some of it from task force members themselves, we were able to get some technological assistance for countersniper operations and additions to their fundamental equipment allowances.

Almost immediately, the units started requesting rifles with more capability than the M16 and the M4. One brigade in the 101st Airborne Division (Air Assault) requested the return of the M14, which was the standard issue U.S. rifle until the mid-1960s, because of its longer range and accuracy with a scope.

So, we took the M14s out of depot, issued them to the unit, and then sent several former snipers to Fort Campbell, Kentucky, to train what the brigade commander called his "company marksmen" to provide over-watch on dangerous roadways and to conduct countersniper operations where possible.

To help these troops on the technical side, the Rapid Equipping Force went out and looked at acoustic and other types of sensor technology that would alert the soldier to the direction of a fired shot. The technology helped them calculate a quick azimuth and distance to where a sniper might be.

Snipers are a very tough problem in urban terrain because of all the different noises and sounds that occur in a city neighborhood, but we were able to allocate money to the Rapid Equipping Force for a device called the Boomerang that can identify the point of origin of gunfire and as these devices continued to develop, we had vehicular-mounted sensing devices and soldier-mounted sensors to help counter the snipers.

The biggest thing that we had going on between 2004 and 2006 was in-country training for soldiers right there in their area of operations by the task force and Asymmetric Warfare Group guys who were downrange with them. The same training was being done for the next-up soldiers back home. All the soldiers were shown how to use the best countermeasures available and how to avoid being vulnerable to snipers.

The former and active-duty snipers they deployed with downrange were the subject matter experts who trained small unit commanders on the employment of their own snipers and how to think like a sniper so they could help their troops stay out of the enemy's crosshairs.

Without going too far into everything we taught our officers and enlisted soldiers, we trained them in some simple counter-sniper tactics like what to be aware of in their surroundings, how to recognize where a sniper might be on the battlefield, and what they could do to counter the invisible threat.

To give our troops an even greater advantage, we looked at alternative sniper weapons, sniper scopes, and night vision systems, and we started training special or designated marksmen who could be sent ahead as a reconnaissance team to counter any threats before an operation. By getting there in advance of a larger element, they could pick out likely danger areas and scan for potential enemy snipers, much like Special Operations forces were already doing.

No area of Iraq or Afghanistan was the same, and every commander had a different experience in his terrain, so those recon missions and any new information learned were sent back to the Asymmetric Warfare Group and the Army Center for Lessons Learned.

The information and best practices were turned around very quickly and sent to units getting ready to go to those different areas.

But many of the tactics, techniques, procedures, and the material solutions we developed cannot be attributed solely to the efforts of the task force, the Rapid Equipping Force, or the Asymmetric Warfare Group.

These agile formations reacted to what soldiers on the ground were telling them. The challenges faced every day by our soldiers and young leaders grew into a wealth of knowledge that informed the development of our strategies as we looked at how to refocus the institutional Army toward the right technology and training to attack this unconventional enemy.

The programs to counter improvised explosive devices, mortars, and snipers were very successful and introduced new technology and techniques that gave our soldiers a leg up.

Soldiers in combat and those returning told the Army what they needed, what systems worked, what systems did not work, and what new tactics were needed in the training base and at mission-rehearsal exercises. The soldiers in harm's way would tell us "this is how they're doing it" and we listened and learned from them.

As agile as this current enemy is, it is no match for the innovativeness and the agility of the American soldier.

*—Gen. Richard A. Cody, U.S. Army Retired*
*Thirty-first Vice Chief of Staff*

# PREFACE: A MOTHER'S GIFT

The day I started writing this book, I didn't start with any typing.

Instead, I spent the better part of the daylight hours rummaging through my war stuff, an assortment of souvenirs, clothing, and travel items tucked away in plastic boxes, tattered envelopes, and dusty Ziploc bags crumpled into a fabric-like softness.

My fascination with the things one gathers on such journeys began in 2002 on my first of several trips to embed with and write about U.S. troops in the Middle East.

But on this day I was after only one small item.

In one of the larger boxes, the clothes I wore to Iraq so many times, though laundered and neatly folded, seemed tired, flaccid, and unfresh. My bright green shower shoes, a pair of flip-flops I bought in Kuwait City's Old Souq for about a dollar, stood out among all the earth-toned garments. I closed that box. What I was looking for wasn't in there.

Inside the second box, my eyes darted around from small bag to small pouch to smaller box before I reached in and started to open them. I felt as if I were getting warmer. My hands sifted through a jumble of flashlights with weakening beams, pens bundled together with crumbling rubber bands, black nylon straps, colorful bungee cords, and clotting bandages sealed in olive-drab foil packages. There were earplugs, knives, lighters, shoelaces, toothbrushes, anti-diarrhea tablets, lozenges, hair ties, and ballistic eyeglasses. I found unit patches from friendly soldiers and enameled achievement coins from their commanders.

There were stale Iraqi cigarettes, old Iraqi money, cardboard PX coins, and odds and ends like Arabic political posters, voting ballots, and a puffy little nylon armband some Iraqi official had worn at a polling place in Baqubah.

Even my favorite souvenir surfaced—a small, homemade slingshot I found in Al Kut in March 2003. It's a Y-shaped piece of a tree branch wrapped in black rubber, perhaps from a bicycle or one of those skinny donkey cart tires. A little square of worn brown leather to launch a projectile is strung into the sling piece.

I spotted the crude weapon sticking out of the dirt in a vast field littered with rusting antiaircraft artillery. I picked it up and put it in my pocket. I've always wondered about the little David who might have tried to take down his own Goliath, an American helicopter, in the early part of the war.

Looking back through my treasures was fun, but the morning quickly slipped into afternoon, and with my laptop beckoning, all this rummaging to put my hands on one item felt more like procrastination.

But I had to find it. I had to find it because it was going to connect me to the one sniper story I knew, the one in which an American soldier who was standing by my side in Ramadi on March 20, 2005, was mortally wounded by an enemy sniper's bullet.

The soldier's name was Spc. Francisco Martinez. His family called him Paquito. He had a mouthful of brilliant white teeth, a generous smile framed by deep dimples and a head of short, jet black hair. His skin was the rich color of cinnamon like so many Iraqis, and his gregariousness drew the attention of their children. His gloves, a black one on his left hand and a white one on his right, were cut to expose his fingertips, and he wore his confidence like an aura.

He quickly came to my side when his commander, Capt. Kevin Capozzoli, told him to keep an eye on me, the visitor. At the time, kidnappings of westerners in Iraq were rampant and usually ended grimly. Most commanders were happy to get media embeds, but none of them wanted a journalist to disappear on their watch.

So Paquito, who had turned twenty only three months earlier, stayed close by, and when he died, we had known each other for four days.

He became one of many soldiers felled by snipers during their deployments in this volatile area west of Baghdad, and Ramadi was notoriously wicked at that time. Dozens of Marines and soldiers had already been killed there, and more would die at the hands of snipers and roadside bomb emplacers before the violence was brought almost completely under control in 2007.

The death of each U.S. service member killed in Iraq or Afghanistan was announced in a Defense Department press release starting in October 2001 when operations began overseas. But nailing down the exact number of those killed by a sniper is difficult because, even though the cause of death was listed on the press release, the only clue that it could have been by a sniper was the phrase "caused by enemy small arms fire." In the case of deaths among Marines, the releases said even less, citing only that the Marine had died "while supporting combat operations."

The word *sniper* never appeared in any of them, I was told, because a U.S. body count chalked up to the work of snipers could have led to an unwanted strategic victory for the enemy.

Adding to the murkiness and the messy nature of combat deaths is the fact that many troops were killed in complex attacks that included a combination of other horrors, like daisy-chained bombs and rocket-propelled grenades mixed with gunfire from several directions.

Still, according to the casualty database maintained at the *Military Times* and culled from Defense Department press releases, the number of potential small-arms-fire deaths among soldiers only for both Operation Iraqi Freedom and Operation Enduring Freedom as of the first quarter of 2010 was 785 out of a total of 3,054 deaths listed as hostile among all service members.

I don't know what that enemy sniper was doing in the hours before he stalked Martinez's patrol, but Martinez was doing what most young Joes do before a mission—checking weapons and water, stocking ammo and dip, and planning new ways to toss stuffed animals to the Iraqi kids who gather around their vehicles.

The day he died, as they prepared to go on patrol, I watched Martinez and a friend test a catapult system for hurling the little toys with their Humvee's flexible antenna. It made me laugh, and it made his father laugh when I told him about it over the phone less than a week later.

Alone in my apartment, about an hour after arriving home following more than two months on a hard trip downrange, my hands turned cold and my body and jaw shivered as I relayed what details I knew of his son's last few days and what I had seen of his death.

Paco Martinez's son was a 13F, the Army job code for fire support specialist or forward observer, whose responsibility it was to call for and adjust artillery fire to support the units engaged in the close fight. He was assigned to Second Battalion, Seventeenth Field Artillery. But when I met him, he was temporarily attached to the scout platoon in Alpha Company, First Battalion, Ninth Infantry Regiment.

They were all part of Second Brigade Combat Team, Second Infantry Division, which deployed from Korea to the growling streets of Ramadi and stayed there for twelve months before they redeployed to their unit's new home at Fort Carson, Colorado.

The Second Brigade soldiers told me they hadn't seen much media in the seven months since their deployment to Iraq, though they didn't blame anyone for not wanting to venture into Al Anbar province. Some listened to why I had come with silent nods of approval, and others said they would never let a woman of theirs go to the war zone. I wasn't anyone's woman at the time, nor had I ever thought of myself that way, but I understood how they felt and told them I thought it was a privilege to be able to tell the stories of soldiers at war.

I was received warmly and made friends quickly, even getting an invitation to "Salsa Night" from an anonymous soldier who left the handwritten invite taped to the door of my hooch. I didn't make it to Salsa Night as I had already accepted an invitation to sample a wheel of cheese that someone's family had sent to a battery commander.

The social events at Camp Ramadi were not that different from some of the recreational activities I'd seen at other bases, but a palpable unease hummed beneath the surface, a kind of shell shock.

There was evidence all around that the camp was a regular target for mortars, rockets, artillery rounds, and rocket-propelled grenades. The indirect fire had killed several people, and there were stories of near misses, such as the case of the lucky soldier in the shower trailer who saw a rocket slice past his face while he was soaping up. The rocket, a dud, never exploded.

The other lurking evil was the enemy sniper, who killed soldiers assigned to observation posts along Camp Ramadi's perimeter, as well as those on patrol in sector. Over time, the snipers learned that if they shot a U.S. soldier in the chest it might just cause a bruise because the body armor was more effective than they thought. So they began shooting them in the face, head, or neck, and in the vulnerable soft areas between the front and back armor plates they wear on their bodies.

That's how Martinez was hit.

It was Palm Sunday around 3 p.m., and the mid-afternoon sun was bright, the sky clear, the air warm. We were walking through an area of Ramadi known as Five Kilo. Soldiers and Marines who have been there wince at the mention of it.

The reason the patrol took place at all was the acquisition of a piece of intelligence indicating that a cop assigned to the police station in that neighborhood was moonlighting as a sniper. Most likely he was moonlighting as a cop.

When Capozzoli and his men arrived at the station to question him, the Iraqis there were cooperative but, not surprisingly, the shady cop wasn't there.

It was the first lead they'd had in weeks and the unit was eager to bust a sniper, but it would have to wait for another day. The soldiers moved on after the short visit and took a ride through the community to check in on some of the neighbors who had become tentative friends.

Maintaining relationships with the Iraqis who governed the areas the soldiers patrolled was a painstaking part of the job for all commanders, and it was mostly done during the day with a heavy security element surrounding intelligence-gathering and civil-affairs teams.

There was an eerie quiet as our patrol of several up-armored Humvees rumbled slowly down a main street of Five Kilo like a flotilla trying to avoid leaving a wake. Paquito and I rode in separate vehicles and walked side by side at various points. As a field artillery soldier, he didn't get many opportunities to go on patrols with the infantrymen, but he took every chance he could get to go outside the wire when they needed more men.

As we walked, we talked, sometimes in Spanish, about his native Puerto Rico, where I had grown up until the age of thirteen.

When three little boys approached us and pointed to our green earplugs, he pulled his out and handed them to one of the boys, signaling that they were good to eat. But the boy didn't believe him and, being the sap that I am, I showed the boy how to put them in his ears.

A couple of blocks ahead, just before Paquito was shot, I saw the boy walking around with those bright green earplugs sticking out of the sides of his head.

We were standing at a T in the road. The infantrymen were in tactical security formation, guns at the ready, waiting for the commander to emerge from a house at the head of the street. I had just snapped a picture of the house when I heard a single gunshot and turned around to see young Paquito lying flat on his back on the ground in front of me.

I felt a wash of horror crawl across my flesh and screamed out his name from some new, alien place deep inside my dry throat, "Martinez!" Trembling and panicked, I watched his buddies run to him to remove his body armor and helmet as they carried him to the Humvee where I was already sitting behind the driver, having been commanded to get into the vehicle by a civil affairs NCO, the only other woman there.

A beaded trail of Paquito's dark blood atop the road's dusty surface marked their short trot to the truck, and then it pooled up and began spreading as they awkwardly maneuvered him into a position at the door to remove his blood-soaked shirt.

Two soldiers swung his limp legs toward the back of the seat and shut the door. As we peeled out of the area, my hands and arms became smeared with his blood as I helped remove his T-shirt so Pfc. Michael Johnson, who was somehow standing in the small space behind the front passenger seat and holding Paquito's body in an upright position, could apply pressure to the bandage.

As we rode back to the aid station, the barrel of an M16 resting on the platform between the two back seats was pointed directly at my right knee. Shit! The safety was on the underside of the rifle, and I didn't want to start messing with a weapon I was only slightly familiar with. Mostly, though, I didn't want to let go of Paquito's right hand, the one with the white glove, because it was all I could do for him.

His forehead was slick with sweat. The ride was bumpy and interminable. I spoke to him in Spanish, my face a few inches from his, my left hand stroking his hair.

"Squeeze my hand," I told him, "*aprietame la mano.*"

"Look at me," I said, "*mirame.*"

"Don't fall asleep on me," I pleaded, "*no te me duermas.*"

"Breathe, my love, *respira, mi amor.*"

Johnson and I grew more desperate as Paquito began to fade.

And then we arrived.

Johnson opened the door, and Paquito's body spilled out onto the gravel in front of the aid station. He was weak, his legs dead. Within seconds he was loaded onto a mesh litter and rushed inside by the combat medics, leaving behind another trail of dark blood.

Johnson and I hugged tightly in a quivering mass of adrenaline, and then he smoked the first cigarette of his life. As the minutes rolled slowly by, my thoughts raced. I could feel the quiet gaze of a small group of soldiers nearby. They probably rode security for us, but I don't know.

How completely out of place I felt. How many times had these men, half my age, been through this? I was a cherry.

I stood near a wall in a piece of shade and waited, suddenly aware that the skin on my arms was taut, painted with Paquito's now quite sticky blood. I slipped into a long-sleeve shirt.

Paquito, his friends later told me, had a thing about the number five, and on each bicep he had tattooed a stylized "5" he designed and planned to use as the logo for a computer graphics company when he got out of the Army. I hadn't noticed his tattoos on the ride from the shooting scene, but when they put his litter into the ambulance that took him to the medical evacuation helicopter, his bare torso and arms were exposed and that "5" showed up in the picture I snapped of him.

When I gave the picture to his parents, who are divorced, they each remarked on how buff their son had become, how much larger his biceps looked. It was hard to watch them examine the last picture taken of him alive.

My plan was to show the picture to Paquito at Walter Reed, because on that late afternoon, while Martinez's life was slipping away, the medical soldiers working to patch him up for the ride to Navy surgeons at Al Taqqadum air base thought he might survive. More than likely it was I who held out hope.

In an e-mail a few months later, Maj. Raj Butani, the battalion doc, described Martinez as "talking and joking" with him and others as they watched his vital signs plummet. Because of that and the fact that the bleeding wasn't visible, some people didn't even know he was in critical condition.

But the sniper's bullet, Butani said, had been catastrophic, ripping through Paquito's liver, a lung, and a kidney, causing massive internal hemorrhage. His chances of surviving, even if he had been near a trauma center in the United States, were slim, Butani told me.

Paquito was just brave and he fought it.

After watching the medevac helicopter take Paquito away, I walked back to the other side of the camp where my stuff was, passing a happy softball game on the way. The players called me over, and I tried to act as if I hadn't just witnessed something terrible.

When I got back to the shady courtyard of the 2-17 Field Artillery's headquarters, First Lt. Ed Kaspar helped me clean my arms with this Army-issue, personal use blood cleanup kit I'd never seen before. In the military, cleaning blood is something people are prepared for. Ed was the battalion personnel officer and was all too familiar with each death as it was his job to process all the paperwork.

Lt. Col. John Fant, commander of 2-17 Field Artillery, was a close friend of my sister and brother-in-law. It was because of that friendship that I had decided to fly to Ramadi at all. John is about six feet five inches tall, and when he walked into the room where I was sitting in silence with Ed and said simply, "Martinez died," he looked ten feet taller. Then he turned and walked out. I sobbed inconsolably while Ed stood behind his famous coffee bar, not knowing the proper response for a crying reporter.

I knew I had to suck it up and pull myself together, but when I rode back to Baghdad that night in a roaring, windy Marine Corps helicopter, sitting alone in the dark, I let myself weep openly for Martinez, understanding, if only marginally, how so many others had felt at the sadness and loss on a night just like this one, at the death of a friend.

The images of the day, the way Paquito's friends stared at me when I stopped by their table at dinner that night, played in my head like a video loop.

There was nothing to be said. He wasn't the first to die, and he wouldn't be the last.

I wrote a version of this story for the *Army Times* and have retold it many times. It helped me sort it out, but it also seemed important to let people know how the death of a soldier unfolds.

As we began the task of finding and interviewing our own military snipers for this book, it seemed important to revisit again because, in some way, I'd like to think that for every U.S. death caused by an enemy sniper, many more troops were saved by the actions of our own American snipers.

A sniper is what is referred to on today's battlefield as a "force multiplier," a term that denotes something that helps double, triple or quadruple the strength, efficiency, survivability, or lethality of a unit of troops without necessarily enlarging that unit's footprint.

A multiplier could be a piece of communications equipment such as the tactical headset radios that double as hearing protectors, allowing sounds—even whispers—to come into the ear canal but shutting down instantly at the sound of a loud noise like an explosion. It's a multiplier because it's a relatively small item that keeps a soldier in action who might otherwise have gone deaf. A force multiplier could be something bigger like a bomb-resistant vehicle that saves several lives at once, or personal gear like eye protection, body armor, flame resistant gloves, or something to be nurtured inside the soldier, like mental and physical health.

In the counterinsurgency wars fought in Iraq and Afghanistan, where protection of the native populace spells the difference between victory and defeat, a small military sniper team—typically a shooter using a rifle with long-range capability and a spotter looking through a powerful custom scope—causes less disruption with a single shot than a platoon of forty infantrymen reacting to gunfire in a crowded neighborhood.

Hundreds of two-man sniper teams have become force multipliers in this counterinsurgency by undertaking one of the most tedious and important missions of the war: lying in wait for hours or days to take out the men who bury in the roadways the bombs that have killed the majority of U.S troops, and the bomb makers who hire them.

Special operations snipers have come up with quick formulas for rapid target engagement without having to adjust their rifle scopes, making themselves indispensable as assaulters in close combat urban raids to arrest dangerous men and in doing so, showing their leaders that they can do more than sit still for the long shot.

This book gathers and updates the stories of today's snipers. The recollections and experiences of just a small sampling of the snipers who have done the job in Iraq and Afghanistan tell the story of everyone's war, a war in which every soldier, sailor, airman, and Marine has had to learn a new way of doing business, employing the finer points of countering an insurgency while stabilizing a foreign population.

Snipers are not eager to jump into the spotlight. Many did not want their full names used in the stories they told us. Many did not want to be interviewed at all. We have respected their wishes and relished the details of their wartime exploits, learning that the art of sniping is more than the "Ping!" of a bullet on a steel target at a firing range.

It is discipline, intelligence, and ruthlessness, a skill as perishable as a learned foreign language. Only with constant practice and everyday use can a sniper stay sharp, and only the most daring men see the mission for what it is: a job.

It never occurred to me, as some suggested back in 2005, that the sniper's bullet that killed Paquito might have been meant for me. That sniper, I knew, aimed to kill an American soldier, a political target easily identified by a uniform, and Paquito was shot by a guy sitting in the back seat of an innocuous looking sedan.

By its very nature sniping is a thinking profession. In a counterinsurgency, the enemy hides easily among the population. Ghillie suits or uniforms other than the officially issued attire were worn by Americans in an attempt to conceal themselves. But, working in a densely populated foreign land, where the enemy had the advantage of posing as a goatherd, a fruit vendor, or a pregnant woman, American snipers had to work hard not only to conceal themselves but also to identify legitimate targets or potentially suffer the consequences in a court of law if they failed.

Their shooting abilities aside, American snipers provide invaluable battlefield intelligence by sitting in uncomfortable hide sites for days, sometimes not taking a shot at all.

The enemy got to kill plenty of Americans, but if American snipers had an advantage, it was their ability to stay one step ahead with continuous training and their focused tenacity, not unlike Paquito's brave fight for his life that Palm Sunday in Ramadi.

Paquito's parents, his father in Texas and his mother, Carmen Hernandez, in Puerto Rico, were gracious with me, as was his grandmother, Mimi Martinez, who had tragically lost a son to gunfire in her early life in front of their home in Santurce. I was worried that they would hate me for publishing the detailed account of Paquito's death. What they were was proud of their son.

In Puerto Rico about three weeks after Paquito's death, Carmen asked that I speak to family and friends at a memorial Mass in San Juan, and when it was over, we gorged on a Puerto Rican meal with her young son and new husband.

It was at that meal that she presented me with a little box, inside of which was the Gold Star she had been given by a general officer in Texas at Paquito's burial. I tried to refuse it. She insisted. I traveled home with it in my pocket.

I found that box four years later, not in one of the plastic boxes with my war stuff, but in my bedroom, in a drawer amid other sentimental treasures. And that's what I needed to see, that mother's gift, on the day I started writing this book.

*—Gina Cavallaro*

# CHAPTER ONE

# GOING TO WAR:
# LESSONS FROM THE HINDU KUSH

In the frigid mountains of Afghanistan six months after the September 11, 2001, attacks on the United States, Sgt. Stan Crowder took a knee on the jagged top of an icy escarpment. Fierce gunfire had greeted his platoon upon landing, and he was already in the crude sights of an enemy fighter as the helicopter that took them there flew away in a riot of wind.

The soldiers had rehearsed. They were told to expect little resistance and were supposed to arrive before dawn, but it was later than planned and the light of a bright winter sun robbed them of the advantage of darkness.

Even before their Chinooks descended to the landing zone, the helicopters' door gunners were ripping through the belts of their M60 machine guns in full engagement with fighters on the ground who were shooting rockets and firing machine guns at the birds. An alternate LZ only two hundred meters away was hot, too, leaving the soldiers little choice but to brave the fire on either one and take covering positions as soon as their boots hit the ground.

Crowder and his partner, Staff Sgt. Jason Carracino, were snipers assigned to their battalion's scout platoon and had just hitched a ride with a rifle platoon with a plan to branch off after insertion. It was March 2002 at the start of a major U.S.-led offensive, and everyone had a role to play.

"A 240B machine gun crew got off just before us. Jason and I went off the back ramp with a ten-foot hover. We looked at each other and we're both like, 'Man! Here we go!,'" Crowder said through an uproarious laugh, retelling the story years later from the comfort of a kitchen table back home and with obvious nostalgia for the hubris of the early days of the war.

He and Carracino each carried more than one hundred pounds of gear for what they calculated would be about a two-day stay-over, watching the rifle platoon and the back side of a mountain pass where Taliban fighters might escape as the offensive put the squeeze on their camp.

Just moments after they got to the ground, while the rifle platoon infantrymen lay prone, regaining their bearings and trying not to get killed, Crowder, from his kneeling position, took two shots at a man wielding an AK-47 assault rifle. The wounded man was jolted but kept firing. Crowder adjusted his aim, took a calculated breath, and finished him off on the third shot, his first kill on the battlefield.

For the next thirty-six hours, the sniper team would stay to help the platoon, getting an introduction to the fighting prowess of the armed men who lived and fought in Afghanistan's majestic and forbidding Hindu Kush.

On 9/11 Crowder didn't even know where the World Trade Center was.

As a kid in the rural town of Pound, deep in southwestern Virginia's mountainous coal country, Crowder led an uncomplicated life, revolving around family, guns, and hunting, not so terribly different from the lives of so many Afghans—except for such American amenities as running water, electricity, and schooling.

The denizens of New York, where terrorists had rained mayhem on the city, likely knew as much about the people of Pound and Afghanistan as the people of Pound and Afghanistan knew about them. But on that day, Crowder and every American in uniform learned exactly where the World Trade Center was and what the attack meant. For him, the excitement of going to war began to sink in.

He was an infantryman assigned to Second Battalion, 187th Infantry Regiment of the Rakkasan Brigade in the cradle of one of the Army's most storied divisions, the 101st Airborne Division, known as the Screaming Eagles, at Fort Campbell, Kentucky. The mobilization for the Screaming Eagles, the Marine Corps, and the rest of the military began almost immediately.

Armed National Guard soldiers were posted at American airports, and F-16 fighter jets flew sorties over the nation's capital. Aircraft carriers were steaming toward the Middle East, and people everywhere waved newly purchased American flags. Support for a war in Afghanistan was strong and widespread.

As it dawned on Crowder that his unit would be one of the first to step foot on the ground overseas, he weighed the implications of going to war, and though his stepfather, a veteran of the 1989 U.S. invasion of Panama who had raised him from the age of four, suggested he think hard about his options, he also answered the question in Crowder's mind about doing his part.

"It's your conflict, man," his stepfather told him. "I had mine, everybody has theirs. It's your turn."

"I kinda felt that way in the back of my mind, but once I heard him say it, I was like, 'Well, all right.' It kind of fell into place. I guess that was just the way it was supposed to be."

## TRAINED AT SOTIC

During his three years in the Army, Crowder had been a fortunate soldier, too, one of only a very few from the conventional side of the Army who had the opportunity to be trained by Special Forces soldiers in the art of sniping.

The course is for Green Berets and other soldiers in the Special Operations community, but back when Crowder was at Fort Campbell, instructors at the Special Operations Target Interdiction Course, or SOTIC, rounded out its class by offering slots to units located near the school. In July 2001, Crowder, who had already been selected to be in his battalion's scout platoon where the snipers get assigned, received one of those slots. Though he expected eventually to be trained at the Army Sniper School at Fort Benning, Georgia, it wasn't a given.

"Back then," Crowder said, "they would send forty guys [to Benning], and five would graduate. It was a heartbreaker and costly. SOTIC was attractive because it was right there at Fort Campbell."

Crowder eventually did go to the school at Benning in 2004, and he later became an instructor there after a tour to Iraq in 2006. But what he learned at SOTIC, he said, was what he took to war with him.

When his unit got orders to deploy to Afghanistan the week before Thanksgiving in 2001, the excitement level among his brothers in arms exploded. "I think I felt like I won the Heisman Trophy! I called everybody. I told them, 'I can't tell you what's going on, all I can say is keep watching the news,'" he said. "My dad said he knew what it meant. 'I got it,' he told me. 'Just don't do nothin' dumb.'"

## ARRIVING IN KANDAHAR AND THE CRASH

The Kandahar air base in southern Afghanistan on January 18, 2002, the day Crowder arrived, was an austere smattering of living quarters—tents, mostly—and brutally cold.

Incredibly, to him, within a few short days of arriving at the compound, he and his partner at the time, Spc. Justin Solano, were given the job to work sniper missions for three months with a Special Forces team at a safe house in Khost.

Along with the enviable mission came the obligatory swagger of superiority. "Some guys who had been on the team longer, one guy in particular, were peeved," Crowder said. Not one to let a good taunting go by, he smugly informed the peeved soldier that "tenure doesn't matter if you can shoot better."

But the elation of getting his first combat mission so quickly would be violently interrupted by one of those things that happen when you're just trying to get somewhere: The CH-47 Chinook helicopter taking the soldiers to Khost to their mission with the Army's elite Green Berets crashed on landing, leaving Crowder practically blind in his right eye and teetering on the edge of getting sent home for good.

The disaster happened in the moments before they were to make a running landing, a method of inserting troops quickly in which the helicopter pilot points the aircraft's nose skyward and angles the rear of the bird downward with the back ramp open during a skilled hover so everybody can run off onto the landing strip.

Crowder was sitting on the port side of the helicopter with his knees smashed against the fuel blivet, a giant rubber-like bubble cell filled with sloshing jet fuel that allows the pilots to refuel in flight and make fewer stops. The bird was packed with troops lining the benches on the sides of the aircraft, and everyone's stuff was piled loosely into the middle. About forty-five minutes out, he said, the door crew did a test-fire, and then the troops got their one-minute warning.

"It was like we'd done a million times in training at Fort Campbell. We were told they would do a running landing, which we had even practiced at Kandahar a few days before," Crowder said.

But the air crews stumbled on the landing order. Crowder speculated that it was because they had failed to perform a pre-flight commo check and were unable to talk on the radios with one another when the first helicopter landed in the wrong place. "When the chalk went to land, bird one landed in bird two's spot, and bird two landed in bird three's spot. I was on bird three," he said, suggesting that the crew flying the third Chinook suddenly had to execute an unplanned landing. "Even if they had an alternate plan, they had no way of communicating it to each other. Bird three, which had almost no visibility because of the sand and dust being blown around by the other two birds, landed on its nose while everyone was standing up."

Crowder was knocked out cold on the impact, and everybody's untethered gear tumbled down on top of him. The helicopter rolled as the rotors turned and the fuel blivet burst open.

When he came to, he remembered seeing the dim illumination from a half-moon, and he instinctively checked for his weapons. He still had his M4 slung across his chest, and his pistol was snug in its holster, giving him some assurance that he could fight back if the enemy was swarming the helicopter. He remembered lowering his NODs just before impact and saw stars in the sky through the back of the angled helo.

But no enemy fighters were approaching the bird just yet. A rescue was under way and people were injured, but no one was killed. Crowder was soaked with fuel, and the right side of his face was numb.

A young soldier on his first ride in a Chinook who was sitting to Crowder's left during the flight had the sense to escape through the door gunner's hatch, but Crowder couldn't move. He was pinned under the weight of the jumbled equipment, his helmet was gone, he was disoriented, and as he started to push through the weight on top of him, he saw lights darting around in front of his left eye, the only one that was working.

The eerie flickers were the sparks of the screaming engines of the dying helicopter. Crowder stumbled toward the rear ramp and dragged an unconscious soldier with him. A Green Beret who treated Crowder's eye also stuck him with a morphine syrette to get him to board a Chinook for Uzbekistan.

Had the unidentified Special Forces soldier not taken care of him as expertly as he did, doctors told Crowder in Uzbekistan, he would have lost his right eye. Crowder never learned the name of the guy, but the solider remembered him when they met several months later. Crowder ate some humble pie when the guy reminded him how belligerent he'd been during the rescue.

In Uzbekistan, under the shock of bright hospital lights, his eye was irrigated and bandaged before Crowder was flown to Landstuhl Regional Medical Center in Germany.

The excitement of war had ended as quickly as it began, and his anxiety mounted as he realized he was getting farther and farther away from the unit and the mission with the Special Forces soldiers in Khost that he had been so pumped up to do.

In Landstuhl he was recuperating with about six other soldiers who had been wounded in the helicopter crash—some more critically than others—and while he was trying to figure out a way to avoid going back to Kentucky, he found a surprising ally in the Air Force surgeon who had tended to his eye wound.

The doc, a former pararescue jumper, not only said that he understood Crowder's desire to get back to the fight in Afghanistan, but he also tipped him off to a bar run by an Irish lady at the end of the road from the hospital and suggested he might check it out. "He knew that infantry guys wanted to stay with their units, could kind of speak the language and understood a lot of what I was talking about, the stuff at the crash site," Crowder said.

The doc and his young patient met daily for medical follow-up and sometimes ate together. Then one day Crowder got just the kind of tip he was looking for—with a little wink of the eye, the doc told him that two C-17s were headed to Afghanistan, leaving the door open for Crowder to make his own decision.

Crowder didn't even have a uniform to speak of. His had been cut off his body during the medical evacuation, and he had no gear, either. Plus, he was expected in the rear at Fort Campbell where the other wounded soldiers were going. Wearing his hospital-issued DCUs, Crowder showed up at one of the birds and asked the Third Special Forces Group soldiers loading up if he could hitch a ride with them to Kandahar. "They gave me some clothes, but I showed up in Kandahar with no weapon or gear," he said.

His gear—a drag bag, a chest rig, and a pair of mini-binos— had in fact been split up between the two guys, peeved soldier included, who took the mission in Khost after the crash.


**OPERATION ANACONDA**
What Crowder didn't know was that the mission to work in Khost with the Special Forces soldiers would pale in comparison to what he and some two thousand other U.S. and coalition air and ground troops would take part in just a few weeks later.

Operation Anaconda was launched on March 1, 2002, in the Shah-i-Kot valley in southeastern Afghanistan south of Gardez, and it remains one of the largest U.S.-led offensives to occur in Iraq or Afghanistan since operations began in each country.

The massive operation took place over a seventy-square-mile area in extremely frigid temperatures that dropped to as low as fifteen degrees Fahrenheit at night in fighting positions that had to be established in mountains with altitudes higher than ten thousand feet. Well-trained Taliban fighters numbered in the hundreds, a considerably higher number than U.S. planners were aware of, and their tenacity as warriors was compounded by their intimate knowledge and mastery of the terrain.

"We were told to expect like a pocket of one hundred or so hard-core fighters, and everybody else would be local to the area. It was the other way around," Crowder said. "There were big-wig hard-core fighters, hundreds of them. They were pretty smart about it; they were just waiting for us to come in."

The mission, he said, "went south really fast."

"We practiced going in at night, but when we got to the Shah-i-Kot valley for the mission, the sun had been out for about fifteen minutes; so we're flying in over villages where there were people outside waving at us."

He was nervous, too, he said, because the helicopter flight was only his second one in country since the night of the crash. And the guy sitting next to him was the same one who sat next to him during the crash.

But Crowder had a lot more on his mind than helicopter crashes when he took that knee on the icy mountaintop, moving solely on instinct to put down the enemy fighter most willing to close with them on the landing zone.

While members of the platoon engaged sporadic gunfire, firing the first live shots of their lives at human targets, Carracino was behind Crowder pulling his M24 rifle out of his bag and checking it over. Once organized and ready to move, the soldiers would march to a blocking position about five hundred meters up, even though it wasn't the plan envisioned by the sniper team.

The wind was wickedly erratic, and there were close shots all around. Crowder was looking south toward an area where he'd heard rounds coming out every few seconds. What he saw was more than rocks and boulders staring back at him.

"I saw an Afghani wearing like a pizza hat, those hats that are rolled up. At first I second-guessed myself because it was all boulders and rocks, I didn't know if it was the guy or not. Jason asked if I had something," Crowder recalled. "I could see more than half the guy and I thought, 'That's kinda dumb,' but then I thought, 'He's probably not alone.'"

With his M4 trained on the pizza-hatted shooter, Crowder took him on. "I put my red dot on him, acquired him as a target. I shot him twice, saw my rounds impact, and it kind of knocked him for a loop for a little bit, but he didn't actually ever go down. He kind of recomposed himself and continued moving forward. So I took another few seconds, went through my breathing pattern one more time and slowed down and shot again."

This time he had adjusted his hold from the enemy's high chest area and beamed his lethal red dot on the man's nose, squeezing the trigger that scored the kill.

"I saw it hit right on the base where the neck and the chest meet, and he went down. It was probably like 125 or 150 meters," Crowder said, speculating that the Afghani hadn't seen him because, as he points out himself, "I'm not a very tall man" and can easily disappear behind a boulder. But he may have seen Carracino, who is almost six feet tall, and the other platoon members behind him.

"It was kind of like really quick and to the point. On that last shot when I saw him go down, I double-checked to make sure he wasn't moving. I was still thinking, 'Why is that guy by himself?' So I was worried about a larger pocket of guys in the rocks," Crowder said.

As he would learn in the coming days, in Afghanistan there are lone fighters in remote positions as well as pockets of guys. The platoon was ready to move out, and there was no chance to answer Carracino's hunch that Crowder had been up to something while Carracino was busy checking maps and other gear.

"About four or five hours later, Jason's like, 'Hey, man, did you shoot a guy down there?' and I'm like 'yeah' and he's like, 'I saw you shooting and I thought I saw a guy down there and then I saw him fall,'" Crowder recounted. "I guess he only saw the third shot."

The rifle platoon started its move toward higher ground, and the Crowder-Carracino sniper team hung back about one hundred meters from the rest of the platoon to make sure no one closed with them. Their plan to branch off was fragged by the intensity of the contact they were all taking, and they decided to stick with the rifle platoon so they could mutually support one another. The men trekked and walked and climbed through low ground and dead space, through wadis and rocks and boulders on the way up from the LZ to the blocking position known as "Diane."

The snipers' planned mission was to stop fighters fleeing the Marzak Camp toward the Pakistan border and to block reinforcements or anyone who was able to get past the rifle platoon from heading to the mountain pass behind the blocking position and higher ground directly above.

The platoon would be the snipers' contingency security plan, the nearest friendly unit. They had expected to operate alone and stay for twenty-four to forty-eight hours. But they stayed with the rifle platoon for thirty-six hours, and ten days would go by before the battalion picked them up.

As the hours wore on, the platoon moved through Taliban country, the soldiers learning that they would have to adapt quickly and anticipate the enemy's movements if they were to survive the assaults of well-entrenched fighters, whose positions had been stationary for decades and who were as much a part of the landscape as the centuries-old rock formations.

"Their positions are so well built, they're not moving around as much or doing a lot of dumb things to let themselves get caught," Crowder said.

He was amused by their crazy fashion choices, a hodgepodge of ancient biblical-style man jammies layered with modern-day cold-weather gear and high-performance designer labels like North Face.

And he was impressed with the unexpected accuracy of their fires. The enemy had only to wait for the Americans to make a move before striking from their well-hidden big machine guns, mortars, and howitzers recessed into the sides of rock face. Wherever the Americans moved, Crowder said, they'd invariably get potshotted by the invisible Taliban.

"We used to find stacks of rocks. One day I pace-counted it. It was roughly one hundred meters from one stack to the next, all the same height and stacked in similar fashion. They weren't painted or anything. They probably had some guy with binos or optics watching, and that's how they figured out their range," he said.

Crowder said he and the platoon found a few positions where bedrock was chiseled in the shape of a base plate or mortar system so that when the enemy took a shot, they would be on target with the first round. "They don't have to set it at all, because it's in rock, not dirt," Crowder said.


## THIRSTY PLATOON SERGEANT

The lessons of exposing themselves to the enemy were made startlingly clear early on, when a senior noncommissioned officer (NCO), apparently thirsty and not just a little bit complacent, took off his body armor and helmet during the platoon's first full day in the mountain.

Perhaps thinking he was at his favorite fishing hole back home, he casually approached a stream of water and within seconds he was nearly shredded by a DShK machine gunner.

"I can't for the life of me figure out why he did that. At this point we had been mortared and grazed quite a few times from the time we reached the blocking position, and the next morning when we came down and reached this position is where this happened," Crowder said. "We would hear rounds for a few minutes, and then you get hit by a few more just on top of each other."

Members of the platoon were on the inside wall of a wadi running east to west. The banks were about seven feet high, and the wadi was about one hundred meters wide. It was a giant riverbed, but only about a three-foot trickle of water ran down the center because the winter snow hadn't melted.

Crowder saw the platoon sergeant approach the water and admonished him against taking such a chance. He knew there was a hilltop just to the west of their position known as "the well" that was home to a couple DShKs (pronounced dish-kah), large-caliber Russian machine guns that could cut a man in half. As the sergeant bent over to scoop up some water in a cupped hand, Crowder said, he could hear the sound of those guns in the distance.

"Boom! Boom! Boom! Boom! Boom! and then I counted one thousand, two thousand, three thousand, and these bullets are coming in all around his feet, hitting the sides of the wadi, he's dancing around and comes running back," Crowder said. "They're all laughing, and then the sergeant told everyone to get their stuff on," but no one else had taken their equipment off because they were about to head out to the LZ to move to a new position.

As if to punctuate the display of terrain dominance, the enemy let fly a new barrage of heavy metal onto the platoon. While the troops were moving out, a mortar sailed in and hit the exact position where they had been sitting. That was followed by the "pop" of a rocket-propelled grenade (RPG), and a young corporal who was standing about fifty feet from Crowder got lucky.

"It hit right at his feet and blew his chest plate out the top of his plate carrier, shredded his magazines. He took shrapnel in his armpit, on the back of his legs and his butt and knocked him a few feet in the air," Crowder said. "The RPG was a dud."


## A RIDGELINE SHOOTER AND READING THE WIND

Another early lesson for Crowder and Carracino was the difficulty of reading Afghanistan's wind at high altitude, a formidable foe that snaps and blows erratically. Short of channeling Aeolus, the mythological ruler of winds, they drew on their training and instincts to get the shot they wanted.

"The wind is insane, between fifteen and twenty miles per hour, and it's crazy, too," Crowder said, describing the conditions on their first day at the blocking position. "The wind will come off the ridge, come down, come back up, hit you in the face. A lot of guys make the mistake of misreading that kind of wind because it's hitting them in the face and they're thinking it's coming straight at them. It's your basic stuff you learn."

Instead of branching off immediately from the platoon as planned, Crowder and Carracino agreed to stay a little longer to help the rifle platoon retain the advantage a two-man sniper team represents—and the benefit of their enhanced optics and weapons.

Crowder and Carracino also knew that minimizing their movement and exposure to enemy eyes after the heavy contact they had seen at the LZ would be smarter than launching on plan—and they could rest and eat. They would help the platoon pull some long-range observation of the vast landscape before them.

They didn't wait long for action. It started day one. A team of 240B machine gunners in a position above the platoon's outpost was receiving shots, inaccurate shots, every few minutes from a gunman somewhere on an adjacent ridgeline. The blowing wind likely kept him from succeeding, but it didn't stop him from trying.

"The way the terrain was, on the other side of the ridge was Khost and then on the other side was the Pakistan border. That ridge looked to be about six hundred meters away, and the top of the ridge looked about nine hundred meters," Crowder recalled.

But he knew distances could be deceiving. Because it all looked so enormous and prominent, he said, "everything looked closer than it really is, plus there was snow and the light reflected on it makes it seem even closer."

The machine gunners fired back across the ridge, but it did nothing to deter the shooter on the other side. At the request of the rifle platoon sergeant, Crowder and Carracino hiked up to a position near the machine gunners. Carracino set up his rifle, and Crowder positioned his scope. They told the gunners to stay back.

The snipers lay side by side, Crowder reading the wind, Carracino relaxing and getting his body position nestled comfortably into the earth. They scanned the ridge for about an hour, looking for all the possible nooks, ledges, cracks, and gaps where a shooter might hide and giving themselves a chance to get used to the wind.

"There was snow, places where snow had melted, there were spruce pines. I wondered where I'd be, what I'd be doing if the shoe were on the other foot. I wouldn't be on the ridgeline because behind it is a big blue sky to show everybody where you're at. I'd probably be a couple hundred meters below the ridgeline shooting down at us at a slight angle," Crowder remembered.

After scanning for at least another hour, the team saw no movement and figured the gunman had retreated. Then "Zip!" a shot whizzed past about five feet overhead. The enemy had refocused his sights on the American sniper team and came damn close, but Crowder was faster. With that one shot, he saw a quick muzzle flash, even though the sun was out, and adjusted his scope to as close to the spot as he could.

"I still wasn't exactly on top of the guy, I figured a little fifty-meter area, yeah, he's right here," Crowder said, explaining how he adjusted the magnification on his scope to bring in everything from the area. After a short while he "saw the outline of the guy from the high chest to the top of the head and what looked like a stick out off to an angle. I kept Jason vectored in between a few boulders."

He focused a little more, "just like we do in training," and identified the stick as a rifle. He saw rocks piled up like sandbags. Carracino quietly said to Crowder that the shooter was at twelve o'clock, directly in front of them about fifty meters up, and said he had seen the flash and was on him.

In one of the only Hollywood moments of the mid-afternoon duel, the sun came across the ridgeline and exposed the shooter. Carracino waited for Crowder's last call to shoot. And now it was between Crowder and the wind, which was constant but with wildly varying speeds. He knew it would be hard to nail it, and they didn't want to miss.

"I asked the 240 guys to give me a three-round burst so I could see the behavior of the tracer. That wind took it for a ride. I told Jason to shoot when the wind was at its lowest so when I say 'go,' we need to go," Crowder said.

He figured out the range and had the scope dialed right around 750 at elevation. He said he didn't dial in for wind, but used scope hold off, a method of compensating for wind.

There are two methods of adjusting for windage and elevation. The first method is to estimate the range and the effect the wind will have on a bullet, then adjust the reticle by dialing the scope. This allows the shooter to aim directly at the target.

The second way to do it is to use the reticle's features, such as mil dots, to adjust the point of aim. This method is known as scope hold off.

"You use your crosshair to judge and the wind was coming from left to right at a constant so we're going to shoot to the left side, a heavy left."

So they waited a bit, saw the guy move slightly every once in a while as if to adjust his own position.

"Jason has no optics, and once the wind slowed down a bit, I told him to shoot immediately. . . . Then I was going to say 'fire' but he shot, which was good, he was right on the guy. It was three inches off his left shoulder. I said, 'Standby.' He did exactly what he was supposed to, he shot, breathed out, re-cycled the bolt, never lifted his head off the gun. The elevation looked good, but the wind needed to be played with so I gave him a correction to move slightly left," Crowder said.

The next shot hit the gunman just above the belly button, and he went down. Crowder considered the shot and wondered if the fight was over. "I thought in the back of my head, 'OK, that's a hydraulic wound, unless we hit him in the spine; he's going to die but it could be a half hour or two hours.' I looked at Jason and said, 'All right man, 750 feet in insane winds with all the climbing and all the stuff all morning, that's good stuff, man.'"

The wide-eyed machine gunners on the hill asked, "You got him?" And I said, 'Yeah, we got him.'"

But the snipers kept an eye on the place they'd sent the shot, and a couple of minutes later, they saw the wounded shooter hunched over the rocks that had been shielding him. He was weak and trying to hold himself up with one arm. Jason shot again and hit the rocks right in front of him. Then he shot one more time.

"That last shot hit the guy right on the right side of his high chest, and he fell straight back and never got back up. We hit him on the second round, and we hit him on the fourth round. "The actual shot was 745 or 746 meters. It wasn't quite 750. In Afghanistan with a 7.62, that's a long shot, especially in that region, it's really long," Crowder said.

# CHAPTER TWO
# A TAUNTING ENEMY

The region of Arab Jabour ten kilometers southeast of the Green Zone in Baghdad is a lush agrarian area where magnificent houses that once belonged to the ruling Sunni elite grace the banks of the Tigris River.

People like Iraqi dictator Saddam Hussein's sons, Uday and Qusay, had their own riverfront houses there, and after the U.S. occupation of Iraq in 2003, Arab Jabour continued to be a Sunni-dominant region that grew sympathetic to Al Qaeda when it consolidated its power there.

"Arab Jabour was where they built their bombs to use on Iraqis and U.S. troops in the Baghdad area," said Lt. Col. Ken Adgie, commander of First Battalion, Thirtieth Infantry, who was tasked in mid-2007 during the surge of U.S. troops in Iraq with taking control of the area. As he described it in a post-deployment executive summary, the unit faced a "determined enemy, an unfriendly population, and difficult terrain."

By the time his battalion got there, the area had for some time been a sanctuary for a variety of insurgent groups that were influenced or forced through violence and intimidation into coming under the umbrella of larger Al Qaeda interests. Al Qaeda paid well and pulled local delinquent kids into its fold, the ones who had been bad actors and petty criminals.

Before the surge and the arrival of Adgie's battalion, the area was only sporadically patrolled by coalition troops, giving the different tiers of the Al Qaeda organization plenty of time to shape and mold ingress and egress routes to their own advantage, creating a custom-made safe haven for enemy operations on a network of trails, footpaths, and canals.

Every main and secondary highway and supply route was dotted with dormant underground bombs, buried there by men with shovels and picks years before Adgie's battalion arrived, then rigged and detonated as soldiers passed through by shadowy figures who knew where they were buried. The area was a support zone for bomb making and a place to stage attacks into Baghdad.

"I lost 153 soldiers on that battlefield, and I've got to live with that the rest of my life," said Lt. Gen. Rick Lynch, who commanded twenty-seven thousand U.S. troops in the beltline of cities, villages, and hamlets across the region south of Baghdad from March 2007 to June 2008. Of those soldiers killed, he said, 75 percent were lost in the first six months and 80 percent were victims of the hundreds of improvised explosive devices buried in previous years.

"They were kicking our butt. There was this constant stress on the battlefield that you were going to run into an IED," he said. But the IEDs were only part of the problem for Lynch, Adgie, and every soldier in the region. The explosion in the roadway was just a mechanism to launch an ambush, a way to get the patrol to stop so the enemy could keep attacking. That's when the troops were vulnerable to snipers.

"Many died in complex attacks with small arms fire, and a lot of that was from a distance, so there were snipers smart enough to know you can't just have an IED and walk away. They refined their skills over time," Lynch said.

Fifteen of the soldiers killed in Lynch's area of operations were in Adgie's battalion in Arab Jabour, where the IEDs destroyed vehicles on the roadways while other types of bombs and mines killed soldiers on foot patrols off the beaten paths. Going on patrol was a crapshoot each time, but one hostile act stands out for its ruthless cunning.

On the morning of August 11, 2007, the two hundred men working and living out of Patrol Base Murray, which was set up in the vacated three-story weekend home of the Hussein brothers, received a visit from the Army's top officer, Chief of Staff George W. Casey Jr., and his coterie of advisors, aides, and security people.

It was a bit of a boost for the troops who might not have imagined that anyone of that importance would spend an hour at their dusty, dangerous slice of the combat zone.

But the good feeling came to an alarming halt when, less than fifteen minutes after Casey's visit was over and his helicopters went wheels up, a Bradley vehicle careered through the gates of the humble patrol base carrying a mortally wounded soldier.

Spc. William Edwards had a wound high on his back squarely between the shoulders. He was less than one kilometer from the patrol base when he popped his Bradley's driver hatch open three-quarters of the way to peer outside, and got shot.

"It was a great sniper shot," Adgie said of the clean hit, which Edwards's platoon immediately surmised had come from a three-story house about two hundred meters away. As the medics and docs in the aid station worked to save Edwards's life, the rest of his buddies from Bravo Company Second Platoon went into reaction mode and headed straight for the house to find the sniper.

If ever there were a good example of an "IED alley" in Iraq, it would have to be the two kilometers of roadway between Patrol Base Murray south to an area of Arab Jabour that was teeming with Al Qaeda operatives. That road was the only hardball road in the area, so any traffic headed north carrying anything heavier than people had to pass through the Americans' checkpoints. It was a narrow road described by Adgie as being "about the width of a Bradley and a half," on a raised levy just west of the Tigris River banks with fifteen- and twenty-foot drops in some places.

The location of the road and the lack of offshoot arteries wide enough for a vehicle left the insurgents no choice but to travel through American blocking positions or sneak past on foot through the hand-carved canals and concrete irrigation ditches to the west of the road.

The presumed sniper house was on the ribbon of land between the road and the river about one kilometer south of Patrol Base Murray, and Second Platoon had surrounded it within fifteen minutes of Edwards's shooting. Four soldiers—Sgt. Scott Kirkpatrick, Spc. Justin Penrod, Sgt. Andrew Lancaster, and Staff Sgt. William

Scates—went into the house to clear it. They entered through the back door.

"There was a trip wire deep in the house at the end of the hallway going into the living room. A pressure-sensitive wire, something under the carpet," Adgie said.

Unbeknownst to the soldiers, the house was booby-trapped with as many as four 155 mm artillery rounds enhanced with homemade explosives. When the first soldier stepped on the trigger, it tripped a circuit and detonated the charge, blowing up everyone in a fiery explosion. Two of the soldiers were instantly killed, the other two died later, a heavy toll that raised to five the number of soldiers the battalion lost that day, all within thirty minutes.

"The explosion was huge," Adgie said. "Structurally the house stood, but it caught fire, then burned for six hours. We had to wait for it to go out and the Navy EOD guys to go in and make sure it was safe before we could get one of the bodies out."

Early that evening, with the scope of the tragedy barely having sunk in yet, the company commander and platoon leader went to the house with an interpreter and climbed an inside stairway to the third floor to see if they could find a clue about the sniper.

On the wall, in Arabic, was a hateful taunt from the sniper himself, a message that read, roughly, "This is where the sniper got your guys." The sniper was long gone and had left nothing behind but the note.

Infuriated by the deadly "gotcha" that had been found, the unit's human intelligence collection team went to work immediately, plying every source in every corner of its battle space to find out who the sniper was.

One of the team's best resources was a small group of Iraqis the battalion called its "Bird Dogs," three men who lived with the unit at Patrol Base Murray and ran a cell phone operation to reach out to a network of sympathetic friends in Arab Jabour. Together, Adgie's report said, "they provided more actionable [human intelligence] information than the task force was able to react to."

Until they were brought in, the men working for Al Qaeda were impossible to single out with certainty because they hid in plain sight among the population. But the three Bird Dogs, who were former insurgents themselves, knew them all, and it didn't take long to pinpoint the taunting sniper.

He was already famous in the Al Qaeda–friendly area for his highly successful and prominent ambush, and a short forty-eight hours later, the U.S. soldiers, with the help of the Bird Dogs, had a name and a description. He was Mohamed Uthman, a five-foot, two-inch tall foot soldier for Al Qaeda who had a reputation for being a murderous criminal. And, no surprise, he was already known as a "high-value target" on a list the Americans had of their most wanted.

"Word on the street was, this is the guy who did it, and he kept on working after that. He was a cold-blooded killer, and he killed more Iraqis than he did Americans," Adgie said.

The mean little sniper eluded capture for months, until one night when he made the decision to go out and kill people with the wrong insurgent mortar team.

It was December 11, four months to the day since he had snuffed out the lives of the five soldiers, and Adgie cleared an Air Force F-16 hot to drop a bomb on the mortar team, unaware that Uthman was one of the teammates. The military found out after a site exploitation team identified one of the dead as the diminutive sniper.

"When Adgie lost those soldiers in that house-borne IED, I flew in and we were on our knees praying and crying like babies," Lynch said. "We learned, but we learned the hard way. If something looked like it might be rigged with explosives, we just blew it up. I wasn't going to allow my kids to go in there again because we'd already lost four."

The house bomb took its toll but strengthened the resolve of the infantrymen to work harder than ever to crush the enemy, and the partnership with the Iraqis in the area, tired of being occupied by Al Qaeda, continued to grow stronger.

The leaders of the terrorist organization had taken over in ways that altered the very fabric of people's lives. Al Qaeda was dictating what people could do, what they could eat, who got to go to school, and it would regularly cut off people's access to water and power. Cell phone use was banned, and they killed people to intimidate others.

A turning point for the cooperation of the populace came in May 2007 when, after services at a crowded mosque, a band of Al Qaeda guys pulled out members of a family, four brothers and eight cousins, lined them up, and murdered them right there to the horror and disbelief of everyone watching. Those killed were the family of one of the Bird Dogs.

The seminal event galvanized the people, and they started to go to U.S. troops with information on wanted men once they saw that the troops had set up shop there and were planning to stay.

The Bird Dogs were instrumental in finding the house bomb sniper and contributed to the capture of many more, but some continued to bedevil the troops, said Lynch. He recalled the death of a soldier in an M1A1 Abrams tank, who, like Edwards in the Bradley, opened his hatch while the tank was on the move and was shot by a sniper from a range estimated at about one thousand meters.

"He's a thinking, adaptive enemy," Lynch said. "They watched our movements, and based on their training, they could pace their engagement on the rate of movement of the vehicle."

Lynch, who was commander of the Third Infantry Division and became commander of the larger Multi-National Division-Center during the fifteen-month deployment, pointed out that the division's brigade and battalion commanders under his command had all been to Iraq at least once before and had come to know the value of having well-trained and equipped sniper teams.

In Arab Jabour, the sniper teams were consistently used to over-watch IED hot spots and other things like long-range cameras placed on elevated platforms. The cameras provided over-watch as well, but the snipers came into play and could shoot from concealed locations if anyone messed with the cameras. More over-watch came from multiple unmanned aerial vehicles and from the aerostat balloon that could keep eyes on a broad area.

"There's clearly a continuing role for our snipers. They found their niche on the battlefield," Lynch said.

# CHAPTER THREE
# "THE NASTIEST FIGHT"

By the time of the big firefight, Sgt. Adam Peeples had already killed plenty of men—bomb planters, getaway drivers, militiamen, and others who openly tried to kill first.

But until that chilly winter night in western Iraq, when so many lethal projectiles were flying through the air that "it looked like the Fourth of July," he said, he hadn't killed an enemy sniper.

It happened on the third night of a major offensive against a slithering nest of Al Qaeda fighters who, for some time, had been lording over the densely populated Ma'Laab district of eastern Ramadi and operating almost undisturbed. They were ruthlessly killing Americans and Iraqis, helping to uphold Ramadi's reputation as one of the most dangerous places for U.S. troops in Iraq.

The city of about a half million people is on the main route between Syria and Baghdad, and from the start of U.S. operations in Iraq in March 2003, it was rife with violence as Al Qaeda fought to establish and maintain its stronghold there.

But this operation would be the beginning of the end for Al Qaeda in Ramadi. It was about to get rudely routed from its cozy urban hideaway by hundreds of dismounted U.S. and Iraqi soldiers backed by the firepower of M1 Abrams tanks, Bradley fighting vehicles, and AH-64 Apache attack helicopters.

As the February 2007 operation was launched, Peeples and seven other men took over a three-story house in the neighboring Askan district at the western edge of the Ma'Laab district, where a giant Texas barrier or T-wall was going to be erected to seal off travel routes between the two adjoining districts.

Two nights earlier, the squad had lost a soldier, Spc. Louis G. Kim, to what Peeples called "a lucky shot" by a machine gunner in a window. So instead of infiltrating the area and entering the selected house on this night through the front door, the team rode in a tracked Brad and climbed through a jagged hole busted open by the vehicle and its 25 mm gun in the side of the house.

What started for the team as a nighttime over-watch mission to catch stragglers slipping through the house-to-house search and to stop Al Qaeda reinforcements from migrating into the fight from Askan ended up as a textbook urban battle—a rooftop-to-rooftop firefight across a ramshackle concrete cityscape that raged almost nonstop over the six hours it took for dawn to arrive.

On the rooftop of the house they had taken over, with the home's occupants cowering in fear one floor below as the team's medic kept an eye on them, the soldiers hunkered low behind a four-foot wall that lined the edge of the roof, dodging hot green tracers that split the cool night air over their heads.

In the first couple of hours, between bursts of enemy fire, the American soldiers fired back with their own bursts—taking cover, then popping up, aiming, and firing before ducking back down again.

The team had what it thought was plenty of firepower. Peeples and his partner, Spc. Craig Stout, had their sniper gear, and the squad members with them had a 240B machine gun, M203 40 mm grenade launchers, an M249 squad automatic weapon, hand grenades, and AT4s. But the gunfire was unrelenting and chaotic, and eventually they had to be resupplied.

The men took positions all around the rooftop and took turns firing and reloading.

"You could hear bullets whizzing by; they were hitting the wall we were hiding behind," said Stout, who was on his first deployment and had been trained as a sniper by his battalion. "It was massive amounts of shooting, but you kind of have the attitude that you're invincible and they're not going to hit you. We would just lay down. I would even stop and smoke a cigarette in the middle of all of it, and I could see the bullets flying over my head."

In fact, no one was hit, and a second over-watch team to the east of their location saw no action at all.

Even with the advantage of night vision goggles and PEQ-2 infrared lasers on their rifles, the men said, they couldn't easily make out the enemy human shapes in the night, only their telltale muzzle flashes, which were coming from rooftops and windows all around. The soldiers tried to shoot the enemy combatants as they saw them run past, like players at a shooting gallery on a summer boardwalk.

"You could see people running across windows and rooftops and jumping roof to roof and over walls. They were running right in front of us in this alley. We had to throw grenades down there because they were coming closer and they were trying to flank us," Stout said.

Stout was using his PEQ to guide the 240B machine gunner onto targets, but everyone had resorted to just aiming at the muzzle flashes.

"I had a universal night sight on there in front of my scope and it was, 'Find the muzzle flash, put two rounds on it, and shift to the next one.' You couldn't see the people, you know," Peeples said.

As the fighting became more and more fierce, the Americans could hear the gunfire getting closer as the enemy gunmen who weren't wounded or dead boldly hopscotched toward them over the walled, flat rooftops and through ground-level courtyards, avoiding the roadways they knew would bring certain death. The two Bradleys parked with their 25 mm guns aimed down the streets that were the enemy's natural migration routes might have had something to do with that.

"There was a courtyard wall that they would have had to scale to get to us, and we had that covered. They never had a hope of getting into our position because there was a north-south running road that divided us from them, and that gave us some standoff," Peeples said.

Precision shooting and grenades kept the most determined insurgents from getting too close. "The guys who came close got killed. Everybody on that roof killed several guys," he said.

Peeples is more than six feet tall, a blond country boy from Griffin, Georgia, who got a BB gun when he was five, started duck hunting when he was seven, and killed his first deer when he was nine. He set out to join the Marine Corps one day in 2002, but an Army recruiter won him over when he caught him first in the hallway. Sniping wasn't a job that Peeples was aware of at the time, but he knew he wanted to be an infantryman.

"I knew going to Iraq was a possibility, and it was something I wanted to do. It was sort of a 'prove yourself' kind of thing, you know?"

On his first deployment to Iraq in February 2004, he was in Samarra with a line company in First Battalion, Twenty-sixth Infantry, Second Brigade Combat Team, First Infantry Division out of Schweinfurt, Germany, the same unit he would deploy to Ramadi with in 2006.

"I did every job you could do in an infantry platoon," Peeples said, remembering his life as a grunt and how impressed he had been with the snipers he got to observe when he helped provide security at a Special Forces team house. It was a whole new world to see soldiers working in a small team with the freedom to ply a craft of precision.

While he was with them, he saw a couple of big fights. "They were right there beside us and it was really impressive watching them work," he said. "They're professional and it's all about finding a target, taking the target out, and moving on to the next one. Those two guys up in a bunker did more damage than the whole platoon."

Before that gig in Samarra, he said, he hadn't even thought about sniping, and now he laughs when asked whether he thought he would die that night three years later in Ramadi as the wild rooftop ride unfolded. Pushing the thought aside with a dismissive "no," he recalled a couple of close calls during the Ramadi battle when some of the enemy fighters came within twenty-five meters of their position and tried to close with them.

The bad guys were so close at one point, the American soldiers could hear them shouting and screaming. The Americans shouted and screamed back. "They were yelling 'Allah akbar,' and we're yelling, 'Fuck you!' and other things you can imagine," Peeples said, "and we could hear them pulling out their wounded, you could hear them screaming. It's a unique sound."

The voices and sounds became an audio map that helped the soldiers gauge their enemy's distance and distinguish their communications by the pitch of those sounds.

"We could tell what they were doing by listening to their voices; some sounded like commands. I don't think the majority of them knew where we were at. They could see our muzzle flashes, but anyone who exposed themselves pretty much got shot," he said.

Describing the engagement as "the nastiest fight I've ever seen," Peeples thinks he might have played an early role in kicking off that fight when he and his team took their position in the Askan district, on the other side of where the blocking wall was to go up.

Peeples believed that many of the Al Qaeda fighters used that district to stage their attacks and the U.S. soldiers could engage them on that side before they infiltrated the Ma'Laab district. His hunch was confirmed almost immediately.

It was late at night, and the main operation had already begun on the ground in the Ma'Laab district. After busting into the house and climbing to the rooftop through an inside stairway, the men began quietly surveying their surroundings. Peeples peered into an alleyway and what he saw through his infrared laser pointer was a fraction of what awaited. What happened next unleashed the heavy metal they would fight for the next six hours.

"I look down and there's two guys right below me not even ten yards away, directly below me and they're both on a knee and they're just whispering," Peeples said. "I had my infrared laser PEQ-2 on my rifle, came over the top, put half a mag into them, and that was it. As soon as I did that, the whole horizon lit up. We just took an unbelievable amount of fire."

On the rooftop with Peeples and Stout was Staff Sgt. Coy Tinsley, the squad leader for the rest of the security team and a soldier Peeples had befriended on their first deployment together to Samarra.

"On my first tour, I think it was just a bunch of uneducated guys who would shoot an RPG just to make some money without thinking about the repercussions," said Tinsley explaining the quality of the enemy fighter he encountered in Iraq.

At the start of U.S. operations in Iraq in March 2003, one of the earliest decisions of the Coalition Provisional Authority—to disband the Iraqi army—left tens of thousands of former soldiers suddenly unemployed and with no way to provide for their families. A rapidly growing and influential Al Qaeda in Iraq quickly capitalized on the misery and resentment of these soldiers by offering them a quick way to make a buck by attacking U.S. forces.

But by the time Peeples and Tinsley were in Ramadi two years later, Iraq had become the place to go to fight Americans and the dumb insurgents had already been killed. Killing Americans was a wholesale business, and the war was in full bloom.

"These guys were seasoned fighters, the way they moved. They had more of a fighting discipline," Tinsley said.

During the rooftop firefight, the heaviest contact they were taking, he said, was coming from the south and southwest of their position. Feeling besieged and potentially outmanned, the team decided to call in air support after identifying several houses where there was a lot of activity.

"There were periods of calm, and it would start up again. After we dropped the big bomb, it pretty much calmed down," Tinsley said, referring to a five-hundred-pound bomb they called in on a house about one hundred meters away.

Over the hours, with some new lulls in the fighting, they were resupplied by the Bradley crew that had dropped them off at the beginning of the operation, one of the advantages of being mechanized infantrymen, Peeples said. "They brought in a bunch of pre-loaded mags ready to go. They brought us a crate of grenades, a bunch of 240 ammo, three AT4s, and the fight just kept on going. You have your lulls of five or ten minutes, and then it would just kick off again."

During one of these lulls, Peeples took the time to scan a building about seventy-five meters away that he believed was the source of a spate of gunshots that were more accurate than most.

"It had started easing off a little bit. We had called in three [guided missile launch rockets] and a five-hundred-pound bomb, and we'd shot three AT4s, so the buildings were pretty devastated. But there were still guys creeping around up there, and we were taking potshots over our heads," Peeples said.

Listening closely to the shots, Peeples figured that there was at least one shooter who was probably using something like an SVD Dragunov sniper rifle. "A couple of shots hit the wall, and I said, 'This is a sniper . . . or he thinks he is anyway,'" he said.

During the fighting Peeples took the universal night sight off the front of his rifle because, at more than a pound in weight, it started to get heavy and he wasn't really using it to find targets that were giving themselves away with muzzle flashes. But he put the sight back on to scan the building he suspected of being a hideout.

Peeples used a customized weapon he built with $2,500 of his own money and parts he mail-ordered from the United States. Using the Army-issued lower receiver of his M16, the part that houses the trigger mechanism and has the serial number on it, he added a twenty-inch match grade Olympic Arms barrel and the Olympic Arms free floated hand guard; a JP Rifles adjustable gas block; a Vortex flash suppressor; an Olympic Arms match grade upper receiver; an ACE skeleton stock; and a cyclic rate reducing buffer spring assembly; and finished it with the Packmire pistol grip that he likes.

"It was an extremely accurate weapon, every bit as accurate as the M24 was. But I went to that length because when you get a chance to get a shot, you don't want your equipment to fail you, you want it to be better than you are. If I had a good shot on a dude's head and I were to miss because the rifle's not good enough to make the shot, then why take the shot?" he said.

With the sweat cooling on the skin of his bare forearms, Peeples propped his weapon up on the wall using his PEQ-2 and with his right eye on the scope went slowly from window to window, using his floodlight setting to look into the rooms through open windows and doors. The PEQ-2 is an infrared laser illuminator with two settings. A broad floodlight for illuminating an area and a narrow stream designed as an aiming device. The infrared light can only be seen with the aid of night observation devices.

It had been a couple of hours since the heavy fighting ended, and the other men, in a relatively relaxed mode for the moment, turned part of their attention to what Peeples was doing. "It was kind of an exciting thing that he did, so we were all looking at him," Stout said.

The night was clear, and the air smelled like gunpowder. Peeples didn't have his finger on the trigger because he didn't expect to see anybody. As he passed over one of the open windows, however, a brief but telling glint caught his trained eye—and he went back to it. This time he switched his PEQ-2 to the narrow setting.

"It went into the back wall, which was white, and the splatter from the laser just lit him up in silhouette. I could see the guy. He had a table set up and a chair, and he had something that he had his rifle sitting on like a pillow or a blanket or sack of sand or something," Peeples said. "I could clearly see a rifle and a guy sitting down. I could tell his weapon had a scope on it."

When Peeples finished his second deployment, he said, his NCO evaluation report listed him as having killed forty-three enemy combatants during his time as a sniper. But nothing compared to the thrill of snaring another sniper, an experience few can boast of.

"It's kind of cool when you can see someone and you know they can't see you. He was close. I could see him back there trying to figure out where to shoot at and where to see us. I can imagine from the shots he's taking at us he couldn't see. It was not accurate fire."

The distance between them was shorter than a football field, and Peeples didn't hesitate.

"From the time I saw him to the time I shot him was six or seven seconds," he said. "It was a head shot, just dropped him. He just fell right on top of his rifle and knocked the table over." Peeples conceded that, even though the enemy sniper's shots weren't accurate enough to kill him or any of his men because he lacked the technological advantages of night vision and laser aiming devices, "he had an idea of what he was doing" and would have been a serious threat had he lived until daylight.

That night was Peeples's chance to take out one of an unknown number of snipers operating in Al Anbar province.

A spate of other bizarre incidents took place within three days of the operation, Peeples recalled, like the time he spotted about eight men, all wearing purple-and-white Adidas warm-up suits, openly preparing to emplace 155 mm artillery shells into a roadway in broad daylight.

Incredulous, he watched as they breached the concertina wire set up on each side of the road, and he tried to call for air fire so he wouldn't have to give his position away. But when he radioed for help, he was told the helicopters were busy so he took matters into his own hands.

Peeples had a whole squad with him at the hide site, and he instructed the 240B machine gunners to set up on the guy carrying the shells so that when he initiated the attack with a single shot at the guy who was the clear ringleader, the others could open up quickly.

"With eight guys in front of you," he said, "you don't want to kill one, you want to kill all of them. I shot the first guy right in the chest, he was about one hundred yards away, and dropped him."

Immediately, one of the 240B machine gunners, whose barrel was poking through a small loophole, pushed through the crappy masonry in the wall and opened up on the group through a bigger hole, as did the 203s.

"The guy that was carrying one of the 155s dropped it, and he was trying to come back out and grab it for some reason so I shot him and dropped him on the spot," Peeples said.

Four were killed, the rest got away, but the action turned into a forty-five-minute firefight with other insurgents hidden in adjacent buildings who popped onto the scene like Clapper lightbulbs, seemingly activated by the sound of gunfire. It wasn't long before backup arrived, though, as Peeples had called a quick reaction force before he took his first shot and it rolled out the gate toward them about three minutes after the shooting began.

"This dude came out of a roof access door, I shot him. Then right below him a guy popped out of a window and one of the Bradleys blew the guy out of the window, and what was left of him was hanging by a leg from a telephone wire," Peeples said.

As bullets pinged all around, one of them zipped through the metal casing of a window he was shooting out of. The brass casing from the round caught Peeples in the face and leg and hit his friend and partner Sgt. Matt Thompson in the hand, leg, and face.

"It felt a lot worse than it was. We were like, 'damn,' and we stepped back from the window. We were both fine, but there was a lot of blood," Peeples said.

As soon as the firing started to die down, he said, the Brads came up, dropped ramp on the concertina wire, and the squad piled in on top of four guys who were already in the troop compartment, which seats five.

On the way in, Thompson got hung up on the wire as the ramp was going up. As it was lowered again to give him a chance to get unhooked, Peeples started to reach out for him when "this dude pops out about 150 yards away and is getting ready to line us both up and the Brad decimated him right there. We got out of there."

In another incident a day later, Thompson and Peeples were in a hide site before a planned operation. The building was adjacent to another site known as OP Hotel, where another team was holed up. But OP Hotel didn't have the bird's-eye view that Peeples and Thompson had down a north-south route, and while they scanned down that road from their site, they saw something that made their jaws drop.

"Holy shit, there were like thirty-plus armed guys on this road, and they were moving tactically in a file, and there were a squad or two crossing the road," Peeples said. It was the first time he'd ever seen a military formation in Iraq.

"One guy pulled security and one guy ran across pulling security, and this threw me off," he said. "There was actually like a big gathering of them, like twenty of them standing around smoking with RPGs on their backs and just chilling, because they knew nobody from OP Hotel could see them. They didn't know we were there," he said.

The men weren't uniformed, but to be on the safe side, Peeples called back to the tactical operations center to ask if there were "friendlies" to the south of their position they might be unaware of, like Iraqi armed forces.

The answer came back "negative," and Peeples also learned that no attack helicopters were available. So he and his team lit up the group, just pummeled it with all they had.

"We unleashed and, I mean, it was just, I mean it was ugly. The guys that we didn't kill on our street, squirted onto the east-west streets and the Bradleys got them. I talked to the guy in the battalion TOC who was doing the [unmanned aerial vehicle] feed, and he said he was flying over and said he just saw bodies all over the roads," Peeples said. "None of them got a shot off, there was probably less than one magazine from an AK that got shot. There were like twenty-five or thirty KIAs."

In their first mission as snipers in Ramadi in December 2006, Peeples and Stout moved into a hide site late one night where they could get eyes on an intersection that was about one hundred meters away. The intersection seemed to blow up under every U.S. vehicle that crossed it, and because it was a main travel route, the snipers were given a chance to put some rounds into anyone messing around with it.

The next afternoon, Peeples said, "I was using a tactical periscope to observe around the mounds." It was cold and windy outside, and when you're sitting in an abandoned building just waiting for something to happen, you get cold. Peeples and the nine men he brought with him were in their sleeping bags trying to shield themselves from the wind. They took turns watching the objective.

"Right at the intersection there was a dude, about a fourteen-year-old kid, with a screwdriver and he was just hacking away at the road. So I zoomed in on my periscope, and he had a blasting cap in one hand. It wasn't asphalt, it was like a hard-packed dirt. He actually had an IED already in there, and he was just trying to get the blasting cap into it so he could run the wire," Peeples said.

Stout fired, hit the teenager in the right neck and chest area, and watched him drop and roll right off the side into a ditch. As if on cue, two other teens they hadn't seen popped out, ran, and jumped into a car.

"They were speeding off, and we're shooting up the car on the way out," Peeples said.

It was critical that the team's first command-sanctioned mission go well, and it had. Peeples and his team did their job and successfully eliminated at least one IED emplacer.

His first experience with an enemy sniper, though, happened before any of his other fights in Ramadi and would end up being one that claimed the life of a U.S. soldier. Peeples was afraid of how his outlook on the soldier's death might sound, but he said it anyway. "I don't mean this in a bad way, but that guy right there saved a lot of our guys' lives," Peeples said of Staff Sgt. Christopher Swanson, who died on July 22, 2006, with only a few days to go before redeployment after a year in country.

It happened during a daytime patrol in the Tameem area of Ramadi on what the Army calls a right-seat/left-seat ride in the days before an area of operation is handed over to the next unit. In this case, Swanson's platoon in Bravo Company, Second Battalion, Sixth Infantry, First Brigade, First Armored Division was leading the way on a combat patrol in which no contact with the enemy had been made as they moved through the area.

As Peeples remembers it, "We're getting ready to go and a squad had moved up to a roof to cover our movement. A guy had knocked out a loophole in the wall up there so he could look through and not expose his head. Swanson looked through it and got shot right through that loophole. That was their last mission, and they took a KIA on that mission from a sniper."

The death, he said, was a tragic jolt to everyone and an eye-opener for him and the soldiers around him, many of whom had deployed together to Samarra where they hadn't encountered a sniper threat.

Like the sniper Peeples would later kill, the one who killed Swanson acted like a trained professional. "The guy who shot the kid on the patrol knew what he was doing. He tracked our movement through sector and knew exactly where to set up on us so he could take a shot. He knew we'd take one of three buildings and set up his shot. He knew about the loophole," Peeples said.

He professed to having learned little about enemy snipers while he was in Iraq, only that he'd heard they would be recruited off the street and given air rifles as a start. But, as with other U.S. snipers, Peeples had also heard that Chechen-trained enemy snipers were in Iraq, and while he was on duty as a sniper, he thinks he may have had another encounter with Swanson's killer.

"He shot an IR beacon off the windowsill from about 150 meters away. He thought it was one of our Kpots I guess. He operated pretty much solely. He killed several Iraqi army guys, and a second lieutenant was shot on a run between two buildings; he was shot through the meat of the shoulder," Peeples said.

He wanted to find the guy, he said, but "I knew that there wasn't really any way that I could go out and try to find him. He's targeting guys he knows are there. He's looking for coalition forces. The reason he's there is because he's looking for coalition forces."

Besides, he said, Ramadi at that time was a target-rich environment populated by insurgents who made themselves more readily visible, sometimes in large numbers, by planting improvised explosive devices in plain view, day and night.

"A sniper's job is to kill the enemy. Bottom line is, that's what you're there to do. Shooting one bullet and killing one guy is great, but when you got eight guys in front of you, you need to come up with some other kind of plan. That's what we did, we did ambushes. Nothing fancy like taking these long one-shots or anything like that. If there was a fight, the commander wanted us up front, and that's where I wanted to be, too," Peeples said.

# CHAPTER FOUR

# OTHER PEOPLE'S HOUSES

In the Army, when the first sergeant asks for volunteers, it could be for something really great, like escorting cheerleaders, or something really crappy, like moving furniture. In the war zone, cheerleaders are few and far between, but Staff Sgt. Rodney Medley took a risk and raised his hand when such a call went out for volunteers in March 2003.

It was shortly after the U.S. invasion of Iraq, tens of thousands of troops were pouring into Baghdad, and Medley, an infantryman with the Tenth Mountain Division, found himself doing what a lot of people were doing: setting up security perimeters and establishing safe places in which to sleep and work.

The adrenaline of the push toward battle had been exhilarating, but the job of making camp was inevitable. On the day he volunteered, he wasn't on combat patrol. He wasn't kicking in doors. He wasn't blowing things up. He was filling burlap bags with sand and laying endless yards of concertina wire. It sucked. Whatever the first sergeant needed, he figured, would be an improvement over doing the kind of work it literally takes an army to do.

His unit—Second Battalion, Fourteenth Infantry Regiment of the Second Brigade Combat Team—was in the early stages of helping to lay the foundation for what eventually became one of the largest U.S. bases in Iraq.

Camp Victory and Camp Liberty grew quickly into a sprawling hive of activity on the southwest hemline of Baghdad and were a short helicopter ride from the Green Zone to the north, where the U.S. embassy and coalition headquarters resided. The camps were contiguous with Baghdad International Airport, which made the area a command post for every kind of unit, including Special

Operations units that commandeered a tactically significant out-building perched atop a lone hill on the outskirts of Camp Victory.

Medley, and another soldier desperate to get out of filling sandbags, volunteered and ended up getting attached to a Special Forces team.

It wasn't cheerleader duty, but close enough.

"We got to go out with a bunch of snipers and help them carry their stuff and pull security for them," said Medley, who was a specialist at the time with three years in the Army. He would spend the next eight months assigned to a team of Fifth Special Forces Group snipers, crisscrossing the country from team house to team house on the kind of adventure most regular soldiers don't get to experience. He never saw one of the Green Beret snipers take a shot, but "I had a really good time with them."

"One time we stayed out in a barn at a farmhouse a few hours and watched what people were doing. It was like a shed full of hay and there weren't that many people, but we'd watch what people there were," he said. Other times, he said, he and his buddy would be dropped off somewhere in Baghdad with the snipers, and they would walk to a location.

Medley provided the snipers' security for the eight months he was in Iraq on his first deployment, and though he said he was treated well by most of the guys and saw a side of the Army that most soldiers don't get to see, the other demands of the Special Forces, like the grueling pace of frequent deployments, didn't appeal to him. His wife was expecting their first baby and he wanted some of the predictability that being in an infantry line unit would give him.

What did appeal to him, though, was watching the snipers at work trying to figure out how they chose their locations and their targets, and it bolstered his desire to be a sniper himself, something he said he had dreamed of doing even before he joined the Army in March 2001.

Medley grew up in Fall River, Massachusetts, and spent the early years of his life hunting and shooting in the woodlands of Maine, a few hours' drive north. The experience of sitting and waiting in those woods, he said, made it easier to envision some of what it would take to be a good sniper.

At seventeen, seizing the opportunity to get out of his life in a foster home and having completed a GED, he got his paperwork ready and left for the Army. Medley was twenty when he found himself pulling security for and learning the ropes from some of the Army's best-trained snipers, "a team of four eyes, four ears, and guns," as he called the two-man team he worked with.

"We bounced from place to place and worked with different groups of people. I saw a lot of Iraq that way," he said.

He never worked with Special Forces snipers after that, but he lucked out when he chose his next unit of assignment in Alaska. It was a brand-new battalion, the Fourth Battalion, Twenty-third Infantry, and almost all positions were open and available for the asking. The battalion was part of the 172nd Airborne Infantry Brigade at Fort Wainwright, Alaska, which endured a sixteen-month deployment to Iraq, one of the longest for a single unit. The brigade left its home base for Iraq in August 2005 and returned, battered and worn, in November 2006 after the grueling rotation, largely in the northern city of Mosul.

Having asked to be in the sniper section of the reconnaissance platoon, Medley and others were molded and honed by their section leader, who had been an instructor at the Army Sniper School. "We did a ridiculous amount of pre-sniper training, and we had a high success rate when guys from the battalion went to the school. If we weren't doing anything active, we'd go out and train," he said.

As a freshly minted sniper, Medley deployed to Iraq as a team leader in charge of two men. But as fate would have it, because he was a leader, Medley would never end up squeezing the trigger on a sniping mission himself, though he fired his weapon several times during his sixteen months in Iraq in other types of gunfights.

"A couple of the other teams took shots from houses. I guess I just wasn't in the right place at the right time," he said, pointing out that the role of a sniper is a whole lot more than squeezing the trigger.

"Everybody watches all these TV shows and movies, and everybody thinks that like somebody comes and tells you, 'Hey, this is the guy I want you to kill,' and it's not anything like that. You go out, you sit somewhere you think there's going to be some suspicious activity going on and you collect a lot of battlefield information and report it. It's a lot of recon," said Medley, who became a sniper instructor at Fort Benning after his deployment to Iraq.

When the sniper team does detect activity, he said, "then you come back and brief your commander and if it is something significant you call up and the [quick reaction force] comes to deal with it."

Medley's sniper section enjoyed the full support of what he described as "a sniper-friendly unit," which he attributed to his commander's understanding of what snipers do. "All we had to do was come up with a mission, and they let us do what we wanted to do. Our commander was good like that," he said. "We'd set up hide sites and pretty much just watch. It was a good time, pretty much watching what people are doing and they don't even know you're watching."

The Iraqis' normal everyday activities would slow down, if not screech to a halt, when the Americans drove or walked through town. Children would excitedly run after their vehicles or swarm the dismounted soldiers like moths to a lightbulb because these big, tall warriors were a curiosity and they had stuff. Sometimes kids could get toys or candy or even walk away happy with a pen. They all seemed to want soccer balls.

But the American soldiers could also be a harbinger of trouble. For soldiers to see Iraqis doing things like sitting outside eating, talking, playing cards or soccer, or playing dominoes on the side of the road wasn't always the norm.

Medley liked to see them doing those things from the hide sites because it meant that they didn't know he and his team were there and they could confidently watch for shady activities that might be hidden among a community's everyday life. Things like people venturing out after curfew or suspiciously moving seemingly random items into the trunk of a car.

"We'd go out a couple of days before and find a house that we thought would be good for over-watch," he said in his thick New England accent, reluctant to elaborate too much on how they chose their houses or how they snuck into them. "I mean, I don't want people to know how we do it. I'm sure they have an idea," Medley said, explaining that there were a number of ways to approach a house, sharing only a few.

"One is on patrol with everyone, and we'd stay behind. That worked for a little bit. We've actually been dropped off a few blocks away and walked in. Also clearing a bunch of houses, we'd stay behind in one of the houses," he said.

Sniper teams can use their own discretion when it comes to identifying a good hide site and then figure out the best way to infiltrate. In a city like Mosul, the variety of choices is limited by a sameness—block after block of buildings that may or may not have already been used by other sniper teams. Depending on the type of neighborhood and what the team was planning to watch, Medley said, he and his team would often take over occupied houses.

About 99 percent of the time, he said, "we'd get into the right house." And that's when the fun part of the job began, even though the soldiers never really knew what they were getting into.

"I'm not going to lie. The first time I did it, I was a little nervous. I was in an area I didn't know. I was in someone's house that didn't speak English, and there was only three of us. It's kind of weird at first, but it gets to be a lot better the more you do it because you know you're doing what you want to do and you're responsible for making sure people in that area are safe," he said.

Medley recalled the very first house he and his team went into. They were scared. The people in the house were scared. It didn't go well at first. "You got four of us come into your house. They're freakin' out and I really didn't understand how to work with the people too well," he said.

The soldiers' experiences with the Iraqi population up to that point were what they had seen daily on the mean streets, a mix of friendly and hostile looks and a complex environment that demanded a man's full 360-degree attention. Busting into a private home was more easily controlled, but in some ways just as complex.

"At first you're the bad guy," he said, remembering how families cowered with fear and then gradually warmed up as the hours, and sometimes days, went by. "When you're in people's houses, they are completely different from what they are on the street when you see them. I met a lot of really nice people. I was treated well in the majority of the houses I was in," Medley said, admitting that he hadn't really considered the human factor when it came to planning a house invasion and that the topic wasn't ever discussed at Sniper School.

Communication was rough at best.

"After a while, if I couldn't get an interpreter to go on the mission with us, I'd just write down everything I wanted to say to the people [before the mission] and I'd have one of the interpreters that I trusted write it in Arabic and that worked out really well. It would say something like, "We're going to sit in your house, make sure there's no bad guys in the area."

He and his team of up to eight men, including some who were there to provide security, stayed in the houses usually overnight, using the facilities as their own and taking precautions against the possibility of a mini-rebellion by any members of the family.

Anyone in the house was herded into one room and patted down, except the women, who were searched superficially with a metal detector. Cell phones and computers were taken away, and soldiers took turns staying in the room with them for the duration of the snipers' stay.

The soldiers lowered their profiles by removing their helmets, and they ate well, too. That is . . . on occasion. Not wanting to get their bowels into a twist from the effects of food prepared to local standards, they accepted chow at times but more often, the hospitality of a hot glass of sugary dark tea.

Medley's commander gave his snipers broad latitude when it came to choosing their hide sites, and the snipers based those sites on what they thought best suited each mission. The occupied houses worked well, but weren't always the preferred place to work because of all the complications and potential danger to the family. The military as an organization is not in charge of deciding where snipers should hide. As a commander, Kauzlarich had his preferred tactics and gave his snipers guidelines on what they could and couldn't do. Medley's commander was not against the takeover of houses and Medley and his snipers used the tactics they thought best suited their mission in their area. So Medley and his team also searched for abandoned buildings, although those exploits didn't always go as planned.

Abandoned buildings, they learned, are not always empty.

"We had gone out with Battle Company, and they picked out this building that looked awesome from the outside," he said. The infantry company enlisted the team to help it put eyes on a turbulent intersection, but Medley and his men were not that familiar with the area so they let the company choose the building.

Even with thousands of troops patrolling the streets for months, the mission in Mosul, a huge city about 250 miles north of Baghdad with an endless grid of streets, traffic circles, bridges, and throughways and a teeming population of almost two million, was to battle a tenacious insurgency that popped up spontaneously and repeatedly. And the teams never really knew if their reconnaissance and sniping missions minimized the number of IED emplacers "because there were so many IEDs," Medley said.

So the vigilance and observations of every soldier on the ground carried a lot of weight, and this three-story building sat on the corner of an intersection where many suspected that trouble was brewing for American convoys.

But the building turned out to be like that perfect empty picnic table in a crowded park. If no one's sitting there, it's probably just masking a beehive or an anthill. It wasn't obvious from the outside that the building was a construction site and that workers would begin arriving at dawn.

"We were in this building for about seven hours. We got there at night, and as soon as the sun started coming up, that's when we started to realize they were working on the house," Medley said. Heavy sweating broke out among the soldiers as a steady stream of construction workers arrived. Each one had to be grabbed, whisked off to another room, patted down, and zip-cuffed.

"We eventually had about twenty workers in there, all hand-cuffed, and it got to where we had to call [to get extracted] because we couldn't take any more people. We were like, 'Hey, we're pretty much compromised; we need to get out of here,'" Medley said.

Docile and compliant, squatting in the room they had been shuffled into, the Iraqis stared at their unwitting American captors as the team waited for a ride out.

"We untied everybody and got out of there. It was not fun at all. I was really friggin' nervous because they wouldn't stop coming, and there was enough of them there to where they could have done what they wanted," he said, once again amazed at how differently people act when they're not amassed on the street and being watched by others. "Fortunately they were all really nice. They just wanted to come and work."

About halfway through his deployment, Medley was pulled out of the sniper section so he could become a squad leader, a key developmental position for any enlisted soldier who wants to keep moving up the ranks. The collateral effect of moving to a line unit was not having to go into people's houses anymore, and even though he said he hadn't befriended any of the people he met while taking over their houses, one of them remembered him.

On patrol about seven months into his deployment, one of the Humvees in their lineup broke down, and Medley quickly set up a security perimeter with his men, sending a couple of his guys and an interpreter into the house in front of them to set up over-watch while they waited for help.

Vehicle breakdowns are sticky. They are one of those interruptions that slap a big fat target on the patrol, and everyone sort of anxiously stands around watching for trouble as they wait for assistance. Medley and his men waited nervously and then, improbably, a little piece of hospitality put a warm blanket over him.

"The interpreter came up to me and told me the guy in the house knew me, which kind of freaked me out a little," Medley said, because he couldn't recall a time when he had used this house as a hideout. His little internal red flag went up.

But he had, in fact, used the house one time, the interpreter explained, seven months earlier when Medley and his snipers were learning the ropes in the neighborhood from the unit they were replacing. The house was the very first one they had gone into on one of Mosul's huge intersections, and it all came back to him once he saw the man who owned the house.

"There were these two houses side by side. There were four teams so we each took a house and had a team with us for backup, and we sat there for about a day and we didn't have anything happen and then left. And the people were really nice," he said.

On this day, all these months later, not only did the man recognize him but he and his family embraced his return by helping him and his men stay safe and inviting him to stay. "They helped us by not throwing a fit or making a big scene; they did everything we asked them to. They made us tea and wanted me to sit down and watch movies with them, and I had to explain that I can't do that," Medley said. "Everybody always thinks that in Iraq the people are bad, and a lot of them are, but when you get them by themselves in their houses, you get to see how they are."

# CHAPTER FIVE

# IN THEIR OWN WORDS

It has been a tradition in the U.S. military to create a sniper capability when it is needed.

The benefit of sharpshooters has been evident since even before the Minutemen decimated the British army retreating from the engagement at Concord Bridge during the American Revolution. But there is a corresponding tradition of destroying that capability when the conflict ends. This was the case in the Civil War, World War I, World War II, and the Korean War.

The war against non-state actors foisted on the United States with the September 2001 attacks, however, was different because we didn't get rid of our sniper capability when the Vietnam War ended.

Almost as soon as that war was over, legendary Marine sniper Carlos Hathcock helped create a formal Scout Sniper training course at Marine Corps Base Quantico in Virginia. The U.S. Army Special Forces started the Special Operations Target Interdiction Course at Fort Bragg, North Carolina, in 1983, which would change its name in 2009 to the Special Forces Sniper Course. And the U.S. Army Sniper School was started at Fort Benning, Georgia, in 1987.

It is almost a cliché that we train for the last war, but in this case it is largely true.

Great lessons were learned during the 1980s and 1990s in places like Beirut, Panama, and Mogadishu about how to fight in urban areas, but there was very little change in the curriculum of the sniper-training courses from the lessons taught by the Vietnam-era snipers.

When the war in Afghanistan began for American troops and was followed a year and a half later by the start of operations in Iraq, both the Marine Corps and the Army had a large number of trained snipers. Only this time we would have an entirely different deficiency.

During peacetime, the emphasis on sniping as an essential capability and the integration of that capability into how units accomplish their missions went to the back burner in the process of training and developing junior officers.

Even now during major training exercises, the role of the sniper is many times not taken into consideration by platoon leaders and commanders poring over maps and juggling all of the other elements of combat power from mortars and machine guns to attack helicopters and unmanned aerial vehicles.

Snipers in every service and of every rank and level of experience have stories of struggling to make their commanders understand what they do. The Army and Marine Corps have created courses for noncommissioned officers and officers on the employment of snipers, and in both cases there's been a sort of "oh, so that's what they do?" reaction from the leaders, some of whom have said the course was one of the best they've had.

The numbers who attend these courses, or even more rare, have some experience in the use of snipers, are very limited. This deficiency has also been reflected in the way snipers are organized within units.

Marine infantry battalions have included a surveillance and target acquisition, or STA platoon, since Vietnam, which has served them well because of their role as infantry. Commanders, after all, easily recognize the need for a reconnaissance element. When the Marine barracks in Lebanon was bombed in October 1983, the STA platoon was almost the only element of the Headquarters Company that was not wiped out because it was deployed in teams out with the platoons on the line.

The Army has experimented with various ways of integrating sniper capabilities within units. Throughout the 1980s the Ranger Battalions, for instance, had sniping as a secondary duty. A Ranger's primary job might be as an automatic rifleman or a grenadier in a line squad, but he could be called on to be a sniper if a mission required it. This was also the case for units as diverse as the

Special Forces and the cavalry scouts. Many infantry battalions did organize sniper sections that would usually also have the role of scouting, but this was at the discretion of the unit commander. The early 1990s brought a spate of intense experience.

The liberation of Panama during Operation Just Cause in 1989 involved many units from the Rangers and Navy SEALs to the Eighty-second Airborne Division and the Marine Corps. This was a time of great experimentation in much of the military as it became more obvious that the next war would more likely than not be in an urban area.

When 9/11 happened, most Army infantry units had small scout sniper sections even if they were not officially authorized.

While the types of conflicts that U.S. snipers are involved in require them to continually adapt both the way they fight and the way they prepare the next generations of snipers and their leaders, what it takes to pull the trigger and be a damn good sniper may never change.

Here are some thoughts from today's snipers about who is right for the job and some advice on how to stay a step ahead of the trappings. Several of the men interviewed asked that their full names not be used. Some of the comments have been edited for clarity.


## ON BEING A SNIPER

SGT. FIRST CLASS RICKY
THIRD SPECIAL FORCES GROUP, SPECIAL FORCES SNIPER COURSE
  INSTRUCTOR
*"It's nothing personal."*
The first time I killed somebody with a sniper rifle at long range was in early 2004 in Afghanistan during an operation we did flying into a Taliban stronghold. The enemy fighters go into these valleys and they congregate until they have about 120 guys, and then they'll send 20 here and 20 there and they'll roll out to safe havens to work in other areas. I was able to take a shot from one ridgeline to another and hit a guy at 850 meters with a gas-operated sniper rifle. To me, I'm not going to say we're desensitized, but to me it's

just a job. It's nothing personal. Our job as military snipers is to interdict long-range targets and targets of opportunity.

STAFF SGT. JIM ARTMAN
THIRD INFANTRY DIVISION, ARMY SNIPER SCHOOL INSTRUCTOR
*"Keep building knowledge."*
The sniper community is small, around 1,200 people at any given time. I would say about five people out of every class, max, continue to build on the stuff and take it farther by going to more schools and continuing to read. I don't drink, dude, and I love it. Like when I go home on the weekends, especially when I first started off before deployment, I had massive amounts of information, I got PowerPoint slides and I read a lot. When I was overseas, I read ballistic charts and every loading handbook so I understood internal ballistics more.

The Army doesn't value that knowledge. It's more for personal growth. All the guys here at the Sniper School thoroughly enjoy it, every aspect of it. I like it a hell of a lot. I don't want to stop doing it, and that's why I want to get out because I know when I get promoted to E-7 one day, I'm not going to be able to keep doing this.

I kind of look at it as someone going through towards a doctorate program. You keep building knowledge over several years until you're really a subject matter expert, knowing everything there is to know about it. You can do this your whole life, and you'll never know everything. It's interesting to me.

I want to get into working for one of those private security contractors and be a designated defensive marksman and experience that type of sniping position because they do a lot of motorcade stuff and protecting of principals and stuff like that. It's a whole different aspect, a different mission than you do in the Army.

MASTER SGT. RICK
THIRD SPECIAL FORCES GROUP, SPECIAL FORCES SNIPER COURSE
INSTRUCTOR
*"I've never murdered anyone."*
Being a sniper pretty much required us to be scouts, to check routes, or look at an area before we hit it if possible so there'd be

less surprises for us. That's what I got paid for, and I didn't mind doing it. I was there to fight a war; I was there to kill people. That's my job, and I have no problem with it.

I'm a Christian man. I grew up as a Catholic but became a born-again Christian at seventeen, and the guy I killed in Afghanistan was about to kill two U.S. soldiers. Some guy came up to me, I guess he knew I was a Christian, and said, "What did you feel when you killed that guy?" And I was like, "Dude, I didn't feel anything but the recoil of my gun." What am I supposed to do? I feel proud. I'm not a murderer, I've never murdered anyone. Even if that guy I shot hadn't been getting ready to kill two friendlies, I would have shot him. He had a gun.

## SGT. FIRST CLASS JAMES GILLILAND
### THIRD INFANTRY DIVISION
***"They're the coolest thing since sliced bread."***
There are lots of schools of thought on confirmed kills. I forbid my soldiers from talking about their confirmed kills. It's to protect them.

Anytime you hand someone an M24 sniper rifle and tell them they're in a sniper section, their ego explodes and they're the coolest thing since sliced bread. They roll their sleeves up, slick their hair back, walk around with their hands in their pockets, and think they're the best thing going. They're too cool for school.

When they're in the woods training, they can do whatever they want to do. But when we get in the Humvee to come back, they're going to be in starched and spits, they're going to 'yes sir' and 'no sir,' and they're going to stand at parade rest or at attention and act like they know something.

I want my guys to stand out for being established and looking sharp, not for their swagger.

While we were overseas, every single shot we did was a good shot, but if we had come out and said, "Hey we just killed fifteen people in three days," people would have said, "You're full of shit" or it would have been, "What the fuck do you think you're doing?"

This granola lady back home asked me a pointed question at a kid's birthday party about whether I'd killed people because I was a sniper. She really pressed me on it.

So I played with her a bit. I told her, "Yeah, I killed more people than are in this room right now. I gave you what you want, have a nice day."

She was appalled, called me a baby killer. I also got an e-mail from a Army civilian [employee] accusing me of being a baby killer.

SGT. FIRST CLASS ROBERT ROOF
NCO IN CHARGE, U.S. ARMY SNIPER SCHOOL
*"I've never hunted a day in my life."*
There's a myth that snipers are all good ol' country boys who've done nothing but hunt and fish all their life. I've never hunted a day in my life. I was raised downtown in a city and spent minimal time in the woods.

STAFF SGT. TIMOTHY L. KELLNER
FOURTH INFANTRY DIVISION
*"A lifestyle, not a job."*
Almost anyone can be trained to be a sniper, but the best snipers are the ones who can't separate their daily lives from their job at home with the family. They see something and the first thing they think is, "Hey, I could use that for . . . whatever." I'm guilty of building a ghillie suit with my daughter Elizabeth as family time. At least the ghillie suit was for her, not that she wanted it. Being a sniper is a lifestyle, not a job.

SGT. FIRST CLASS MICHAEL RACH
SEVENTY-FIFTH RANGER REGIMENT
*"We're ninjas."*
Most people think of sniper teams as shooters and spotters who infil and assassinate. The way Rangers operate is, everybody's pretty much a shooter, there's no spotter in an urban environment. You're covering a large area, you're shooting and doing it all on your own. There are two snipers with a couple of privates for secu-

rity, a four-man rollout. The goal is to set up a hidden place before the platoon arrives at the objective. When you're the lead, it never looks the same on the ground. We're a small element operating on our own at that point; we're ninjas.

SGT. FIRST CLASS ED
TENTH SPECIAL FORCES GROUP, SPECIAL FORCES SNIPER COURSE
INSTRUCTOR

*"You're basically conducting an ambush, just from a little further away."*

I used ghillie suits some in Samarra, Iraq, but it wasn't for the traditional stuff like hiding in brush and camouflaging myself.

There were these ruins we'd crawl up into and hide in. They were old embattlements with parapets and all kinds of stuff. We'd walk out there from the team house. Ninety percent of the time in Iraq, the people in the town are watching for us on the roads, not the countryside.

I had a ghillie net I would drape over my hat with my nods down, and it broke up my outline so it didn't look like a helmet. I also had a really nice ghillie suit that I had made that I would wear that broke up the outline of my shoulder so when I was pressed up against some of the corners of the old ruins I kind of blended in as opposed to giving that nice sharp outline and that worked pretty well.

Being a sniper doesn't always mean you're going to take a shot, even though that's what people think. In the military, there's a lot more being cold and wet than there is to shooting anybody. When you're sitting and you're looking for somebody through a sniper rifle, you're basically conducting an ambush, just from a little further away. So if you've ever been laying behind a 240B machine gun for eight hours and seen nothing and had to pack up all your shit and walk away with your head hung low, it's the same thing for a sniper.

It's also what you do when you come off the mission, too. One thing about being in a small group like we are in Special Forces, before we go on a mission, I'll spot-check my team but I don't have to go around like I would do with a private checking his magazines or his water to make sure he's completely topped off. There's no time for that. I expect that as soon as one of my guys comes off mission, before he does anything else, before he takes care of himself, he gets his kit ready to go out again. You'll occasionally see people who aren't that way. Complacency is probably the biggest thing that gets people.

## SGT. FIRST CLASS JOEY
## THIRD SPECIAL FORCES GROUP, SPECIAL FORCES SNIPER COURSE
### INSTRUCTOR
### *"A sniper can be hellacious."*
It hasn't happened since Vietnam, but we're there to demoralize the enemy. That's one of the things we brief the guys we teach here at the school. A sniper can be hellacious. One guy shoots the lead man in a pack of ten, and now everybody's scrambling to deal with that guy, and then he caps another guy and slides out of there, and they don't know where it's coming from.

We're there to create confusion and interdict targets with precision fire and take them out.

By comparison, a police sniper is there to end some sort of situation that's taking place. He's there to put an end to it if he gets the opportunity to shoot, to deliver precision fire to end some type of hostage or crisis situation, whatever it may be. We're there to create confusion.

## SGT. FIRST CLASS CHRIS
## THIRD SPECIAL FORCES GROUP, SPECIAL FORCES SNIPER COURSE
### INSTRUCTOR
### *"The commander takes a risk every time."*
You can't take for granted that your commander knows your capabilities or when to use you. A sniper needs to understand his own capabilities and limitations because he needs to be able to brief that to his commander and brief it well. If you want to go do a sniper mission in combat for real where there's obviously a risk,

and the commander takes a risk every time he sends out his troops, there's no way around that. The sniper has to be able to articulate to his commander in favor of and against a mission. He has to look at that and understand whether the risk is worth taking. The weather is a huge a part of that. If they can't plan for air cover or medical evacuation, they won't send you out. So if you can make the commander understand you've got the capabilities to perform a job and you can sell him on that job, then you'll be put into action and used much more as a sniper.

## Capt. Ken Noack
### Officer in Charge, U.S. Army Sniper School
*". . . the most underused assets in an infantry company."*
Snipers are like mortar systems in the Army. Every commander has them, but only about 5 percent know how to effectively use them. Mortar assets are probably the most underused assets in an infantry company. Snipers are right behind them.

## Cpl. Neal Brace
### First Battalion, Sixth Marines
*"You have to have the dirtiest, dirtiest mind."*
You have Marines who become snipers and think they're badasses and they've proved it their whole life by playing football and acting tough and they want to assure everybody that they can kill somebody. You also have Marines who are stuck in the platoon, who don't really want to be there but they do it because they're protecting their buddies. Then there's a couple of guys who see a moral justification for this war and have no problem being somewhat of an executioner because they see a larger goal. I'm kind of in the middle of those last two. But in terms of what snipers know they have to be, you have to have the dirtiest, dirtiest mind because you have to be able to get into the enemy's head and think about where he's going to go and what he would do if he were trying to kill Marines. A lot of times Marines will say, "If I were an insurgent I would kill them all by throwing a grenade over the wall," and we would all just die.

# THE RIGHT STUFF

LT. COL. RALPH KAUZLARICH

COMMANDER, SECOND BATTALION, SIXTEENTH INFANTRY, FIRST INFANTRY
DIVISION

### *"They have to be good all-American kids."*

I wanted to make sure our snipers had physical stamina and endurance, no nicotine addictions, a psychological evaluation to make sure they weren't crazy, that they weren't going to get into a bell tower one day and start shooting Americans, and make sure they had the ability to pull the trigger. It takes a special person who has the ability to do that. Typically they have good eyesight, they're farsighted, and they've got to be quiet by nature, reserved in the way they do things, thoughtful. You can't really have a whole lot of hang-ups. They have to be good all-American kids willing to do what snipers do and get beyond it. Otherwise you get guys who develop PTSD and can't sleep. To pull the trigger they have to possess the mental and spiritual strength to deal with what they've done.

SGT. FIRST CLASS PETE PETERSON

SNIPER SCHOOL INSTRUCTOR, AUTHOR OF SNIPER EMPLOYMENT LEADER
COURSE

### *"I didn't want anyone who was lazy."*

My sergeant major told me to start a sniper section for the battalion, that I could have any E-5 or below. This was at Camp New Jersey in Kuwait. I put flyers out, and forty-five guys showed up.

I gave them a test on Kims, target detection, watched them load up rucksacks and make a packing list, checked if they had range card skills. I did a little mind test on them, too.

I had them map out some targets and told them they had to walk four miles to this target. And it's hot out, and they're wearing kit.

I parked the truck they were going to look for about three hundred meters out, but I wanted to see who was going to be like, "Okay, I gotta get this done," or who was kicking dirt about walking so far and just really kind of weed out who wanted to do this.

Light infantry scouts are the best and heavy mechanized scouts are 19 Deltas and you earn that title by going to Fort Knox, Kentucky, and going to school. The criteria are like being able to tie your shoes. There's no selection process, and light infantry scouts are selected.

I had a little interview with the top seven men. We didn't take any psychological tests, but I asked them some personal background stuff, like what kind of sports they played. You can learn a lot about a person by what kind of sports he plays or the kinds of things he likes to do, how he carries himself, how he takes care of his equipment. You want to look at whether a guy's rucksack's all torn up and jacked up, is his web gear tied down or not tied down. I made a packing list and had them dump it out to see if they had it all. If they didn't have some items, I thought they were lazy. I didn't want anyone who was lazy.

If they were a habitual smoker and smoked so heavy it was going to be a problem because they were without it, that might be a problem, but I smoked off and on for years so I don't think it's a disqualifier. What I did tell them was, whatever you do continuously, if you drink coffee every morning, you better keep on drinking coffee before you go out and shoot. Don't change up your habits just to shoot, because that's when you start not being able to handle what you're doing if your body starts thinking about that caffeine.

None of them had been to sniper school. I taught them everything they were going to learn in Kuwait. We went shooting with Nineteenth Special Forces Group guys who were also in Kuwait and they'd all go learn stuff with them. They helped us with some techniques.

TROY CARTY
U.S. ARMY SNIPER SCHOOL, SENIOR INSTRUCTOR
*"It's not always one shot, one kill."*
For the most part, people see the image of a sniper as being the Mark Wahlbergs out there in movies like *Shooter*, and it's just not true. Hollywood puts its own spin on things. It's not always one shot, one kill. . . . Sometimes it's two shots, one kill.

There's always been this aura around the sniper community. It's such a small, tight-knit community, and most outsiders, when they look in at it, they don't really understand what we talk about, they don't understand the recipe. When we're talking to each other about positions, when we talk about scope adjustments, about how we operate, about minutes and other technical things, they don't really understand so they're like, "Okay."

Everybody wants to be a sniper for different reasons. It could be the desire to set yourself apart and be part of something different. It could be seen as kind of a romantic job, but that's because there's little known about it—it kind of has a mystique about it. The down and dirty of it is not really romantic.

The overall outcome of our job is to find and kill the enemy, and we do it in a much different way than an infantryman in a line platoon does. We will sit in a position, wait for the enemy combatant to come out. Once he presents himself and it's a viable target and we're authorized to take the target out, we take him out. Most of the time the combatant had no idea we were there.

Infantrymen go out in team or squad size elements, and they find a silhouette and when you look through the sights of an M16 or an M4, it's quite different than looking through a 10-power optic. You're actually looking at an individual. For the infantryman, in a way it's a lot less personal.

A proper candidate is a soldier who's a good performer, a highly motivated, highly disciplined individual. You want a soldier who has a tremendous amount of patience.

They do need to be qualified with their weapons systems; they have to be a pretty good shot. We will refine them when they get here to the school, but if they're not proficient, it's hard to get them up to par.

A psychological evaluation requirement has been around almost since the opening of the school in 1987 and is done by the unit that sends the soldier. They do have to be physically fit, and age doesn't really have anything to do with it. It has a lot more to do with the disposition of the individual, their personality.

They have to be a team player, and it helps to have a soldier who understands how the Army works. They need to know the theme of operations, how their units operate, how infantry operations are conducted. They need to have a little experience under their belt before they come here.

For young soldiers, it's not necessarily a setback to lack that knowledge and experience; they can still learn and be effective. It really has to do with the soldier's ability to pick up that information and learn. Some are better at reading books, but most often soldiers learn hands-on.

### Sgt. First Class Chris
### Third Special Forces Group weapons sergeant, sniper instructor
#### *"Someone who can think on his feet."*

Being a sniper requires a lot of patience, somebody who has a level head, who's calm and collected because when you're operating on your own or in small groups like we do in Special Forces, you have to have that, especially when things are going wrong. It has to be someone who can think on his feet and is willing to operate on his own. People think they can do that, but when you're in that position and there's only a couple of you and you know it's going to be twenty or thirty minutes before someone can come and get to you, it requires some confidence in yourself and what you can do, that you can take care of yourself. Another big thing for us is somebody who has trust in his partner.

### Sgt. First Class James Gilliland
### Third Infantry Division
#### *"Being a sniper is not that much different from being a hunter."*

For me, a pre-qualifier was whether the guy was a hunter because if so, then he'd already have some field craft or personality skills built in. People say sniping is 10 percent shooting and 90 percent everything else, and that's absolutely true. You have to be able to figure out situations and know how to get out of a situation if it's not working.

Hunters have already had to think through these types of things. Being a sniper is not that much different from being a hunter, except for differences in, like, you're not going to eat one of them.

There are similar scenarios, though. You've got to set up your weapons, choose the ones that will best suit you; you've got to zero, clean, and maintain them. You have to know what your weapon would do under different conditions just like a hunter would, and you have to select your personal kit just like you'd do in a hunting scenario. You have to decide what you need with you based on the amount of time you're going to spend in the woods, make decisions about how much stuff to bring, how much weight.

Patience is a good quality that comes from people who are generally hunters. I know I've got it.

When it comes to choosing guys who've got the will to kill another man, you could probably sit in a room full of ten people and figure out by just talking, the conversations you have with them, probably, whether they could kill. Of course, that's the end state of everything infantry. Someone, if you do your job, is going to die. You're not going to get away from it. It's going to happen.

### SGT. FIRST CLASS ED
TENTH SPECIAL FORCES GROUP, WEAPONS SERGEANT, SNIPER INSTRUCTOR
*"It takes hundreds of times . . . to know what you're doing."*
For us, a sniper's got to be someone who has some experience. As a sniper you're in a support role when there's an assault but you're not a static guy. You have to be the guy on the ground that says, "I gotta move right now," and you may have to split your force at that time and push guys over or move yourself.

But without that heads-up and someone who's watching and listening and has been on the ground and been put in situations like that, you don't know whether to trust him. It takes hundreds of times of doing that to know what you're doing. We did raid after raid when I was a Ranger, it's all skill level 1 stuff, nothing fancy. For us you're working in much smaller forces.

One time in Samarra, we stayed in our hide for two-and-a-half days, even though we got compromised. We went in at night and got compromised around midday the next day by some kids who came upstairs to our hide site. We stayed anyway. We had a squad of infantrymen on the third floor and because we were over-watching a poll site during the first elections, they kept us there because they figured if everyone knew we were there, maybe it would lessen the chance someone would try something and people could come through and use the polls. Normally we would have been pulled out. But that's the kind of thing a sniper has to be ready to adapt for.

We packed pretty heavy with automatic weapons and grenade launchers. It was a pretty good site. We did actually shoot somebody out of that hide; it was a pretty good shot. He was two blocks away. They were out driving after curfew, and the warning had been put out on loudspeakers so they knew. This vehicle came speeding out around a corner moving about thirty miles per hour, and I saw it when it was about two or three blocks away.

He actually made the corner and almost got away, but I got him just as he made the corner. All these women started crying; we called quick reaction force. Certain areas became, I wouldn't say a free fire zone, but there was a curfew.

## ON ENEMY SNIPERS

**Lt. Gen. Rick Lynch**
**Commander, Multi-National Division Center, Baghdad 2007–2008**
*"They refined their skills over time."*
The enemy was smart enough to know you can't just have an IED and walk away. They refined their skills over time. I routinely would see an IED go off and then hear small arms fire that wasn't necessarily adjacent to the IED, but he was a ways away because he's a sniper. We didn't see any foreigners. In some cases they were immersed in the population, which impeded our ability to do counterfire.

SGT FIRST CLASS KEVIN

THIRD SPECIAL FORCES GROUP, SPECIAL FORCES SNIPER COURSE
INSTRUCTOR

*"You catch a sniper . . . through intelligence or by watching for a shot to be taken."*

People throw the term "countersniper" around a lot, and that's a very difficult thing to do. People who don't know what they're talking about say, "You just look for movement and you look for target indicators," and that's all crap. If you're in a city with a million people, there's a lot of movement and a lot of target indicators. That term is thrown around a lot, but no one really knows. The way you catch a sniper is through intelligence or by watching for a shot to be taken. All that other talk, that's all TV stuff.

TROY CARTY

U.S. ARMY SNIPER SCHOOL, SENIOR INSTRUCTOR

*"Nobody knows more about snipers than another sniper."*

Countersniper operations are discussed in the school. If there's a lot of variables involved and you're trying to go against another sniper and the commander's planning for a countersniper mission, he should leave that up to the snipers; he wants his most experienced snipers to take on that task. Nobody knows more about snipers than another sniper. All around the world in every country that uses snipers, all the snipers train the same way. They learn basically the same fundamentals, the same techniques. The only thing that's going to change is the way their army operates, how they're employed. But every sniper is trained on core skills, their marksmanship, their field craft.

SGT. FIRST CLASS ED

TENTH SPECIAL FORCES GROUP, SPECIAL FORCES SNIPER COURSE
INSTRUCTOR

*"Enemy snipers are definitely working in a target rich environment."*

Poor snipers don't last very long. The ones that were any good did a pretty good job of engaging targets, and not necessarily from any long ranges, but they did well in concealing their hide sites. For Iraqis it's a lot easier to move among the people. The guy who blends in has much more freedom of movement than we do. It doesn't take that much to make a good hide site, especially in an urban environment if you know what you're doing. They can isolate a target, pick a window, and all they have to do is maneuver into a position so they can see that one target and shoot him from one hundred meters away. Nobody has seen that shot and he's taken out the only person that could have possibly seen him, and it was maybe even when their back was turned or they weren't looking at the sniper in case he missed. He takes that shot and he leaves. No one would have a clue. It doesn't take a whole lot of skill to shoot someone in the face at one hundred meters. It's just some good basic tactics and they have to get good at it that way because they don't have a range and they can't collect data at eight hundred meters like we can.

And, the enemy snipers are definitely working in a target rich environment when it comes to U.S. troops. All the Americans are wearing a uniform that blends in absolutely no place except the uniform factory or the gravel parking lot. So they're all targets out there.

SGT. FIRST CLASS CHRIS
THIRD SPECIAL FORCES GROUP, SPECIAL FORCES SNIPER COURSE
INSTRUCTOR

**"We shot some white boys in Iraq."**
The American targets are standing out there a long time. The way the regular Army operates, they will make soldiers stand somewhere forever in the middle of the road, as if to say to the enemy snipers, "Hey we're going to stop here and operate a checkpoint for the next *eight* hours . . . please shoot me or blow me up. I'm standing here and I have no protection and not much more than the body armor I'm wearing."

It didn't take them long to figure out that they can't shoot the guys in the chest so they waited until they turned sideways and shot them in the side or in the face. It's not like it's hard to shoot your average U.S. soldier who's manning a checkpoint.

The snipers are probably not from Iraq.

I know we shot some white boys in Iraq. I know I shot some redheads, guys that look like me that don't belong. Same in Afghanistan, those guys stand out. They're absolutely either foreign, foreign trained, or Iraqis trained by foreigners. Not necessarily snipers, but definitely foreign fighters.

It's not hard to figure that whole thing out. It's no stretch to think that those guys could have been trained by foreign countries especially during the Iraq/Iran war. I've heard the name Juba thrown around; it could be like William Shakespeare, though. He could have been real, but did he write all the plays attributed to him? I'm not sure.

STAFF SGT. RODNEY MEDLEY
U.S. ARMY SNIPER SCHOOL INSTRUCTOR
*"A guy up there shooting everybody."*
In Mosul in northern Iraq, it was mostly movement to contact. There was a guy up there who was shooting everybody, including Iraqi police and army, shooting people in the leg, avoiding the plates and going for the sides and head. It didn't bother me until fuckin' one of my guys got shot. I always thought this won't happen to me, but when a guy gets shot right next to you, it's real.

# CHAPTER SIX

# RANGERS: SNIPER ASSAULTERS

Soldier for soldier, the Rangers have probably seen more combat action in the war on terror than any other group in the Army. As it should be. Their storied existence is peppered with tales of secret missions and harrowing battles that require a special brand of stamina, speed, and lethality.

But if there's one thing that has changed for the Rangers in the war on terror, it's the role of the Ranger sniper.

Once misunderstood as long-shot loners and sometimes left behind to tend the fire, Ranger snipers have earned a front seat on the urban assault train over the course of thousands of raids on high-value targets in Iraq and Afghanistan, and the presence and numbers of Ranger snipers have increased as the military looks at the prospect of open-ended conflict anywhere in the world.

"I remember when I first became a sniper, I had a platoon sergeant kick me off the Humvee, saying he'd rather take another case of Mk19 ammo than a sniper. Nowadays it's, 'Get rid of the Mk19 and take the sniper,'" said Sgt. First Class Joe Lynch, who spent five years as a sniper in the Seventy-fifth Ranger Regiment's Third Battalion at Fort Benning, Georgia.

At the start of U.S. operations in Afghanistan in 2001, each of the Seventy-fifth Ranger Regiment's three battalions was authorized to have seven snipers, or about two per company. Even that was an improvement over the era of operations in Panama and the first Gulf War, when snipers were simply members of line squads who had the additional duty of carrying a sniper rifle when a mission required it.

The recognition during operations in Iraq and Afghanistan that snipers could do a lot more than lie on their bellies and take the long shots turned into a race to whip up more of them so each company could have its own team.

It's not unlike the trend seen outside the Special Operations community in the regular Army, where commanding officers, most of whom still receive no formal training in the use and capabilities of snipers, watched them in action on the battlefield and saw how they could reap the benefits of this tactical tool—professional observers who could also kill with precision.

Some commanding officers in the conventional Army were more savvy than others and gave their sniper teams the leeway they needed to execute their piece of the mission—largely the over-watch of enemy activity such as roadside bomb planters in Iraq and stalkers in the mountains of Afghanistan.

But because an officer's career path takes him through a variety of jobs and units to get his promotion card punched, he is rarely the keeper of a unit's lessons learned. That job belongs to the NCO corps.

This is especially true in the Ranger Regiment where, because the mission is steady and soldiers tend to stay in the regiment longer than soldiers in conventional units, the strength and institutional knowledge resides in the continuity of the NCO corps, and those lessons of battle can be handed down among a tight-knit group of operators.

Ranger snipers, whose tactical evolution in places like Baghdad became the norm for a generation of those NCOs, earned a more valuable position in the organization by gaining the freedom to develop stronger urban tactics and learning how to sell themselves to their commanders.

Their presence on every urban assault is now expected.

"The team and squad leaders from those early days have all seen the necessity for snipers, and now you have platoon sergeants who won't want to leave on a mission without their snipers," Lynch said.

Traditional sniper reconnaissance missions were frequent on Lynch's two early rotations to Afghanistan, where he would go on long treks into mountain hide sites to act in direct support of targeted missions and keep an eye on enemy activity. But as the war evolved there and in Iraq, the regiment created dedicated reconnaissance sections that freed the snipers to be used more as sniper assaulters, particularly in Iraq's complex cityscapes.

Unlike regular Army units, whose commanders have specific areas to control and patrol during year-long rotations and whose missions center on countering the insurgency in that area, Rangers serve a strategic role along with other Special Operations units in the hunt for high-level leaders in terrorist organizations like Al Qaeda and the Taliban throughout the entire war zone.

Once Iraq heated up in 2003, Afghanistan became the place for young Rangers to gain some combat experience and iron out their combat jitters by going on their first missions there. By the fall of 2010, the drawdown in Iraq was planned to be under way, and the force strength in Afghanistan, where for the bulk of eight years the mission was carried out with less than fifty thousand U.S. troops, was slated to climb to almost one hundred thousand troops in an effort to crush the Taliban's resurgence.

"It's kind of ironic," said Sgt. First Class Michael Rach, who was in the sniper section with Lynch during the same five-year period from 2003 to 2008. "Back then Iraq was for the more senior guys, and Afghanistan was for the younger guys. Now the opposite is true."

When Iraq kicked off, Rach said, the Ranger snipers didn't know what their role would be. They practiced conventional stalking in the woods, quiet movement techniques, and avoiding leaving telltale signatures behind.

"All those things are important, but operating with the platoon in an urban environment, the first time we didn't really know how to do it. Every night it had to be fast, and we didn't know how to support these guys. For us to be helpful, we had to assume some risk," Rach said. "Sometimes we would be a whole block away because the objective building was so tall. You're hopping from roof to roof and you have no idea what's going to happen—we really didn't know, but thank God nothing ever did."

The shift in focus for the Ranger snipers changed the way they trained. The days of lying prone and firing out to one thousand meters morphed into exercises tailored to emphasize rapid target engagement combined with fast and accurate information gathering of conditions of the objective.

"As we started learning more in Iraq, it was the quick, close-range shots and being able to target discriminate as fast as you could because you're the eyes for everyone. There's a lot of communication, a lot of recon in a different way because you have to be very observant and all your target detection skills come into play," Lynch said.

Over time, he and Rach adopted their own approaches for the assault, and sometimes their experiences coincided. They were given permission to describe some of their tactics as long as the descriptions took place under the close supervision of an Army public affairs officer, and they were prohibited from discussing details of how and with whom they operated.

Typically, the two said, Ranger snipers did not follow the conventional Army tactics of going out into a sector of the city to set up a hide site a day in advance of a raid. Rather, because their missions came down so quickly and were always time sensitive, the Rangers moved with and were part of the assault, much like Special Forces snipers were.

"Regular Army snipers, they hole up, make a hide. It's more a traditional role because their mission is more traditional. [Rangers] don't deal with the insurgent piece like the regular Army does. We do the terrorist side of the house. It's a different role in the war on terror. We do run into insurgents at times, but that's not our focus," said Rach, who quit Stephen F. Austin State University three years into getting his degree through the ROTC program because he thought he wasn't "mature enough" to be an officer. Besides, he said, "I wanted to be a shooter."

Rach, a lean, blue-eyed son of Hemphill in the heart of East Texas, enlisted in the Army in August 2000 before starting his fourth year at college. He was assigned to the Seventy-fifth Ranger Regiment after basic training, Airborne School, and completing the Ranger selection process.

Ranger school came a few months later in 2001, and at the end of swamp phase in Florida, while waiting to return to Fort Benning to graduate, he saw the September 11 attacks on TV.

"I saw the second plane hit. We were stoked because it was like, 'We're going to war.' We would talk to people who had been in twenty years, and they said all you do is train. How lucky did we get?" Rach recalled. "I hadn't even been in a whole year, and I was going to war."

But the rush they all felt to deploy turned into a three-week wait that seemed like an eternity to him and the other Rangers, and when they did jump into Afghanistan in October 2001, he said, "it was anticlimactic."

"No one knew anything about war. There was this urgency to get back to the unit. Now we know it's a process," said Rach. "It was a couple of years before I really started getting into some action. It wasn't until Operation Iraqi Freedom."

In Iraq, the snipers became de facto assaulters with better equipment and more training who could shoot out to longer distances than the guys on the ground. And because they climbed to a higher point somewhere near the raid site, they were able to eliminate threats from above and they became the eyes and ears for the ground leaders, reporting everything they saw to commanders getting ready to do a breach.

Unlike the regular Army's traditional configuration of operating as a shooter/spotter team, the Ranger sniper teams moved as two shooters and never had fewer than four men on a team. "It's shooting out to three hundred meters, you have your gas gun, it's close range, and you've got to both be shooting on four sides of a building, so you got a couple of guys for security," Lynch said. "I think it would be dumb to go out with less than four men."

Before an operation, Lynch liked to study aerial imagery of the target area to figure out the best places to climb to the roof on the exterior of a nearby building while the rest of the platoon moved into place.

Rach's infiltration method was to tag along with a squad leader and then find a place to set up, not worrying so much about the target building itself because it was already everyone else's focus. "It was usually a threat from somebody on a roof who could pop up and drop a frag down in the courtyard, so I was trying to prevent that and anybody coming off the objective," Rach said.

Getting to the rooftops usually meant scaling a two- or three-story building like a ninja, but the maps weren't always as precise as the plan and the buildings could be completely different from how they appeared on paper, so quick adaptation on the ground constantly came into play.

Then there were other surprises, like reaching a rooftop and being confronted with a common aspect of life in the Middle East. People—lots of people—sleep outside to avoid their stuffy, unvented rooms downstairs. "Me and Mike have been on buildings where there were more people sleeping on the roof than we had bullets in our guns. So, they're not bad, they're just kids and people sleeping so you just sneak by," Lynch said.

In the summer, the Rangers tiptoed every night through as many as thirty sleeping people, and if they stirred and had to be treated with force, the reaction was never what the Rangers expected.

"You'd think they're terrified, but they're not. They're so jaded, they're not freaky about shots. I think Iraqi males have a lot of bravado, that 'you don't scare me' kind of thing. They make it a point not to show any reaction at all. If it were me, I'd be dancing," Rach said.

Unless someone was an obvious threat, by being armed or having a cell phone or something they were hiding, the Rangers said, the people who were found awake were more likely to cooperate and help the Rangers stay alive if treated with finesse.

One time, Rach recalled, he and a private reached a roof that, to their surprise, wasn't covered with sleeping people. But there was an enclosed upper room. Inside they found a fat, middle-aged man, his wife, a couple of kids, and an elderly man and woman.

Rach brought the two men out, flex-cuffed them, and looked through the room, but he knew the platoon was getting ready to assault that building next and he didn't want them to blow open the door. Rach asked the fat man, who spoke some English, to take him downstairs and unlock the front door so the platoon could come in.

"The guys just came in and it turned out that he was, like, the dude we were looking for, the fat guy."

The man wasn't as much of a threat as a younger, more nimble man might have been, but Rach's choice to treat the man in a more civil tone was the result of a commonsense technique he learned on the job from another colleague, one that took into account the fact that when you're an army of two, the security situation required a wiser approach.

Rach learned how to play a different role. "As an assaulter you're like AAARRRRRGH!," he said, describing the war-faced, badass approach it takes to breach and assault on a raid.

But as a sniper in a small team on a rooftop, a quiet approach is required. Rach said he was working "with [a guy] in another Special Operations unit, and he kind of taught us to get out of the 'line' mentality because you're a small element. You can't go in guns blazing and being an asshole because you're by yourself so it's a lot better."

He recalled watching this mentor in action on a rooftop one night when a bunch of Iraqi men started coming up from inside the building to their position.

"He'd pull them off to the side, flip his nods up, and start talking to them and be real calm, and a lot of times they'd be like, 'Okay.' They'd be bad guys, but a lot of times when you climb up the outside of a building, you're not always going to be climbing back down. You might have to knock on the door. That happened a couple of times with us—we banged on the door, and they'd come up and we'd go downstairs."

The Rangers are not trained to break bread, feast on goat, or drink tea with the locals, so the need for Ranger snipers to assume higher levels of risk by moving with as small an element as possible demanded the learned behavior of killing when killing was necessary but also the ability to gingerly coax someone into doing what they asked.

A chance encounter with a bystander was sometimes better handled quietly.

"When you're trying to sneak up on a target, they have weird sleep schedules. There could be someone standing there in the courtyard and they see you, so you just make a "shhh!" signal and ask how to get to the roof. The guy walks you to the roof, you flex-cuff him, and then he sits there and watches you do your mission. You're not compromised," said Lynch, a straight talker with an air of confidence that belies his boyish face and slight build.

He was born in Egypt to a Brazilian mother and an American father in the shipping business whose work took the young family all over the world to countries like Thailand, Indonesia, and Singapore. Lynch's fascination with the military was at least one source of discord between him and his father.

"My dad was such a hippie. I remember getting in trouble when I was a kid for wanting to play soldier. I would make a bow and arrows and go out and try to shoot people I didn't like," he said.

When Lynch was a teenager, he and his brother broke away from their father and fled to the United States, where they worked in construction and lived with friends in North Carolina until reuniting with their mother in Brazil. Lynch was eighteen when he won a silver medal for Brazil in tae kwon do in the Pan American Games, and he was twenty when he finished high school. He considered joining the Marines but was persuaded by his brother, a cavalry scout at Fort Carson, Colorado, to become a soldier instead.

After graduating from Ranger School in March 2003, Lynch went on his first deployment to Iraq immediately. By the time he went on his second deployment, he was a trained sniper and continued to train in sniping and scouting techniques at Marine Corps and Special Forces schools, where shooters are forced to think outside their comfort zones and consider all unusual possibilities on urban missions.

On another rooftop mission in Baghdad, he said, he had already flex-cuffed a man when the platoon leading an assault on the next building over found out that they had the wrong building. This meant that Lynch would have to move one building over to coincide with the platoon.

"We already had this dude, so we walked him through his own house, walked out the door, handed him to the guys as they went into the next house, and it turned out that was the house they had to hit. I was like, 'It's already clear. We walked through.' It was the guy they were looking for. It's a risk," Lynch said.

But a polite rendezvous is not always what's needed. Lynch and Rach each killed plenty of bad guys from rooftop positions, like clueless jokers running right toward them, their arms loaded with weapons.

"We racked up a ton of kills when we were pulling security like that because there were people in alleys and side streets taking off out the back of the objective. The platoon didn't need for us to put eyes on the front of the building; they needed cover for adjacent rooftops and lower buildings. Sometimes a guy would come barreling over the wall, and he didn't know you were there, so you'd blast him," Rach said.

Coordination in the tight spaces and time lines around an objective relied heavily on cross talk among the experienced Ranger NCOs leading elements of the assault force who understood what needed to be relayed in the tense moments before and during an operation. For this, Lynch would bypass the ground force commander and speak directly to the squad leaders, making sure that they had the information they needed as the assault progressed.

"I would try to tell them, hey, there's this person in the courtyard, the door has a padlock on it, you're not going to get it open, to get it unlocked stick your arm through here, or there's this many people on the roof, try to be able to tell them stuff like that. We used night vision, but you're also not that far away that you can't see," Lynch said.

As they ramped up their skills in Iraq, the Ranger snipers put just as much of a premium on spending time educating their leaders on what they bring to the fight, advertising themselves and continuously pushing to show what they could do. Old friendships with platoon sergeants played a role, but so did taking officers out to the range for a few hours or coming back from a sniper competition with a first-place trophy.

"Our platoon leader knows he's the guy with the radios and does tactical planning, but the platoon sergeant is the one running the platoon with the boys and coming into that mentality as an officer here is already a plus," Lynch said.

Before becoming a platoon leader or company commander in the Ranger Regiment, officers must have already served in that role in a regular infantry unit so the experience level is comparatively very high.

Lynch and Rach took the time to find out which platoon they were going to be assigned to, and they would go there to talk with the platoon sergeant and platoon leader, maybe have drinks with them and begin the process of getting comfortable on a personal basis. That way, when it came down to explaining what snipers can—and cannot—do on a particular mission, the conversation took place on more familiar territory.

"You're going to have that commander who says, 'Go up in a helicopter and take a shot at 1,500 meters,' but it doesn't work that way," Lynch said.

Rach recalled a time in Ramadi, a violent city about seventy-five miles west of Baghdad, when a battalion commander approached him about conducting a countersniper mission to get an enemy sniper who was running around killing people.

"I told the commander of the company, I'm not doing that. To send somebody out on this guy's turf and try to hunt him, I was like, 'This isn't Hollywood,' and he agreed and managed to save us from going out and getting killed," Rach said.

Trying to hunt down an enemy sniper who may have grown up on the city's streets, every day looking at the buildings and the people, would be almost impossible, especially in a city like Ramadi with a population of more than a half million people.

"One of the dumbest things I've heard a ground force commander say on the radio . . . was, 'Okay, snipers, go into countersniper mode,'" Lynch recalled of a classic operation in which everyone in the assault was facing the target when the assault was happening. After the assault, when the snipers had faced outward to protect the target from anyone coming in, Lynch heard the comment.

"There's five million windows out there, you can't possibly expect me with my two guys to watch 360. There's that mentality somewhere that they feel such a benefit that they don't realize that the benefit has its limitations."

Almost every Army Ranger has been on ten or twelve deployments since 2001, and even though the months they've spent with their boots on the ground add up to about the same number as many soldiers in the conventional Army, their experiences are another story.

By the age of thirty, Lynch could no longer deploy because his legs had been jacked up by impact injuries from jumping and running, sometimes while wearing more than eighty pounds of gear on his back.

Lynch went on nine deployments of about four months each, while Rach had eight deployments under his belt. Over the course of those deployments, they went out on as many as three direct action missions a day. That amounts to thousands of missions per individual Ranger. And these were not the kinds of missions that soldiers in the regular Army were used to doing, in which their unit arrived in country, got settled onto a forward operating base, and was handed the reins after a period of orientation. Instead, Rangers live in a fast and furious world where they own no land, fall in on equipment, and often have missions waiting for them before they even arrive.

"I've done missions the day I get off the plane," Lynch said, describing how there were also times when he and his boys would come off a mission, sweaty, dirty, and out of breath, only to be told to clean up and prepare for a customs inspection before a plane ride home the same day.

"By the time you're halfway through a deployment, you're burned out, but you find the will and you're doing what you signed up for. That's why people are Rangers, they want to take it one step above. And it's fun, you're going after high-value targets; you don't get the credit but you go after it," Lynch said, referring to the dearth of war tales that have come out about the Seventy-fifth

Ranger Regiment's exploits in Iraq and Afghanistan because of the high level of secrecy in which the unit operates.

In nearly nine years of war, the Seventy-fifth Ranger Regiment, which at 3,700 soldiers is about the size of a brigade combat team, had lost twenty Rangers in Afghanistan and eighteen in Iraq through the first half of 2010.

Neither Lynch nor Rach deploys anymore, having moved on from the sniper section and, eventually, the Ranger Regiment. It took each of them some time to come down from the high of a job few people can imagine.

"My last two deployments I found myself wanting to go, and then after a month, I was like, fuck, why am I here?" Rach said. "Once I stopped deploying for about a year, the withdrawal was gone, it was a good time. I'm ready to move on and do something else."

Lynch said he missed the Ranger sniper life, too, and felt terrible when he was unable to deploy at first because the rest of his team was out there in the fight. But the weight of his kit was unbearable. Then there are other times when he realizes it's kind of nice after nine deployments to have a life back.

"It was fun. My wife keeps trying to get me to skydive, saying it's the ultimate thrill," he said, adding wryly, "Skydiving is for people who've never been shot at."

# CHAPTER SEVEN

# OPERATORS AS TEACHERS: LESSONS LEARNED AT RANGE 37

Six rotations to the war zones in Afghanistan and Iraq with the Third Special Forces Group qualify snipers like Sgt. First Class Chris to teach the advanced skills they've learned to other Special Forces guys.

None of the Green Berets like to leave their Alpha teams to take an assignment at the Special Forces Sniper Course at Fort Bragg, North Carolina, for a couple of years because it means being away from the action they've been living since going to war in 2001.

The men who work at Range 37, where the course is taught, get to go home to their families every night, reacquaint themselves with their children, and take a rest from the grueling pace of operations overseas. When they're asked about being away from the war zone, however, they get a wistful look in their eyes and exhale big puffs of yearning as they recount their exploits.

In the same breath, though, they explain enthusiastically that the yearning they have is to go back and use the additional skills they've picked up from each other while teaching at the school— and get back into the action, of course.

"I will honestly say I thought I was a pretty decent sniper before I came to teach here, but having spent time here has made me a much better sniper," Sgt. First Class Chris said.

He and the other Special Forces soldiers who were interviewed did not want their full names used because of the sensitivity of the jobs they do and, some said, to protect their families.

Chris explained that he improved his knowledge and skills by getting the chance to mess around every day on the range with different scenarios and by learning new and better ways to do things from other Special Forces snipers. "As much as I'd rather have stayed on a group or team, I have learned a lot of stuff here I will absolutely be able to take back to a team and share the knowledge I've gained here."

In the case of Sgt. First Class Chris, he teaches a course on rapid target engagement, which he did a lot of on his own rotations but has never been associated with the traditional sniper role or previously trained at the school.

It's the learned skill of how to effectively kill multiple hostile people quickly when there is no time to reset the dials on an optic before each shot.

In the wars that American snipers have fought since 9/11, in which there is no front line, no uniformed enemy, and tightly packed urban areas, the snipers in the Special Operations community have developed a more prominent role for themselves with their ability to act as an integral part of an urban assault, pushing ground commanders to pay attention to what snipers can bring to bear on the battlefield.

"People think being a sniper is about laying on his belly or sitting in a hide site somewhere making a shot out to five hundred or six hundred meters, which is clearly part of what we do," Chris said. "But, especially in urban environments, the fight is more close-in, and a lot of times you're going to have multiple targets that have to be engaged very clearly so you don't have the time to calculate range and data and dial stuff onto a scope or look in a book."

The sniper instructors have put together formulas with a little help from their ballistic computers, some quick mathematical formulas that guys can do in their heads while they're looking through their rifle scopes to come up with a solution that lets them shoot quickly and engage consecutive targets without setting dials on their guns. The fact that snipers use mathematical formulas is not secret, but those formulas are not discussed outside the sniper community because the enemy could use the information to improve his own shooting.

The formulas discussed in broad terms by Sgt. First Class Chris and others, he said, can and must be done quickly because snipers on the urban assault have to be able to shoot targets that pop up unexpectedly, even out to six hundred meters. They have to be able to get a first- or second-round hit and make follow-up corrections if they miss.

Rapid target engagement is generally applied in an urban setting where snipers take rooftop positions on buildings within a block or two of the main objective, but it has also come into play in the rural villages of Afghanistan.

"We were in Afghanistan one time and had a fairly large force moving towards us, about fifty or sixty guys on foot in a village. Something like that would lend itself to that, whether you're in the open or not, moving from one target to another without having to adjust the gun," Chris said.

Chris, who had more than one engagement of that kind, said that when the shooting begins and the bad guys start going down, "the rest of them don't always scatter." They'll keep shooting, so a good sniper will continue to find and kill targets who keep moving.

"When you combine accurate fire on an enemy with the fact that you're closing the distance, which is something the enemy doesn't expect, it's violence of action, which is one of the tenets of close-quarters combat or anything like that. It's speed and surprise. If you can get all three, it's great. You're moving forward and engaging targets, using cover, moving at the right times, moving with your buddy, all the basic things. Combined, it works," he said.

At Range 37, the sniper instructors can test new shots or tactics at any time, and they do, because they have tailored this 130-acre fenced compound to their needs and have complete autonomy in what they do there and when. "This facility is incredible, and it's ours. When we want to go down and run and gun, we can do that. I don't have to go down to range control and request this range nine months out and coordinate with five different people. We call range control, we open our range, and go down and shoot," Chris said, comparing their ease of operation to the cumbersome process that units in the regular Army have to go through to get a firing range reserved for training.

Another advantage of Range 37, he pointed out, is that everybody who goes to the course is an experienced operator, "so when we've got guys running through the shoot house with loaded weapons, their pistols hot, the whole nine yards, that's something you're expected to be able to do as a SF operator. We expect the guys can do that safely. We don't have privates running around here."

Sgt. First Class Chris and his fellow sniper instructors were given free rein to develop courses that tapped into their specific areas of expertise, and the school now morphs constantly as lessons from the battlefield arrive at their doorstep. Nothing is done in a vacuum because tactics, techniques, and procedures continue to evolve so every theory, idea, and exercise is tested before it is brought into a classroom.

"You can talk theory all you want, but if you can't show it with a bullet going downrange it has no credibility. We shoot it first, and it's usually a step above what they're going to be doing, so we teach them a step below that and that also gives them confidence that it's not just smoke and mirrors, it's not do as I say not as I do. Right after we teach it in the classroom, we go to the range and shoot it and we put it into practical application," he said. "Range 37 is one of the few places in the Army that actually teaches true hardened combat skills to soldiers."

The course builds on the fundamentals of long-range shooting because the basic tenets of precision rifle work carry forth over time and will always be taught. But other skills are developed and layered into the program of instruction in response to actual lessons learned by the operators and discussed in after-action reviews.

Sgt. First Class Chris recalled one such lesson, pointing out that the mistake he made was not necessarily related to the sniping mission, but to the infiltration. In hindsight, he concluded that he should have fallen back on basic maneuver tactics that every soldier knows.

It was a mission in 2004 to snatch a high-value target in Afghanistan on a night so dark it was hard to see even under the power of night vision devices. Chris was one of twelve snipers and other shooters assigned to go into a village before the main assault force. The group planned to split into three-man teams and set up their positions on the rooftops of four houses, lock down the houses, and provide cover as the main assault came up.

The infiltration plan was inconspicuous. About sixty guys loaded into the back of a couple of big trucks, the kind of local truck that went in and out of the team's firebase all the time with supplies. They had the local drivers stop and let them dismount when they were most of the way to the village.

The men set up on the near side of the river and lined up their reference points, and everything went according to plan. The advance team of twelve went ahead, walking across a river that was about three to four feet deep, and moved toward their designated houses, setting up an L-shape around each house.

"As we were crossing the river, there was a cornfield between the target house that I was going to with a couple of guys. Instead of going through it on our way to the target, we chose to go around it. We were trying to be as quiet as possible," Chris said.

The infiltration was still going pretty well, except for an unarmed man who came upon his team. They grabbed him, covered his mouth, flex-cuffed him, tied him up, and sat on him. Almost simultaneously the team at the next house was compromised and had to shoot an armed man who was getting ready to shoot its members.

"Even with a suppressor that's still a pretty obvious sound at night when that supersonic crack of that bullet goes off," Chris said.

The men got into a pretty good gunfight after that, but the assault force hadn't moved into position yet. While the gunfire was coming at them from the village to the front, he said, they started taking fire from the cornfield behind them, about 30 seconds into the shooting. Bullets were zipping all over the place, and the teams were caught in the middle of a cross fire.

"It was all because we had failed to clear that cornfield on the way to that target. If we had bothered to look through it, we would have seen the guys sleeping there. They were posted out away from the village, and they were sleeping in the cornfield when we walked by," he said.

Chris's team killed a couple of the guys in front of him, but now they had to turn and fire in the direction of where the assault force was beginning to head. He called the force by radio and found out it was just approaching and was still low on the riverbank.

"Stay where you are," he told the assault force, then shot the two men in the cornfield with his MK12, a Navy special purpose rifle. "It was certainly not something I needed a sniper rifle to do. They were probably maybe fifty meters away; it was quick and up close. They didn't have the equipment to see, and I could barely see them. They were just spraying rounds in our general direction."

After that, the assault force moved up and blanketed the area on the original plan, stopping the enemy with superior firepower and killing about twelve guys. The Americans took about a half-dozen casualties from small arms fire and rocket-propelled grenades during a solid firefight that was complicated when a U.S. Apache attack helicopter strafed them.

"I have no idea to this day how nobody was killed that night," Chris said. "We had 30 mm high explosive rounds coming into our position."

The mission to snatch the man they wanted ended up netting only the guy's cousin, who was also on the list of wanted men, which was not uncommon in such raids. The soldiers were used to hitting certain targets multiple times without getting their man.

But what stuck with Sgt. First Class Chris about that night was the cornfield. "I should have at least maybe looked down some of the rows with my high infrared floodlight and scanned them real quick to see if there was anyone in there, or something, anything, made at least a little bit more of an effort to slide over there and at least check it out. We just blew it off. We never should have walked by," he said.

What Chris teaches is new to the sniping community, but not necessarily new to the Special Forces community. It is a type of sniping used in the context of counterterrorism and interdiction, but it's also a capability that is maintained for specialized missions within other types of Special Operations units like hostage rescue.

One of the more conventional skills taught at the Special Forces Sniper Course is the art of the hide, although one of the people who taught it was anything but conventional.

He was born in the mid-1960s in the city of Dundalk in the Republic of Ireland, six miles south of the border with Northern Ireland and equidistant between Dublin and Belfast. He arrived at the start of what became known as "the Troubles," an almost thirty-year period of violence and conflict that spilled across Northern Ireland's borders into Ireland, England, and beyond.

What that meant for young Sgt. First Class Kevin was a boyhood in the shadow of bombs, bank robberies, and dangerous, angry men who were waging war on the other side of the border. As he explained it, "In every counterinsurgency war in the world, the bad guys go across the border for safe haven, go back to hit their targets, then come back. So my town is where they all lived."

The war taking place across the border became a daily part of Kevin's life. The men, members of the Irish Republican Army, prepared their bombs and trained in Dundalk, and recruited young people, often by holding their funerals in the street at the close of the school day in the hopes of eliciting the children's sympathy as they walked home.

"The IRA attempted to recruit everybody as a kid. They'd bring you into this thing called 'Young Islander' and you'd march in a band in IRA funerals," said Kevin, who never marched with them.

"What they were doing was regimenting the young minds early—you're marching, they put you in uniform, they militarize you and give you a sense of pride, and once the young men have proven themselves on a couple of little jobs, then they do more and more," he explained. "Going to jail for a couple of years was almost a prerequisite to getting anything decent. They'd train you there."

The young man from Dundalk came to understand terrorism and insurgency as a kid, but his destiny was not with the IRA. He joined the Irish Army infantry corps when he was eighteen, was stationed in his hometown, and for two years patrolled the border with Northern Ireland. After getting a taste of the uniformed life, he switched to an Irish special operations unit and became a sniper doing counterinsurgency and counterterrorism missions in his own country, though he never fired a shot there.

In sniper school in Ireland, he learned what everyone there learns most: basic skills that don't require the use of bullets. "Here [in the U.S. Army] we have millions of bullets so we do a lot of shooting, but in Ireland you don't have the facilities, ammo, or money so you concentrate heavily on field craft and stalking and all those basic skills. They become very, very good at those and not as good at shooting," he said.

As a sniper, he deployed to Lebanon in the 1980s where he took his first shots, but back in Ireland, he said, "It's a weird situation. It's not like a combat zone. All you're doing is aid to the civil power, protecting the police who are unarmed. They're running around on the Northern Ireland border with no guns and you're protecting them."

By the time he was twenty-six, Kevin's path to becoming a Green Beret slowly began. He left the Irish Army; worked in Mogadishu, Somalia, as a contracted bodyguard for less than a year; and, through a lottery drawing, obtained a green card to become a legal resident in the United States. He arrived there, got married, and after a string of crappy jobs, joined the U.S. Army.

"I was a recruiter's dream because I didn't know anything about the Army. I had been an NCO, and now I was starting at the bottom," he said.

Still, he reenlisted so he could go to Germany with his son and his Swedish wife. She had overstayed her holiday visa and had to leave the country after Kevin went to his chain of command for help and they reported her.

Eventually he got his U.S. citizenship so he could go into the Special Forces, was assigned to the Third Special Forces Group in 2003, and went straight to Afghanistan, with three trips to Iraq every year after that. In 2005 he went through the Special Operations Target Interdiction Course and brushed up on his sniping skills, getting back to what he really loves to do.

"When I was a kid, I was sitting in the back of my house with a camouflage net over me shooting rats. I read a lot of books about Vietnam and felt I could really relate to those people," he said.

And later, as an instructor at the Special Forces Sniper Course, Kevin drew heavily on what he knew best when he was a sniper in Ireland. "One of the things I teach here is hide classes, like digging into a hide and sitting in there for seventy-two to ninety-four hours for reconnaissance and taking a shot if necessary," he said.

In the mid-1980s, when Libyan leader Muammar Gadhafi was believed to have shipped huge amounts of weapons and munitions to the IRA in retaliation for Great Britain's assistance to the United States in bombing Tripoli, Ireland was faced with the dilemma of trying to unearth these weapons caches presumably hidden all over the country.

"Now the IRA, instead of having a couple of guns here and there and homemade explosives, they had Semtex, proper commercial explosives, millions of rounds of ammunition, AK-47s, surface-to-air missiles, they had everything they ever needed," Sgt. First Class Kevin recalled.

Kevin and his fellow snipers went to work infiltrating the IRA's training and storage areas in the rural mountains of Ireland to find the underground bunkers and to take out targets of opportunity as the IRA members were trying to learn how to use these foreign weapons.

"We would go up and infil on a Thursday night and dig in the hide and set up and stay there for ninety-six hours and interdict them and catch them. We did a lot of that type of mission and became really good at it, and that's why I teach it here because guys in the American army don't do that kind of stuff too much," he said.

He didn't work as a sniper in Afghanistan, where the classic hide site he learned to master in Ireland might be a consideration, but during his deployments to Iraq, Sgt. First Class Kevin worked regularly as a sniper assaulter in Baghdad.

There, he learned a lot about what a sniper can and can't do for a hide site in an urban environment. Hiding in an occupied home was difficult and something he never did without his team's Iraqi counterparts, whom they had trained themselves. The Iraqi counterterrorism forces could shoot, but more important, they could interact with the family and make sure they knew they would be treated well.

Weapons and cell phones were taken away, the house was checked, and the Iraqis would see if anyone had a job and would be missed if they didn't show up to work while the snipers did their over-watch.

"You have to know the culture of the area you're working in. Iraq's a weird place because no one's got a job so it's not uncommon to have fifteen people come and visit the family in the house before nine o'clock in the morning. There's a whole slew of intricate problems you have to deal with," Kevin said.

The team would stay up to twenty-four hours if it worked out, and "sometimes they'd feed you. They're not hostile, and you pay them. There's a fund set up for that or for any inconvenience or damage," said Kevin. "You don't want to create more terrorists. We're not going in and kicking in doors and beating innocent people."

More often, however, his urban sniping activity was on the assault, providing cover for a breach team on the ground from the highest building in the area where they could dominate the fight.

The rules of engagement changed from time to time, but the threats, which might not have looked clear-cut to the untrained eye, were very clear to the American snipers.

Every time they went into the poor, densely populated area of Sadr City in eastern Baghdad—and at one point, Kevin said, they were the only people going in—they would get into a huge gunfight.

"The people who lived there were so used to the sound of gunfire," he said, "I'd be shooting a gun off a roof, and there'd be people sleeping below me that don't even budge. The brass is falling on them and they just lay there sleeping."

But not everyone slept. As soon as the shooting started, a lot of people would run to the roof with guns and cell phones, making themselves easy targets for the snipers who had the advantage of night vision devices and suppressed weapons. "I don't want to argue rules of engagement, but a guy with a cell phone on a roof looking at an assault force can be considered to be holding a weapon. He can trigger bombs, call in reinforcements. Each guy has to make that determination for himself," he said. "Everybody in Sadr City has a gun, and when the gunfights started, everybody became a combatant because everybody's shooting at you so you gotta do what you gotta do."

His Irish background notwithstanding, Sgt. First Class Kevin was no different from the other instructors at Range 37 and the other Special Forces soldiers who eventually have to put in a couple of years on the training side of the house. For him, his passion was for the direct-action missions, the type of missions he did in Baghdad.

But like the other operators who were teachers at Range 37, he was pleased and surprised at how much he learned by coming off the battlefield for a while.

"I want to go back to that sniper team because I've got sniping in my blood. I was a good sniper before I came here, and I've learned so much since I got here. I can't wait to go back and pass that knowledge on."

# CHAPTER EIGHT
# HIDDEN IN PLAIN SIGHT

When his skin gets tan in the summertime, Master Sgt. Rick's olive-toned complexion turns the color of dark, toasted tobacco. His jet black hair is streaked with silver, his thick eyebrows don't quite meet in the middle, and his brown eyes can be soft and mean at the same time. His smoky Mediterranean-cum-Arabic look was the perfect camouflage in Iraq for scouting and reconnaissance missions, which are the bulk of a sniper's job. Master Sgt. Rick's look confounded the Iraqis. They were sure he was one of them.

"I finally told one guy after three weeks of working with him, I told him, 'I'm an American.' The guy said, 'You're an American?' And I was like, 'What did you think I was?'" said Master Sgt. Rick, who is, in fact, of Cuban descent, a 1960s baby, and the first in his family to have been born in the United States.

With a more finely tuned ear, the Iraqi who doubted him might have also figured out that Rick was a toughie raised on city streets and had an accent that would make Tony Soprano feel right at home.

The Iraqis tried to trip him up to get him to reveal his true identity. "They would ask me stuff to see if I would answer them, but I couldn't. They wouldn't believe it, especially when I had a full beard and got dressed up in their clothes," he said.

And that is what made Master Sgt. Rick a boon for his Third Special Forces Group team, which relied on his dangerous reconnaissance missions for the highly accurate intelligence they yielded.

Using his natural physical disguise and a dingy, floor-length dishdasha, or "man-dress" as it is called by U.S. troops, he went about as far out to the edge as a man could go before getting killed on the streets and alleyways of Baghdad to scout for sniper sites or gather intelligence in advance of a direct action hit by his team.

After his daring recon trips, he helped write assault plans with the details he had gathered and also acted as primary navigator to the sites he had canvassed for the assault team.

He stayed alive by hiding in plain sight—not with a ghillie suit, but with his own face and the help of his ballsy Iraqi driver, who assumed great personal risk to help the Green Berets do their job.

Rick did not speak Arabic, but was able to gather physical and visual intelligence while his driver picked up what he could by doing the talking.

"He saved my life a lot of times when we would stop at certain places where people would start talking. He would just chime in, and I kept my mouth shut because the jig would be up if I opened my mouth. He'd smoke, he'd exchange cigarettes, he'd take the focus off me," said Rick, a medical sergeant and sniper instructor at the Special Forces Sniper Course at Fort Bragg, North Carolina.

At least once, however, Master Sgt. Rick busted out of his passive Arab observer role like the Incredible Hulk and came close to blasting two men on the spot with a mini-shotgun he carried for quick action on the street. To this day, he said, he still wishes he had shot them.

It was April 2004, a year after insurgents began killing scores of passing U.S. troops by blowing up their vehicles with crude, remote-detonated, improvised explosive devices that were buried in roadways, strapped to trees, and bolted onto highway guardrails.

Cruising around in a little Toyota Corolla that looked like any local Iraqi car to the unsuspecting eye, Master Sgt. Rick got a tap on the shoulder from his driver, who pointed to two men who were busy banging on a guardrail on Route Tampa, a main supply route for convoys chugging through Baghdad to points north.

Pissed off and suspicious as hell, he told his driver to go down about one thousand meters, loop back the opposite way, and stop in an area at a distance from where they could watch the two men but not arouse their interest.

"So we're watching these guys, and this convoy is approaching the base. When the guys see the convoy, they stop working. They sat on the guardrail acting like they weren't doing anything. Their behavior changed drastically," he said. "After the vehicles drove into the base, they went back to working on the rail, and I said, 'Okay, these guys are up to no good.'"

They were just outside the sprawling Camp Victory complex just north of Baghdad International Airport. Master Sgt. Rick ordered his driver to pull around to where the suspicious men were and, screeching to a halt in a cloud of dust and pebbles, the Special Forces soldier dressed as an Arab came out of the passenger side of the car with his mini-shotgun pointed at their heads, standing less than ten meters away.

"They freaked out. They turned around, and their eyes got real big. I had my finger on the trigger, and my gun was off safe, and I told them not to even move. They made a gesture to run, and I don't know if they understood English, but they knew better than to run," he said. "If they had taken half a step, I would have shot 'em in the face."

But he couldn't shoot them and he knew it. The Iraqis he was with and the backup guys in a truck behind them went to work scanning the area and found no weapons or explosives. The two men were patted down, cuffed, brought in for photographs and interrogation, and then released, clearly aware of the restrictions that the rules of engagement placed on the U.S. troops. They knew that without weapons or explosives present, there wouldn't be enough to hold them, much less kill them.

"My gut feeling was they were guilty; there was no doubt in my mind they were the enemy. But if I had shot those two guys, I could have gone to jail," Master Sgt. Rick said. Still, he said, he feels as if he may have saved at least some American lives with his recon mission. The two men, and others like them, he concluded, would think twice before working in that area again.

"They were probably like, 'Dude, these guys came out of nowhere and they were on top of us before we could react.' It was a lesson learned for them that they are being watched and they're not as slick as they think they are," he said. "We can be pretty slick."

Born in Miami, Florida, Rick grew up in New York and Philadelphia and joined the Army because he felt a debt of gratitude to the country that had given his parents shelter when they fled Fidel Castro's Communist takeover of their native Cuba. Fiercely patriotic, he calls the United States "the best country on the face of the Earth," acknowledging that it has its problems but "nothing I've ever seen a Communist dictator fix."

As a young man he became a foreign car mechanic, a machinist who rebuilt engines and transmissions, did welding, and developed a professional standard that he found lacking in his first enlistment as a mechanic in the Army Reserve.

His skill level was far above the Army standard, but he was married now and had a baby boy on the way. He needed to make a living, and if he didn't serve his country then, he thought, he'd miss the chance forever. So he switched to active duty and, instead of the infantry job he wanted and didn't go for because it would have meant returning to basic training, he became a medic.

As it turns out, his background as a mechanic helped him become a good Army medic and later a Special Forces medical sergeant, also known by the Army job code 18 Delta, one of the most prestigious and difficult-to-attain jobs in the military. Special Forces medical sergeants are trained to a level far above the average Army medic and are often the only medical assistance.

In the early days of the war in Afghanistan, the few Special Forces medics who were with the Northern Alliance fighters as they routed the Taliban were the only medical support for an entire army, performing multiple battlefield surgeries from abdominal wounds to amputations.

"I was all over it," he said, "I really had no problems with it. I learned by process of elimination and by asking questions because I had to have those skills as a mechanic. Plus when I went to school to be a mechanic, I learned how to memorize. In physiology and anatomy I learned how to memorize, too."

He would also excel in the surgical nature of sniping when he went through the Special Operations Target Interdiction Course in October 2001. After that, Master Sgt. Rick and the rest of the Special Forces community began deploying on regular rotations, doing the bulk of the heavy lifting in Afghanistan and sustaining a brutal pace of operations in Iraq when the war began there in March 2003.

As did most Special Forces soldiers, Master Sgt. Rick, who didn't want to use his full name to protect the identity of his family members, deployed to both theaters, straddling the vastly different demands of each war zone—Afghanistan's rural, unforgiving terrain, ancient customs, and skilled Taliban fighters were 180 degrees from Iraq's Arabic culture, urban infrastructure, and Al Qaeda influence over disgruntled citizens.

In Iraq, hide sites in occupied houses worked only if a long list of conditions was met. And it never was, especially in a densely populated place like Baghdad, where turf was intermittently owned by good guys and bad guys. Pulling off a house hide site was difficult at best, even for the Special Forces soldiers who invested the time in getting close enough to know who was who and what took place in which neighborhoods.

"You'd find an area that you thought was abandoned, but it really wasn't abandoned. You could stay there a short period of time, but somebody would come by and take a look, like children or somebody else," he said.

One time when he was a team sergeant, he sent a couple of his guys into a building that appeared, and in fact was, abandoned. It was dark, rundown, and empty. The snipers were to set up a hide site with some Iraqi soldiers and stay there for a period of time to over-watch a factory area.

A grim discovery forced a change in plans. "They got in there and found the bodies of two people who had been tortured and decapitated. It was an empty building, but the [bad guys] were using it," he said.

Master Sgt. Rick is not afraid to kill.

As a kid, he said, his life was so violent that he believed he might eventually have become a killer because he was "a wild street kid from New York," a renegade on a path to ruin who got into plenty of fights, hurting people and getting hurt. At the age of seventeen, though, his life changed when he abandoned his Catholic upbringing and became a fervent born-again Christian, dedicating his life to Christ and burying his head in volumes of history books and the Bible.

Through religion, Rick developed a deep belief and conviction in the righteousness of killing people who are out to destroy others and their way of life.

"There's a fine line between murder and killing, and there's a lot of good examples in the Bible of good men killing people. They were warriors. King David comes to mind, as do Jonathan, Gideon, and Joshua. There's a right time when you need to defend yourself and some of these sissified versions of Christianity don't fly in my book," he said.

In Iraq and Afghanistan, he approached his job with a purposefulness that few who share his vision dare articulate and that he believes is necessary to keep hatred against Americans from reaching U.S. soil again as it did on September 11, 2001.

"I tell ya, I see the enemy still lurking in our country. I take examples from George Washington and Patrick Henry. They knew there was a need, and this is my generation. I'm up to bat, and I intend to hit a grand slam, to leave a legacy for my son and future grandchildren," he said. "But it isn't going to happen by me being wishy-washy and sensitive about the feelings of people who want to kill us. It's just the way it is."

In the summer of 2003, he killed his first man, a man who was about to kill two U.S. troops on a hillside in Afghanistan. Master Sgt. Rick and his partner had been hiding on a ridge in the northern part of the country for a couple of days while soldiers from the Eighty-second Airborne Division and Tenth Mountain Division and Special Forces teams were battling Taliban fighters.

They froze their butts off at night, and all the time they were bored. There hadn't been anything for them to do but watch and keep the ground guys informed of any threats they saw from their vantage point. It was a classic over-watch mission, and it behooved them to stay concealed while the battle raged in the valley.

On the second day, though, as the sun came up, his partner tapped him on the shoulder and pointed to a man trekking along about a mile and a half away.

"We saw a little spot moving. We were watching him for a long time. There was a man wearing a man-dress walking through all the dried-out riverbeds. His right arm was locked to his body, and he was balancing himself with his left arm. We could tell he had something under there. It was obvious he was concealing it," he said.

The sniper team called the guys on the ground with information about their sighting, and two U.S. soldiers set out to confront the man. As they approached him, the man raised his right arm and pulled his gun out.

"He fired a little burst as he started raising the gun, and I shot him from about 160 meters away, right through the back. He was down on a little valley road on the bottom. He had no idea we were up there. He thought the only people there were the two guys approaching him," said Rick, who shot the man with his SR-25 semiautomatic sniper rifle.

Later, when the sniper team talked with the two soldiers who had approached the suspicious man, they said the man had smiled as he raised his weapon. "One guy said he just dropped, but he twitched a little once he hit the ground, and one of the guys shot him with a squad automatic weapon," Rick said.

After his first kill, Master Sgt. Rick went on different types of missions during his Afghanistan rotation. A few months later, on the Pakistan border a few hundred meters inside Afghanistan, he was positioned on a sniper site with five other guys.

To their south, two teams of Navy SEAL snipers set up their own positions as designated by a plan to over-watch the traffic and activity on a road network between the two countries. Each team infiltrated its position in separate helicopters around the same time of night and walked from their landing zones to their respective sites.

The infiltration had gone smoothly. It was quiet, but not for long. The SEAL team that was positioned between Master Sgt. Rick's men and the SEAL team that was farthest south got into a firefight on the first night.

"We watched the firefight all night long. We stayed quiet," he said, remarking wryly that when he returned after four days on the mountain, he was told "that they had purposely put us in there expecting a compromise. Gee, thanks, you know."

But the gunfight wasn't their problem. There was no point in helping the SEAL team with its firefight at the expense of giving themselves away. No, the Special Forces team was compromised on its own, quietly, in classic fashion by a woman walking up the mountain with a donkey in tow. The team's pucker factor went sky-high. There she stood, unarmed, looking at them. They looked back at her, and it was quiet.

Should they shoot her?

"She found us in the morning when the sunlight came up, and she freaked out. She didn't yell, but she froze in her tracks. She got really close to us. We saw her coming, but there was nothing we could do. We were hoping she would bypass us, but she came right at us, kind of figured it out, and at that point we knew we were in trouble," he said.

They didn't do anything to her. She turned and walked back down the mountain, throwing the team into its own freak-out mode, albeit a quiet one. After being compromised, they expected an attack. After all, the woman had presumably returned to her village with valuable intelligence, and they assumed it would only be a matter of time.

"I told my guys, you know what, we're going to have to start shooting at some point, so let's get ready because she went back and is telling everybody there's six Americans up here, so be extra alert," Rick said.

They were armed to the teeth and had with them an Air Force tactical air controller who could call in air support if they got into a fight and needed big guns.

But nothing ever happened and besides, the weather was pretty nice. They watched the team to the south of them get into firefights all day and the following night and did what snipers do when they're on a four-day over-watch mission.

They mostly lay prone, watching the roadway through binoculars and scopes, keeping notes, eating sparsely, and making their water last as long as they could before one of them had to venture out to fetch water they'd hidden on the way up.

In a hide site that a sniper plans to return to someday, Rick said, he won't leave a trace, including human waste. "You shit in bags and take it with you, or if you know you're never going to return to the area, you can dig a hole. If you know you have the ability to move from your setup, you go, do your business, and come back," he said.

In the setup they had for this road over-watch mission, the terrain allowed for them to pull off a little bit and relieve themselves, cover it, and leave it. But nobody was eating enough to produce the urge.

"You carry whatever food you can and mostly you just go hungry, you don't eat as much. You make it stretch with power bars and that kind of stuff. We carried a lot of extra water and used most of it walking in," he said, having carried more than 120 pounds on his back during the infiltration and walk to their position.

As the hours ticked by, the team watched the roads and saw plenty of oddball activity that was difficult to nail down under the rules for shooting, frustrating Master Sgt. Rick and his men.

"I've seen them come from the Paki side in the middle of the night and drive across into Afghanistan. From the ridge we were on, we could see a long distance and there was a town on the Pakistani side; you could see a vehicle come with no lights on," he said.

The pattern repeated itself openly. A series of flashing signals from the town would be answered by a corresponding series of flashes from the car's headlamps, and then the car would pull into the Pakistani village, stay for about thirty minutes, then drive back across the border to Afghanistan with the lights off.

"They would continue to drive off without lights on for a period of time until they felt it was safe and then they'd turn the lights on," Rick said.

This went on during the hours of darkness, but on their third day on the ridge, they had a live one—or so Rick thought. It was another situation like the one in Iraq when he knew in his gut that the men he was watching were part of an attack but were off-limits because they weren't carrying weapons.

About nine hundred meters from the team, over a ridge near the border, the snipers saw a radio antenna first, then a guy holding the radio. "I wanted to shoot him, but he was too far, the wind was too high, blowing about fifteen to twenty miles per hour, and it was a long shot," Rick said.

The Air Force tactical air controller, who had heard a couple of Apache attack helicopters in the area, called to them and asked for an overflight of the area where the radioman was so they could get a better idea of what was going on. The pilots buzzed the area and saw three men who waved at them in a friendly gesture from a squatting position. They saw no radios in their hands, only smiles and waves.

But Master Sgt. Rick knew better, and he wanted to take them on. The situation, he felt, required an aggressive response.

"They had a radio and there's a firefight going on, and I'm thinking this is their forward observer. They're giving direction, and they know where the SEAL team is," he said.

The pilots circled for a few minutes and asked the team if they should shoot because they didn't see any weapons or obvious threat. "I said, 'Yes, kill them,' but the warrant officer who was with us said, 'No, don't kill them,' and he outranked me," Rick said. "My justification was, you're on a ridge with a radio that looked to me like one of those old Russian radios, and there's a firefight going on not far from us. I'd say, 'Bad day for you.' If you're not guilty, you're stupid."

The pilots eventually returned to whatever mission they were doing before the Special Forces sniper team called them over.

"They would have engaged if we had given the word, but we didn't," Rick said. "I can't fault them for leaving."

Master Sgt. Rick's attitude toward Afghanistan, which he called "an armpit," was colored largely by the way women are treated there. Of all the things he saw in combat, he said, of all the people he and others killed, "nothing bothered me as bad as when I got to Afghanistan and saw those women in burkas because it's absolute slavery. I just don't see how people can treat other people like that. That infuriated me more than anything else, I don't know why. They were walking around in their own personal cell. It sickened me. I didn't trust the men."

Afghanistan, he said, "literally reminded me of pre-Christ times, biblical times. The only time you knew civilization was around was when you saw a vehicle or a helicopter.

"It's frozen in time. They still cook off of cow patties, which is probably not the healthiest thing," he said, expressing his sorrow for the women and children and how timid they were around military people, which he figured was a throwback to when the Russians were there in the 1980s.

In addition to being a sniper, a medical sergeant, and an extraordinary reconnaissance asset, Rick's specialty on the team was his proficiency in the high-tech equipment that Special Forces has steadily acquired and put to use in both theaters.

As a sniper instructor at Fort Bragg, he taught scouting, photography, and video, mapping out routes to and from targets. "It wasn't really taught in this course when I went through. The technology is new, but we were never really teaching it and now we teach it. I was available, I had already retired. There's nothing better than doing a job you know," he said.

## CHAPTER NINE

# THE HIDE SITE: THREE STORIES

When the first Gulf War began, there were many units whose mission was what Special Forces soldiers called "special reconnaissance."

These included certain Special Forces A-teams as well as Army long-range reconnaissance and surveillance, or LRRS, units and Marine Force Reconnaissance teams.

Special reconnaissance meant infiltrating deep into enemy territory according to an established doctrine that dictated up to a certain number of kilometers, and pulling surveillance, or putting "eyes on," an important terrain feature such as a road intersection or a main supply route.

The idea behind special reconnaissance was to establish a secret observation post, or hide site, close enough to the terrain feature or other objective to be able to observe it but far enough away that no one on it would ever expect you to be there and catch or compromise you.

This doctrine had been developed over the years since World War II with the assumption that we'd be fighting the large conventional armies of that era. In Europe, for instance, the LRRS units planned to go to ground and let the Soviet juggernaut roll over them before establishing their surveillance positions in the enemy's rear.

Unrealized was the fact that this doctrine presupposed a disinterested populace. This was, after all, doctrine written by an army that had known almost twenty years of peace following the withdrawal of the major units from Vietnam.

The last time U.S. forces had fought in large numbers in a foreign desert was during World War II when we battled against German and Italian forces in a region populated by North Africans who had no dog in the fight, so to speak. The doctrine was to be tested soon after the air war commenced in the Gulf War in 1991.

In August 1990 the U.S. began the movement of a half-million troops to Saudi Arabia where they staged along the border with Iraq in response to Saddam Hussein's invasion of Kuwait.

As part of that action, various American and coalition Special Operations units were given the task of searching across Iraq for Scud missile launchers, which were showering their deadly payload on civilian neighborhoods in Saudi Arabian and Israeli cities.

One of these units was the storied British Special Air Service or SAS. The plan for its initial insertion was to fly hundreds of miles into the Iraqi rear and establish surveillance on the main roads exiting the Baghdad area.

On the first night of the mission, several teams were to infiltrate by helicopter and then continue their infiltration by foot and establish hide sites overlooking the main and secondary travel routes. When the first team got into the area of its planned infil, it flew over the terrain and realized that it wasn't going to work. Even from inside the helicopter, the team members could tell that the barren landscape offered little chance of remaining hidden. The second team landed but it called for its helicopter to return almost as soon as the bird flew away. It also determined that the chances of success were small.

Only one team that night continued on with the plan. That eight-man team, which would be known to history by its radio call sign Bravo Two Zero, was compromised by a little boy herding goats on the first morning of the mission. The men on that ill-fated team were forced to evade capture and try to escape more than two hundred miles to the border with Turkey. But it was futile. All save one were killed or captured in the attempt.

The doctrine that dictated the planning and execution of that mission was flawed partly in assuming the terrain would be more forgiving. But the more colossal oversight was the failure to take into account the people of the region and the way they live.

The little goatherd understood that those foreign men weren't there to fight other foreign men as was the case in North Africa during World War II. He and his family understood that they were there to fight Iraqi soldiers, at the very least, or them.

For people raised in the United States or Western Europe, it is easy to imagine remaining concealed while very close to civilization, partly because these areas don't have nor do they tolerate nomadic tribes. Few people in these regions make their homes outside the offerings of a robust infrastructure and, at least in America, walking to and from anything, except in a major city, simply put, is rare.

Most Americans leave their homes by getting directly into their cars and driving to the parking lot where they are headed. Even children stay inside more and more and watch television or play video games rather than roam the countryside playing.

In the Middle East and Southwestern Asia, this is not the case. People in these regions live on the land, walking distances wildly unimaginable elsewhere.

Today's sniper teams in search of a hide site can probably count on someone like the goatherd who compromised Bravo Two Zero walking in on them eventually, even in what seems to be the most remote reaches of desert.

In Afghanistan's natural environment, Special Forces sniper teams perform a combination of missions, from over-watches of people and villages to direct assaults to providing covering fire for a force package. Watching the approach of a goatherd and gauging his intent is part of the job and the risk. Getting compromised happens all the time.

"Just when you think you're not on a goat trail, the goat herder happens upon you. He sees you, you flex-cuff him, and you leave. Somebody finds him a few hours later. He says, 'The Americans were here, they flex-cuffed me, and they left.' You're a fool if you stay in that area," said Sgt. First Class Joey of the Third Special Forces Group.

Another aspect of society in America and Western Europe is the prevalence of a multiethnic society. It's easy to blend in, especially in larger cities, regardless of ethnicity. As was the case in Vietnam, the fairly homogeneous societies of Iraq and Afghanistan make American and coalition soldiers stand out like redheaded babies in a Chinese maternity ward.

The Green Berets have learned plenty of tricks to staying concealed during their thousands of missions in the mountains, hills, and wadis of Afghanistan.

One is dressing for success. They have worn and continue to wear a mixture of clothes, and they never, ever wear the Army's digital camouflage pattern, known as the universal camouflage pattern. The ineffectiveness of the pattern, which was fielded in 2005, for the variety of terrains in Afghanistan was recognized early on by Special Forces troops.

Among the items they've worn is the popular Multicam pattern, which was even authorized almost begrudgingly by the regular Army in 2010 for all soldiers headed to Afghanistan.

"Early in the war we wore a mix of civilian clothing and local garb like blue jeans or man jammies or whatever the locals were wearing. We all had beards back then and didn't cut our hair for a while so we were shaggy as we could get," Sgt. First Class Joey said. Still, he said, the locals always knew they didn't belong because the villages are tight—they all know each other, and they can spot an outsider from more than a mile away.

This challenge carries over to urban operations in Iraq as well.

"If you drive a car into a neighborhood in Iraq, everybody in that neighborhood knows every car. So you may get away with it once, but you're definitely not going to get away with it twice. On a second pass to get a photo or something, somebody's going to know," he said.

By the same token, if villagers in Afghanistan see an outsider milling around a mountainside where there is usually no one, they're more than likely going to check it out and they'll do it with guns in hand.

Protective equipment is optional in some cases, and for the unforgiving, vertical terrain in Afghanistan, it can even be a disadvantage. Soldiers deploying to Afghanistan began wearing the lighter plate carriers when it was acknowledged, after years of fighting that often took place on the face of a steep hill, that the heavier gear bogged down a soldier, inhibiting his speed and agility. The gear also created an untold number of musculoskeletal injuries.

Special Forces soldiers, who work in small teams and have more flexibility in what they wear, shoot, and carry, opted for the lighter gear years before the conventional Army did.

"In a city, you better have body armor on, but in Afghanistan, there's been times we've been without body armor because at 11,000 feet, if you think you're going to climb a mountain with body armor on and be worth a darn when you get to the top or if you think you're going to chase some half-naked Taliban guy down a foot trail with body armor on at that kind of elevation, you're mistaken," said Sgt. First Class Ricky of the Third Special Forces Group.

That kind of flexibility for Special Forces soldiers, whose missions are stacked toward the snatch-and-grab variety versus the intersection over-watch type, was critical when it came to time-sensitive missions, which happened more often than the long-lasting hide and wait missions.

"These targets don't stay in one place for a very long time. The reality of dropping a sniper team kilometers away out of earshot of a helicopter and having them walk through that type of terrain and over-watch that target, if you want to really catch the guy, is not always realistic," Sgt. First Class Ricky said, pointing out that a long infiltration also has logistical concerns with provisions, depending on the length of stay. "The two-man sniper team crawling on their belly up to take a shot on a guy is, I'm not going to say unrealistic, it's not the norm these days."

### GUTS, GUNS, AND GARBAGE

Cities get smaller and smaller when you're a sniper in need of a loophole. The more hide sites you find and use, the fewer there are for new missions. And it's especially hard when you stand out to begin with.

With the exception of a few who have certain physical traits, American infantrymen walk, talk, look, and smell like Americans.

Not to mention the American uniform, an instant identifier the enemy has no obligation to wear.

When Sgt. Derek Balboa was faced with finding a hide site for an over-watch mission on the outskirts of Mosul, a city of nearly two million people in northern Iraq, he and his partner went to the most unpleasant, outside-the-box idea they knew of.

It was a disgusting way to carry out a mission, but the wet, rotting, offal-laden garbage dump—in which they spent three days lying on their bellies—ended up being the crown jewel of hide sites, the king daddy of concealment.

Okay. It should be mentioned that they did get compromised by a peripatetic goatherd, but Balboa said he still considered the mission a success because the reconnaissance, planning, and execution of the dump-as-hide-site concept was proven.

"All that together tells me that the idea would work," said Balboa, an affable young patriot from Illinois who quit his job as a construction worker and joined the Army on the spot when he saw the television images of New York's twin towers crumbling to the ground on 9/11.

When he decided to serve his country, he hadn't envisioned the part with the stinking trash pit, but the day he and his partner came up with the idea—"we'd heard about some Marines or a British team doing it"—they enthusiastically started outlining their plan.

The mission itself, to over-watch a surveillance camera, had become an occasional standard with Balboa's leaders, a method of baiting criminals into the sights of their snipers by placing a real, or sometimes bogus, camera on a utility pole or some other high spot and waiting for someone to come along and shoot at it. And they almost always did, even though it was announced to the public that there were snipers in the area who were authorized to kill those who tried to disable the cameras.

"Messages had already gone out in the media that if anyone was caught messing with the cameras, it would be necessary for us to use lethal force. Other sniper and recon teams were engaging guys who did this so they knew there were going to be consequences," said Balboa, who noted that the knowledge that snipers were watching an area generally had a calming effect on the enemy.

"It demoralizes the insurgency because they know you're out there, and nobody wants to move; your stomach's going to be clenched just walking around. Even if there wasn't much going on and we weren't catching them, we were still denying them freedom of movement on the battlefield. I didn't like the fact that they knew I was there, but just by my sheer presence we might have saved someone's life."

The realistic-looking decoy cameras were usually made with ammunition cans painted black with some kind of cylindrical "lens" and were then affixed to a visible point overhead. The baiting idea was hatched when the battalion's intelligence section kept reporting that other surveillance cameras they installed at known areas of trouble were being regularly shot and disabled.

A camera was posted alluringly on the southwest end of town in a poverty-stricken area, a corner of Mosul with a mix of tumbledown tenements and crumbling abandoned buildings that overlooked a vast garbage dump from about four hundred meters away.

In Iraq, many garbage dumps are simply empty lots or fields that are covered with various layers of waste and refuse and sometimes, especially in an urban area, abut neighborhoods. The people who live there walk into the field and dump their garbage.

It was perfect, almost too perfect.

The recon a couple of days before they set in was done in broad daylight, and the sniper team got a good look at—and a good whiff of—the squalid place it was thinking of calling home for three days. The gritty reality of the plan sank in like the *Titanic*.

"These buildings were horrible; there was just nothing. I looked at my buddy, and we started looking out in the trash and we're like, 'I don't know, man.' We're both thinking the same thing. I was like, 'I do not want to be sitting in this,' but the commander was all over it. We're like, 'Sure, because you don't have to sit in it.'"

Beyond the dump to the south was a hardscrabble wasteland that disappeared into open desert. They could infiltrate from there.

In the dump itself, the sniper team saw the same thing at the same time—a section with two piles of trash and an open area with a backstop, a dip that looked directly toward the target they wanted to watch. The closest buildings were a good five hundred meters away and were on a slight hill. The chances of being seen because something looked out of place, they thought, were slim.

"Most people in the country don't have jobs. They know what their neighborhood looks like, and they're pretty much clued in to their habitat. But they're not clued in to their trash," Balboa said, pointing out that the landscape in the dump changed with the wind and the rummaging of goats, "so we could move stuff around and it wouldn't matter."

They took pictures as they drove away and went back to their planning table to nail down the details.

"Everybody was all into it," Balboa said. And even though the excitement was palpable, they realized it was dangerous for a human to burrow into the layers of refuse in any garbage dump, much less a Third World dump where raw sewage was mixed with animal entrails, household waste, and all kinds of foul schmutz.

The snipers saw and smelled rotting food, goat guts, goat heads and blood, feces, rusted-out cans, gas canisters, "and just about everything you could think of" in their planned hiding area. "The smell was, I don't even know how to rate that. It's probably like your blue cheese mixed with the end-of-the-day smell at a slaughterhouse. Dried blood and guts and after sitting there a few weeks it ferments and you get the flies," Balboa said. "I was worried more about hepatitis or even malaria, there were flies everywhere."

They considered sitting directly in the trash but quickly discarded that idea.

"I didn't want to get any of that stuff near me," he said. "The other option was to use cold weather gear and ponchos and lay trash on top of us, with no dug out, just something in between us and the trash." They ended up adopting something closer to the second option, using a piece of plywood instead of poncho liners.

With two men for security, the sniper team was ferried by Stryker around the edge of the city from the desert side. They then walked into the trash pit under night vision optics from the cold, open desert, a moonlit trek of about a half-mile, far enough away that the vehicle drop-off would not have been noticed.

"We walked in from out in the middle of nowhere," he said.

Their plan was to dig a shallow pit on what looked like a mini-saddle with a downward slope in front. The pit would be wide enough for the four of them to lie prone on a slight, upward incline and look out toward the camera through a loophole in the strategically scattered trash. Their position would be hidden on either side by the two humps of trash and concealed in the rear by the backstop where their feet would rest.

For the walk-in, each of the four men either carried something or pulled security. They hauled two pieces of plywood, two two-by-fours, a shovel, and "everything we needed to be in there for three days." Each man was armed with an M4 rifle, and the sniper team had one M24 rifle that would lie between them in the hide.

They soon found their choice of shovel lacking. After pulling off the top layers of garbage with their noses wrinkled against the stench, they discovered the ground was rock-hard. Trying to dig with their shovel, a version of the e-tool with a small pick, was like using a plastic spoon to break up a pint of frozen ice cream.

"We thought it would take only a couple of hours to do our digging because we thought we'd just move the trash out of the way and then just dig a little. But the ground was so hard; it was dry, hard clay," Balboa said.

They started their unexpected hard labor at the front end of the hide, making it narrower toward the back where their feet would go. To say it was slow going would be an understatement. "Ridiculous" is how Balboa described it. They were working so hard and sweating so much, each man had to take several breaks to drink water.

"While three guys pulled security, one guy was digging real fast, breathing hard and heavy, and we did that rotation for like two hours, and we had only enough room for two guys. We were just really going at it," he said. "I couldn't believe this was happening. We're sitting here with all the trash moved out, but the ground is so hard. We did the best we could in the time we had."

Army Sgt. Ryan Coffield in Kuwait in January 2005, before his 3rd Infantry Division unit headed to Ad Duluiyah, Iraq, a town sixty miles north of Baghdad.

This photo was taken of Army Sgt. Ryan Coffield on October 2, 2005, by a soldier in a Humvee two stories below during a mission in Ad Duluiyah, Iraq. He snapped the photo a moment before Coffield was shot in the neck by an enemy sniper who was standing about 150 yards down the road and probably had almost the same angle on Coffield as the photographer. Coffield saw the sniper just before he was shot.

*At a forward operating base in south Baghdad in spring 2008, before a joint patrol with Iraqi national police, Sgt. Stan Crowder cradles his M4 rifle customized with a LaRue Tactical stealth upper receiver, Magpul butt stock, and a Chip McCormick match trigger. The scope is a Leupold Mark 4 with 5.56 mm bullet drop compensation. Snipers like Crowder, a weapons expert, spend their own money to trick-out their military-issue rifles for better performance.*

In September 2003, at the Syrian border northwest of Mosul, Iraq, Sgt. Stan Crowder shot and killed the man pictured in the crosshairs of his rifle. He and the rest of the sniper section with 1st Battalion, 187th Infantry, 101st Airborne Division, had been sent on a reconnaissance mission to the area based on reports from family members of legitimate Iraqi border guards who had been killed and stripped of their uniforms. The impostors, including the man in the photo, had taken the dead men's uniforms and their posts and were allowing contraband and fighters across the border. Crowder and his teammates killed three before the battalion engaged the border crossing with a full-on assault.

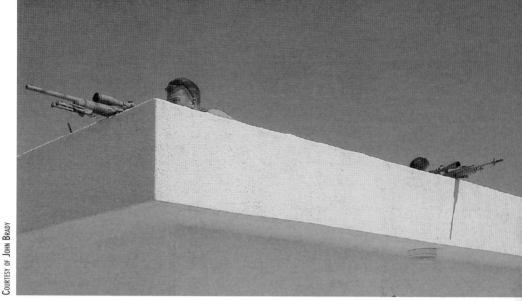

*Army Sgt. John Brady, left, and Sgt. Andrew Furman, crouched behind the wall of a rooftop in Mosul, Iraq, on April 9, 2004, to fend off attacks on their forward operating base. The attack was part of an insurgent uprising that also saw coordinated attacks in several major cities around the country on the same day.*

*(Clockwise from top left) Staff Sgt. Timothy L. Kellner, Sgt. Ben Redus, Pfc. Chris Lochner, and Sgt. John Nebzydoski pose in May 2006, near Iskandiriyah, Iraq, before an all-night trek to overwatch a house southwest of Baghdad. They ended up killing a high-value Al Qaeda target who controlled the entire area between Baghdad and Syria.*

*Army Rangers Sgt. 1st Class Mike Rach (left) and Sgt. 1st Class Joe Lynch stand in front of a Stryker vehicle with their M110 sniper rifles in northern Iraq in 2005. The role of snipers in the 75th Ranger Regiment and Special Forces teams evolved during the wars in Iraq and Afghanistan into one of a sniper assaulter in which multiple targets are engaged quickly at various distances during a raid or assault.*

*Snipers from 1/6 Marines (from left): Cpl. Corey Canterbury, Cpl. Joel Alvarenga, and Sgt. Justin Cooper, pose before a mission in Ramadi, Iraq, in 2005. They took over what they thought was an abandoned building to over-watch a highway, but in the morning the college administration staff that worked in the building began arriving for work. After detaining about forty of the workers, the Marines realized they had to let them go and then got pinned down in an all-day fight.*

*Cpl. Joel Alvarenga of 1/6 Marines stretches over a wall to get a shot with his MK-11 semiautomatic sniper rifle in western Helmand Province, Afghanistan, in July 2008.*

*Cpl. Joel Alvarenga (looking at camera), Cpl. Tim Senkevich (sitting), and Sgt. Justin Cooper of 1/6 Marines, on duty in May 2008 in western Helmand Province, Afghanistan, on a mission they called "reaper farm" because of the number of kills they and nine other snipers racked up from their hide site in an abandoned farming complex.*

*Marine Corps Platoon Commander 1st Lt. Jason Mann kneels in front of a memorial for Sgt. Justin Cooper, a sniper who was killed May 19, 2008, in an ambush in Afghanistan while assisting an infantry platoon. Mann, leader of the Surveillance and Target Acquisition Platoon, 1/6 Marines, was killed two months later when the building he was in at their forward operating base collapsed.*

*Sgt. 1st Class Jim Gilliland, who claims the longest shot in Iraq—1,250 meters—with an M24. 7.62 mm sniper rifle, is shown in July 2005, at OP Hotel in Ramadi aiming a .50 caliber sniper rifle from a top floor window. The observation post was used by a number of sniper teams to scan the roadways and intersections of a city where buried roadside bombs killed hundreds of soldiers and Marines.*

From inside a hide site set up by Army Sgt. Derek Balboa and Staff Sgt. Rey Fernandez in a trash field in southwestern Mosul in 2006, the team could see these dogs rooting around in the garbage; they only saw the snipers when the snipers shooed them away. On the soldiers' second day in the hide site, a goatherd came within a couple of feet of them, slowly realized he was being watched, and ambled away. Though compromised, the team remained concealed for another day.

Army Sgt. Derek Balboa in a self-portrait inside his hide site in a garbage dump in Mosul, Iraq, in late 2006. He and a partner, Staff Sgt. Rey Fernandez, dug an earthen pit in a field covered with gag-inducing trash, where at night the temperature fell to thirty degrees. During the three days they stayed there, it rained and they never got to take a shot.

Sgt. 1st Class Pete Peterson mans his M24 7.62 mm sniper rifle from the hatch of a Humvee at the beginning of the war in Iraq in March 2003. On the tire next to Peterson is an M240 general purpose machine gun. The soft canvas doors and rooftops, open backs, and thin windshields would soon be replaced by heavy armor kits and ballistic glass as the enemy started killing U.S. troops with buried roadside bombs.

*Marines in the Scout Sniper School fire from a seven-hundred-yard position at Marine Corps Base Quantico in July 2009.*

*Roasting under the heat of a spring-time sun in Salman Pak southeast of Baghdad in 2007, Sgt. Mike, a Third Infantry Division sniper, used a ghillie suit during missions in the subtropical marshes near the Tigris River.*

*Master Sgt. Rick, a Special Forces team leader, poses with his sniper rifle before a mission in Tal Afar, Iraq, in 2004. During missions in Baghdad, he often did his sniper reconnaissance missions in full Arabic garb, and, with the help of his driver who did all the talking, got away with it because he looked like an Iraqi though he spoke no Arabic.*

*Third Special Forces Group sniper Sgt. 1st Class Chris, far right, prepares to go on a mission with his team in Iraq during one of two rotations he did there. As an instructor later at the Special Forces Sniper Course at Fort Bragg, North Carolina, he and the other instructors said they drew on lessons learned to teach other snipers and improve their own skills.*

*On a mission in Baghdad in January 2005, Special Forces sniper Sgt. 1st Class Jason wears a patch with the initials "D. E." on his left arm for his friend, Capt. Danny Eggers, who was killed May 29, 2004, when the two were on a mission in Afghanistan.*

*On one of dozens of missions in Ramadi, Iraq, between 2006 and 2007, Sgt. Adam Peeples (left) and Spc. Craig Stout posed for a souvenir photo of themselves on a mission at one of several observation posts in the violent city, an Al Qaeda stronghold for much of the war in Iraq.*

Around 4 a.m., before first light caught up with them, the men decided to stop and get into position. The space, as it turned out, could only accommodate two men. It would be Balboa and their sniper section leader, Sgt. First Class Reyes Fernandez, whom they called "Fern."

"We did rock, paper, scissors to see who was going to go in there. My partner Gus lost, but he wasn't too worried, because it ended up raining and they were sitting in a building," Balboa said.

Fernandez and Balboa placed the plywood with the back end jammed into the backstop and propped it up as an overlay by placing a two-by-four near their shoulders and one by their lower legs. The rest of the wood was dug into the two side trash humps, and the whole thing was covered with the garbage they had removed earlier.

On the slit that looked out toward their objective, Balboa hung a discarded grain sack he found in the dump. It was great camouflage because it was perfectly fouled up like the rest of the detritus around them.

Before dawn, they had settled into their earthen hide, wearing their uniforms under their wet-weather pants and listening to the sounds around them, still keyed up from the nightlong activity of burrowing in. And there was that nervous exhilaration, "that sort of puckered-butt, hoping-nobody-saw-us feeling," Balboa said.

They weren't cold, yet. And they weren't wet, yet. They were just happy the plan had worked out mostly as they had wanted. Having the two men in a building over-watching their trashy position had actually turned out to be a better plan, as time would tell.

For the first few hours, they watched the camera and stayed alert, but the excitement of living like Oscar the Grouch started to fade. Around noon, it began to get cold and clouds rolled in.

It was autumn, around the time of Ramadan, the rainy season. Naturally, around 8 p.m., it started raining and continued to rain for eight hours. Now Fernandez and Balboa were lying on squishy wet ground with a puddle of putrid water creeping up beyond their boots.

The men began sharing their misery by radio, joking with each other about their hide sites. The smugness of having a dry building to sit in was gone for Gus and Brian because the roof had caved in under the weight of the rain. Balboa told them he couldn't take a shot even if he wanted to because he was shivering like a poodle.

And the prolonged exposure to the cold, wet ground was causing him to hesitate.

"I couldn't pee. We laughed about it later. After like the seventeenth hour, I started talking to my camera because I was getting delirious," Balboa said.

Besides the shivering cold, the culprit for his biological problem was a boulder he couldn't get away from that was pushing against his kidney. He scooched as far from it as he could, in Fernandez's direction, turned onto his side, and "went."

"So now I was laying in my own urine. That's the way it is. In sniper or recon, even in the infantry, you do things outside the box, mission or situation dictating, you put it out of the way. I've done spooning when I want to stay warm," he explained.

The urine wasn't that bad, he said. At least it was his. After the rain the sides of their hide started to deteriorate and little pieces of trash were seeping in, slithering down next to them. "I'd pick it up and throw it out the front or stuff it into the side, or I'd see something hanging that was all black and green and I was like, 'I don't even want to touch that,' so I'd shove it up in the crack like, 'Ew, what am I touching?' Probably somebody's, like, I just think the worst," he said, recalling the details with a scrunched face. "I'm like, this really sucks, this is not how I figured it to be. We were supposed to have a kill by now and get out of here, not stay here for a full three days."

But there they were on their second night. It was about twenty degrees, and their first unwanted guests showed up.

Fernandez and Balboa could hear some rustling behind them, some movement, but they couldn't see that it was a pack of about ten dogs rooting around with their noses. The guys in the building had eyes on them, and as the dogs went about their scavenging, they started to come around the sides and to the front of the hide. One of them lifted its head up and looked right at Balboa.

"I kind of made a little 'click' sound and looked him in the eye, and he ran off. To me it meant I did a really good job, because if the dogs didn't even know we were there and couldn't smell us, it was good," Balboa said. "It was that much more reinforced when the guy came and literally walked on the wood and our position."

It was a goatherd that the other team saw from about 1,500 meters out. As he slowly made his way closer over the course of an hour, the team watching him felt sure he was unarmed, but everyone was nervous. This was the perfect hide site; it wasn't supposed to be compromised.

The guys in the building on the radio told Balboa and Fernandez that "if the guy even flinches or farts sideways, we'll light him up."

Balboa and Fernandez prepared themselves by lying on their backs with their weapons at the ready between their legs and the soles of their feet on the plywood, positioned to kick it upward and come out guns blazing.

"The guy had his goats. He was just meandering and didn't know or think anything of it, and I'm like sweatin' bullets. We went silent on the radio; we're sitting there breathing heavy," Balboa said, estimating it was about 10 a.m.

The man wandered toward their hide. First the snipers heard rustling, then, footsteps. The man was walking on their plywood, and the snipers could hear him. Tension filled their hearts as the man bent down over the front of the hide.

"We see him, then we see a sandal, then another sandal, and we were like, 'This guy doesn't even know we're here.' He stepped right in front of our loophole, which was about twelve inches," Balboa said.

The man fished around in the right-side trash pile, then took another step down the gently sloping trash pile in front of the hide, putting himself about chest level with Balboa's M24, which was aimed at the man.

The goatherd squinted his eyes and focused on the crude opening, but the hide was dark so he couldn't tell what he was looking at. He stepped closer. Then he stepped closer again, craning his neck a little.

"Now he's like two feet out, and I stick my barrel right outside the grain sack, which is twelve inches from my face. I put my face out just enough so he could see it was an American soldier and an American gun. I didn't want him to think we were insurgents because some people care and would tell the Iraqi police who would come and shoot the place up," Balboa said.

Balboa gave him a slow nod, and the man quickly backed up and kept his gaze fixed on the American sniper. "His eyes got real big. He looked at us, backed up, and kind of walked away," he said. "I didn't say anything to him; once he saw the barrel, he knew."

The team in the building watched the goatherd mosey on down with his goats and go about his business. "He obviously didn't have any insurgency ties or tell anybody because we stayed there another twenty-four hours," Balboa said.

Dogs and goatherds aside, the team did eventually get a nibble near the bait. It was midafternoon on their second full day there, and they were still nervous they'd be overrun, not fully believing the goatherd was an innocent passerby. Even the chain of command knew they had been exposed but told them to stay put.

A young man drove up close to the pole where the camera was, riding a beat-up moped-style bike. Both teams had him in sight. The team in the building was about two hundred meters away but didn't have a good shot. So the trash team snipers said they'd take a shot from their four-hundred-meter position if the guy gave them cause.

"I have him in my crosshairs. He got off his bike, opened up the bike seat, took out what looked like a pistol, and cocked it. All he had to do was point it at the camera, and I would have been able to do my deal," Balboa said.

Instead, the man sat on his bike, looked at the device a couple of times, looked down, looked at it again, and either thought twice about it or got scared and drove off.

Shot denied. One more night in the pit.

Around midday the next day, the boys from A Company rumbled up to within four feet of the hide site in a Stryker vehicle and dropped the hatch for the snipers. By this time Fernandez and Balboa were close to hypothermia. And that wasn't all.

"They were hooting and hollering about coming to get us, and then when we got in there, they were like, 'Oh my God! You guys stink so bad,' like to the point where the whole ride back, guys who normally try to stay behind the slat armor because of the IEDs were hanging outside the hatch gagging and stuff," Balboa said.

As he headed toward the vehicle, he snapped a couple of pictures he could use later for training other guys.

The team wasn't happy about being extracted in daylight, but in keeping with the warning to any locals who might have been watching, the commanders wanted people in the area to see that their snipers could be hiding anywhere at anytime.

For those idiots who might think the threat was gone and come in and shoot the camera anyway, the commanders left the building team in place to take care of them.

Balboa burned his uniform, cleaned his snivel and wet-weather gear, and washed the boots he'd been wearing for seven months, not wanting to discard a good pair of boots, even stinky ones.

"Even though we got compromised and we exfilled during the day, I still consider it to have been a very successful sniper mission. The only thing that didn't work out is we didn't get four guys in there," Balboa said. "The training aspect of it is thinking outside the box. You can only use buildings so many times."

By 2005, when they made their trash-pit hide site, he noted, a lot of American snipers had used a lot of hide sites in Mosul.

The trash pit was a new frontier for them.

"From that position we could see everything in front of us. We could see the corner where the cars came in, and we could almost see the building our buddies were in," he said. "I consider that to have been a success."

## HIDING IN THE WILD, WILD EAST

Millions of miles were driven over the years on Iraq's roads by tens of thousands of uniformed and civilian road warriors who slipped behind the wheels of trucks, tractor trailers, and Humvees to keep the war machine supplied.

Tons of stuff like boots, bullets, and fuel; shampoo, chow, and water; vehicle parts, aircraft parts, and weapons parts was moved around on Iraq's main routes and secondary roads from Basra to Baghdad, Musayyib to Mosul, and Karbala to Kirkuk.

During the surge of 2007, when the number of troops in country was close to 150,000, the highest level of the war, more than 475,000 tons of food and several thousand tons more of construction material such as concrete barriers, steel, and wood were shipped to Kuwait from the Defense Supply Center Philadelphia, then taken over land by truck hundreds of miles into Iraq.

It was a part of the war that rarely made the front page—or any page—of the newspaper in more than seven years of the U.S. presence in Iraq. Still, that log train never stopped, even when the going got rough, even when the drivers and their security escorts were killed by crude, homemade bombs that exploded as they passed through, detonated by low-level cowards hiding in the shadows with cell phones and garage door openers.

The bombers didn't get as many as they might have, however, and lost a lot more of their own, denied their evil deeds by people like Sgt. Ray, a First Infantry Division sniper who did his part by killing several bomb emplacers on the main supply routes of eastern Baghdad and coming up with innovative ways to be where they least expected him.

"We were in a very sporting environment," he said of the area around Forward Operating Base Rustamiyah on the south side of the infamous Sadr City, a forsaken section on the east end of Iraq's capital whose more than one million residents were steeped in poverty, soaking in sewage, and surrounded by Mahdi army militiamen. Sadr City's troubles were many, and they spilled over its boundaries to feed a level of violence that refused to be tamed for years.

It was on the eastern and southern flanks of this part of the city, which looks like a perfectly rectangular grid when viewed on a satellite map, that Sgt. Ray and his team of snipers worked at night to watch over and keep safe the U.S. supply convoys that rumbled through.

The big supply routes—the north-south Route Pluto and the roughly east-west Route Predator—were like highway boulevards, split roads with two lanes on each side, divided by a canal, sewer trench, or concrete island of some sort.

Along that divider, the commander of Second Battalion, Six-teenth Infantry built a series of concrete observation towers in early 2007 about every quarter mile, with some standing sentry over traffic control points. From these makeshift towers, Iraqi police armed with AK-47 assault rifles could watch the traffic points and provide security for their counterparts on the ground. Except on the nights when snipers like Ray and his crew arrived.

"We would just pull the Iraqi police off the tower, get them to pile their cell phones into a corner and their AKs into another corner, tell them to pull out their mattresses, drink tea, smoke, whatever you want. We'd say, 'We got security tonight,' and it got to where we didn't even need an interpreter anymore. They would just get down and hand us their stuff," Sgt. Ray said. "They really enjoyed that."

And the Iraqis weren't the only ones who enjoyed it. Ray's security element, usually soldiers who didn't get a chance to get off the base much, welcomed the foreignness of hanging out with the Iraqis—while they kept an eye on them. "We would take sup-ply clerks or someone from another company. They would drink tea with the Iraqis, have fun. For some reason soldiers like to drink tea," he said.

The snipers were grouped into two teams of five, with three people in each tower and two people on the ground. They only worked at night and never hid in the same tower twice in a row.

While the tea was brewing downstairs, Sgt. Ray and his team would watch for trouble brewing on the highway. The towers were really just six-foot-wide vertical culvert pipes with a ladder on the inside to climb the twenty feet to a circular ledge. From there the snipers could watch and take a shot from a standing or squatting position through little windows that measured about eighteen by twenty-four inches. Above them were eight more feet of pipe with a vented concrete seal at the top.

The main supply routes they had to keep bomb-free were two of the biggest in Baghdad, and notoriously bad for attacks. The sniper towers were something new, and they worked.

"We had to be very creative in how to use snipers in Iraq. You can't sit on top of someone's house because there could be retribution for the people who own the house. I built towers all over the place," said Lt. Col. Ralph Kauzlarich, commander of the 2-16 Infantry, a unit under the First Infantry Division's Fourth Brigade Combat Team.

"It was harassment, if you will. Psychologically it really scares the insurgents when someone gets shot and, believe me, everyone hears about it and they tend not to go into that area anymore."

At first, Sgt. Ray recalled, Kauzlarich was leery of sending his snipers out in sector without a full complement of infantrymen for security. But as the snipers found success and developed their own intelligence, they gained their commander's confidence.

"We did our research. We found what we thought was a dirty mosque. We set up around it and shot some people moving weapons in and out of the mosque. After that it became 'Okay, now you guys are starting to contribute to the battlefield,' so he took us off the security detail and kind of took the leash off for a couple of months," Ray said.

He placed his snipers in adjacent towers so they could have eyes on the same objective while covering for one another if something went wrong. They had multiple angles on the same target and the advantage of aerial surveillance from an aerostat blimp at their base, which gave them even more intelligence and a sharper, broader view of what they were seeing.

The wider roads in the east were the ones that could accommodate the size and speed of the larger supply trucks. Because of their location on the city's fringes, the roads were also magnets for bomb emplacers who, Sgt. Ray said, were more willing to take a chance to place their bombs on the highways than in the inner city.

"On the road you have plenty of area for shrapnel to land before it goes into friendly areas, so you'd see a higher percentage of devices on the open roads or a road next to a junkyard or soccer field than you would on a road with apartment buildings on both sides," he said.

The snipers ran the tower mission three times a week and took at least one shot every other week. They were up against the same types of bomb emplacers who had always been willing to do the job, disgruntled and desperate locals looking to make some money. But by the time Sgt. Ray's battalion got there in February 2007, a new and more deadly kind of bomb known as an EFP, or "explosively formed projectile," had been in use for at least a year.

The first improvised explosive devices, or IEDs, were mostly made of artillery rounds scrounged from the vast stockpiles left by Saddam Hussein's army. Those types of bombs are technically known as blast mines because the raw blast from the mass of explosives is what affects the target vehicle.

Later on, the enemy made the blast mine more effective by increasing the amount of explosives. But U.S. troops began seeing a more deadly device in 2006 when plastic explosives were placed on the back of a cone of metal, usually copper, and affixed to a roadside tree or a guardrail at the height of a Humvee door. When detonated, the force of the blast inverted the cone to form almost a dart of superheated metal capable of penetrating even very substantial armor.

While the city was under curfew in the early morning hours, miles-long convoys with the heaviest trucks barreled through on the darkened roads that skirted that eastern edge of Baghdad, their drivers praying they could dodge those EFPs.

"I had a very specific area that I had to control and make sure it remained EFP-free. The dumb bad guys would make themselves available to get a bullet, and we would provide them with one. On the road at night, we'd see them down there, and we'd shoot them out of their sandals," Kauzlarich said.

The tower missions had a direct effect on the safety of the convoys, and violence on the roads was kept at bay. But an even more important part of guarding the truckers, and more difficult in its execution, was the job of going after the insurgent nerve centers to kill or capture the elusive bomb makers, the bomb planters, and the men who made it all possible with money, supplies, and more money.

Those larger-scale missions were planned and executed by the battalion—sometimes in concert with another nonmilitary government agency—and a larger complement of infantrymen and air assets, depending on the size of the operation.

Sgt. Ray, who was reluctant to use his full name, in part to secure his family's privacy and safety, played his role as a sniper in support of those secret direct-action missions, nighttime raids on the homes of known high-value targets.

The 2-16 Infantry arrived in its area of operations and wasted no time in hitting back with a strong show of manpower and a willingness to crush the violence, as the surge intended. After a few raids in which the suspects were either killed or captured, a spate of direct fire attacks on the infantry's base would happen like clockwork.

"Every time we shot or captured someone big like a finance guy or a bomb maker, the locals shot rockets at us twenty-four hours later," Sgt. Ray said. The attacks were generally lame, but the attackers were predictable in their timing, so the sniper section hatched a plan to go after them.

The local thugs, presumably hired by the henchmen of the captured or dead guy, were firing their rockets from trucks driven onto a field near the Diyala River. Surrounded by high ground, the field was a good launch site. But there was a weak point, and Sgt. Ray and his boys found it on a satellite map. One side of the field was open to the river, on the other side of which was a wide-open area where the snipers could easily hide and probably get a clear shot.

There was only one small hitch they had to overcome.

Because commanders in Iraq each had a specific area of operations delineated by a dark line on a map, simply crossing the river into another guy's territory was dangerous—unless that commander knew about the mission—because it could lead to U.S. troops firing on each other.

Even though it was during the height of the troop surge, the commander in charge of the area across the river was stretched thin for manpower and considered the area near the river—the farthest edge of his section of operations—quiet. And it was, which made it perfect for the snipers. The guys launching the rockets from the field assumed there would be no risk of getting caught as they rarely saw an American patrol on the other side of the river.

After an exchange of messages between the commanders clearing the way for the sniper op, the snipers waited to launch.

Using the same satellite map, they had chosen what seemed to be a good hide site, a natural depression in the earth that looked as if it could have been an old, worn crater from a rocket or a bomb. It appeared to be practically isolated except for two small villages on either side.

It was around 10 p.m. the first time they went there. Bravo Company had captured someone of interest so the likelihood of a rocket launch looked probable.

The snipers left their base with five gun trucks armed with a long-range advanced scout surveillance system and a .50-caliber machine gun and crossed the river on a bridge a few miles south of their crater. They took Route Crow, a main road north, and at a bend in the road, the patrol slowed down so the sniper contingent could slip out while the Humvees kept rolling about a mile past the crater.

Still an unknown, the crater, which they had only seen on a satellite map, ended up being pretty good. It was about three feet deep and twelve feet wide, enough space for the six men on the team—two shooters; Sgt. Ray; the team leader, on scope; and three men—to watch the network of trails behind them.

The soil was soft, "kind of like Midwestern topsoil," Ray said, and the hole was symmetrical, with a lot of grass around it that would help conceal them. They infiltrated the site by following the river right to it.

Behind them were Route Crow and a network of footpaths to an open area. There was a trail between the two quiet, sparsely populated villages, which were about two hundred meters apart, much closer than they looked on the map. The snipers' hide site was dead center between the little clusters of houses.

"It was really a luck game," Sgt. Ray said. But it worked out perfectly for the first night's mission, though not the mission they expected. The enemy launched no rockets, but the snipers shot two guys laying a bomb on the main road into Bravo Company's combat outpost.

"It wasn't the target we wanted, but an equally important target," he said.

Buoyed by their success, they pulled the crater mission four more times and were able to nail it at least twice when the rocket assailants were there, killing an unknown number of them. They also isolated and captured a rocket truck.

They started infiltrating at night ahead of planned raids or snatch missions and stayed hidden in the crater for a full day, doing the part of the job some outsiders might think of as the glamorous part. It was summer, and the weather in the crater was hot and uncomfortable. The beating sun soared to 120 degrees and baked the soldiers into their body armor as they lay flat and waited for nightfall. "We couldn't drink a lot of water. There's nowhere to urinate, and you can only carry so much, maybe three quarts for an all-day affair," Ray said.

The snipers had wanted to wear something other than what Sgt. Ray called their "glow-in-the-dark ACUs," but they didn't receive permission. "We're not Special Forces, we're just a regular unit. We asked for bongo trucks and local vehicles and asked to dress like Iraqis over our body armor, and we were told that would put the locals in danger," he said. "Erring on the side of safety, if we did get contact, I'd rather have armor on me than nothing. We shot in helmets, we shot in full kit."

They put branches and leaves on top of a thin canvas Sgt. Ray had, and as uncomfortable as they were in biding their time, the missions at night went off without a hitch.

Until the fifth mission. And it happened to be the one in which they took a new platoon leader with them to show him just how dangerous their work can be.

"I was trying to show him what we do, show him how we move," Sgt. Ray said. "He thought we were lazy because he'd only seen us on the raids. He thought we went over the top of a rooftop and laid down. He hadn't seen our sniper-only missions before."

A crazy infiltration route and a dose of humble pie contributed greatly to the young lieutenant's education on snipers. "We wanted to break him off so we gave him the .50-cal and two magazines of ammo. He was carrying about sixty-nine pounds on top of his body armor," Ray said.

They started their infiltration by being dropped off three roads farther away from their usual point on Route Crow and approached the crater site in a big, sweeping U-shaped route before making a bold five-kilometer hump to get into place.

"We hit every irrigation ditch, every sewer ditch, every uneven terrain we could possibly find," said Sgt. Ray, who was point man and as such was the first to arrive at Route Crow where he took a knee and checked security like a hawk before pushing across with his team. As he performed his stop-look-listen drill, Ray didn't notice right away what the lieutenant was up to. Exhausted and demonstrating just how wet he was behind the ears, the lieutenant decided he would take a little rest.

"He did a rucksack flop like he was in Ranger School instead of taking a knee and pulling his weapon up and pulling security in his sector. He just laid down like a parachute landing and was using his rifle as a back rest as he pulled out his canteen," Sgt. Ray said. "I had to go over and slap him upside the head and tell him, 'This is the real deal,' that he had to take a knee like everybody else. We had a lot of problems with this particular lieutenant, but he started to realize there's more to being a sniper than just laying on a rooftop."

And then the officer got his next lesson in sniping—how a hide site gets compromised.

After the team crossed Route Crow and moved through a series of cornfields below one of the little nearby villages, it settled into the crater, which had become wonderfully familiar by now, almost too good to be true.

Lying in their usual positions, one of the guys told Sgt. Ray that there was "something funny" over by his place. It was funny—like an exploding cigar. "It was a 155 mm artillery round with a wire sticking out right in the middle of our circle. So it was time to go," Ray said.

He cut the wires on the bomb, and they all made a run for the gun trucks after calling for a ride home, leaving the crater for the last time, their newly educated platoon leader in tow.

The tower missions continued after that, and the only time it got quiet, Sgt. Ray said, was during an unexpected cease-fire called by Mahdi army leader Moqtada al-Sadr in August 2007 that was supposed to last six months.

But for Sgt. Ray, the quiet wouldn't last that long. Within a week of the announced cease-fire, after eight months in country, he was being medically evacuated following his miraculous survival of an EFP attack that critically wounded two other soldiers in his Humvee.

It happened on September 2 when, after a night of training at a firing range a few clicks away from their own base on Route Brewer, Ray and some of the other snipers decided to combine a reconnaissance mission at daybreak with a run for breakfast at Forward Operating Base Loyalty just west of Sadr City, where the chow hall was superior to their own.

Taking the usual security precautions, the group of snipers rolled out of the firing range around 6 a.m. in four Humvees with the intention of videotaping the route to FOB Loyalty so they could study it later for possible new hide sites.

Sgt. Ray rode shotgun, which he hated. He is taller than six foot five inches, which might not matter in a roomy, commercially sold Hummer, but in a tactical Humvee, the front passenger seat is crammed with stuff like a computer screen that, among other things, tracks "blue" or friendly forces, and a bulky radio console. On top of that, the seat is not readily adjustable.

He rode with his knees up to his chest.

A rarity in the sniper community, Ray had been a member of the Presidential Escort Platoon in the Third Infantry Regiment's Old Guard at Fort Myer in Arlington, Virginia, for almost three years before being assigned to the 2-16 Infantry.

"I was one of the sword guys," he said of his first duty assignment. He was also one of the short guys. "Our group was six-foot-six to six-foot-nine. If you were shorter than six-foot-five, you were kicked out of our platoon."

During his assignment in the Old Guard, Sgt. Ray did missions like Ronald Reagan's funeral in 2004 and George W. Bush's second inauguration in 2005. He did general officer retirements at the Pentagon, and state dinners and head of state visits at the White House, and he lined the perimeter of the Rose Garden with the Marines during presidential speeches.

"We were the lawn statues, the pretty boys standing out in the grass," he said. He volunteered to walk the solemn vigil at the Tomb of the Unknowns at Arlington National Cemetery when the platoon in charge of that mission had its Christmas party. All the while he educated himself on the art of sniping by reading everything he could.

Ray was only too happy to leave behind the trappings and duties of Washington's ceremonial life to do his part in Baghdad, and as the four Humvees weaved their way through the serpentine wire barriers at a checkpoint on Route Brewer that early morning, he was brutally cut down by the same guys he hunted at night.

"We took nine EFPs into our truck," Sgt. Ray said, still amazed that he was alive years later to tell about it.

Two projectiles burned through underneath the dash, piercing the blue force tracker and his radio, knocking them out; one stopped in his ballistic glass window; one went into the air intake and one into the engine; one went through his door and burned into his stomach, and another sliced across his back and took off the sniper's leg in the seat behind him; one flew past his chest and took off the 40 mm grenades on his vest before taking off his gunner's leg and zipping under the driver's arms above his lap and out the door on the other side; and the last one hit the gun turret. A tenth projectile grazed the top of the cab.

"I thought I was dead, I thought I was cut in half and bleeding out at the time," he said. "I refused to let them take care of me because you don't treat the dead."

Sgt. Ray had an EFP stuck between his armor plate and his groin pad. The searing hot projectile had burned through the groin pad and one of those big riggers belts.

"I felt that heat and thought that heat was the feeling of something going straight through me, and I didn't want them to drag my body out and leave my legs in the truck," he said.

The whole time the mayhem inside the Humvee was unfolding, the gun trucks were being attacked with small arms fire from behind concrete walls. The 240B machine guns the soldiers were fighting back with were not able to penetrate the wall. So the snipers went to the tail hatch of their Humvees and pulled out their Barrett .50-caliber rifles, which punched right through the walls, killing more than fifteen enemy fighters.

In the attack, Ray was struck by the door handle to his right, which hit the sheath of his femoral artery and had to be surgically removed from his hip. Another of the copper slugs seared a hole the size of a large hand through his groin pad just below his belly button and burned its way through flesh and fat to the muscle layer. The muscle and flesh from his right hip to his spine were burned through by another slug that came in through his side armor plate and deflected off his back plate. Plus, he had a concussion and his arm was broken in three places.

The snipers never got breakfast that morning, and Sgt. Ray was medically retired by the Army because of his injuries.

He's not sure how many rocket guys were killed from the crater hide site, but the enemy stopped using the field as a launch pad for their direct fire missions. Instead, they began launching mortars from somewhere inside the city.

"We enjoyed the fact that they thought they had a safe spot because the other unit never patrolled over there," Sgt. Ray said.

The team had effectively denied the rocket launchers their terrain and forced them to resort to a more inaccurate way of attacking.

He didn't get to do everything he wanted in the Army, like trying out for Special Forces or continuing to work as a sniper. But Sgt. Ray made a difference to the road warriors who drove their tons of supplies all over Iraq for years after he left.

## WITNESS TO CONTROVERSY

In July 2002, less than a year into U.S. operations in Afghanistan, a secret operation was planned to bring in a high-level Taliban leader.

He was known to frequently visit his ancestral home in the village of Deh Rawood, about 250 miles southwest of Kabul in Uruzgan province.

Men from Army, Navy, and Air Force Special Operations units were brought in from other areas of the country to take part in the major operation, which would unfold over the course of a few days before a well-timed snatch-and-grab raid took place.

Air support for the ground operation included an AC-130 gunship and a B-52 bomber, and in the ridgelines around the village, teams of snipers, observers, and communications specialists would burrow in and generate intelligence in the days leading up to it.

"Our job in a situation like that was not to interdict the target in question. Our job was to observe and to report and to corral anyone who tried to come through the mountain passes and attempted to escape," said Sgt. First Class Ricky, a sniper with the Third Special Forces Group.

He, several Navy SEALs, and other Third Group snipers were on different teams of eight to twelve men that were broken down into smaller teams and positioned on adjacent mountain ridges a few hundred meters apart. They could see the passes nearest their hides, and they could also see the same things in the village from different angles.

Deh Rawood is a cluster of small village compounds on a valley floor at about eight thousand feet in elevation where a pattern of streams and irrigation canals flows near the larger Helmand River running through the valley. About 1,500 meters away and above the valley, the observing and reporting teams were tucked strategically into the ridgelines.

"The village is more urban in the center and starts to get more rural out to about six hundred to one thousand meters to the base of the mountains. There were a lot of irrigation ditches in the fields, and on the back side of the mountains, there were vast opium fields. They would bring all the opium to this village for sale and move it down the rivers," Sgt. First Class Joey, another sniper with the Third Special Forces Group, said.

The teams infiltrated at 10 p.m. by helicopter, far enough away that the sounds of the helicopters' rotor blades chopping through the air wouldn't compromise the mission before it even started. They then embarked on a sweaty, punishing slog on hardscrabble terrain for at least two miles, each man carrying three or four gallons of water, which weighs twenty-four to thirty-two pounds, and humping rucksacks filled with not only what they would need to live without resupply for the duration of the mission, like food, but also radio equipment, batteries, and the munitions they would need for the fight. Each human pack mule was carrying more than one hundred pounds.

"It doesn't sound like a long walk, but in that kind of terrain and carrying that kind of weight, it's slow because of the rocks and steep terrain," Sgt. First Class Ricky said. "You're carrying guns, everyone's under night vision, and you're walking all night until damn near when the sun comes up."

That kind of trekking with that amount of gear would lay the average person out for days. But on a mission at war, where the timing of the teams' arrival on the ridges was critical and being compromised would mean certain disaster, there was no room for a weak link. Every man was physically fit and capable of carrying his own weight. Everyone was switched on high, and the level of adrenaline pumping meant the men had to force themselves to chill out after the extreme feat of just getting there.

"In that situation, for the first forty-four to forty-eight hours, you really have to make guys lay down because they want to stay up, they want to see what's going on. They're jacked up from the infil, and you have to tell them, 'Hey, go lay down, get some sleep man, because your turn is coming and in eight hours my ass is going to sleep,'" Sgt. First Class Joey said.

Now that the challenge of reaching the hide site without getting caught was finished, a well-rehearsed chaos began with the swift unpacking of gear and each man finding his place to settle into the craggy ground before sunrise.

They had to become a part of the landscape, go into still-life mode by either lying down or crouching in the rocks, moving very slowly and avoiding positions that would create a silhouette against the sun. Succumbing to primitive caveman desires to start a fire was out of the question.

"We like our jobs and doing what we do. It definitely takes a different kind of person to sit up there for days on end in Indian land watching over targets with bad guys walking all over the place and trying to figure out who's bad and who's not," Sgt. First Class Ricky said.

Goatherds, he said, may not walk right up to the hide site, but they may see it and the sniper has to figure out his next move. "Now you have to weigh the risk. He's fifty meters away. Do we lay here or do we freakin' bug out, what do we do?" Sgt. First Class Ricky said. "I've been lucky, I've rolled the dice a time or two, and he either didn't see us or he didn't tell anybody he saw us."

And there were the more stressful tasks of resting, sleeping, biding time, and keeping calm, which take the patience and maturity of seasoned operators who can endure the restrictive and uncomfortable environment in the intimate company of a bunch of other people.

It was rocky, and the wind could turn a man's skin to leather. When the sun went down, the temperature dropped more than twenty degrees, which, after a humid ninety-degree day, made for a frigid night under the stars.

Basic bodily needs, like eating and eliminating waste, were not afterthoughts. In fact, for some it was a tactical art form.

"That's part of the reason we go through all this training like Ranger School and some of the other schools that deprive you of sleep and food. You just learn to operate under those types of conditions," said Sgt. First Class Ricky. When people are lying in a hide site for several days, they move so little that the urge to eat is lessened—and so are its effects.

"I'll tell you what we did for sanitation. We would pop Imodium, and it stops you up so you don't have to defecate for five days. Of course when you get back, that's a whole 'nother story," he said with wide eyes and a convincing nod.

As the hours turned to days and the moon and the sun came and went, layers of different priorities were at work around the clock and each team member had a specific task. The sensitive operation involved communicating with the other services and coordinating reports on what they were seeing.

"You had guys on glass looking at targets, you had guys on the computer making products to send back, you had guys taking photos and uploading them into the computer and labeling them with a new labeling system," Sgt. First Class Joey said, explaining that over the course of the snipers' many deployments to the war zone, the digital equipment they used for observation and reconnaissance grew increasingly more sophisticated. They had to learn it all, sometimes while on the job.

Some guys did old-fashioned sketching with one hand, while with the other hand, they used the latest laser range finders to build quick-reference range cards in case they had to take a shot.

At a distance of 1,500 meters from the village center, the Special Operations teams weren't at firing range and they couldn't identify individual faces, but they could see a lot of other things, like routine human activities and obvious hostile actions; they could see guns and the types of vehicles coming and going from the village complex.

The teams used a tagging system to give every vehicle a code and tracked parked and returning vehicles, how long they stayed, who was in them, whether they carried guns and what kind, and whether the vehicles were loaded or unloaded and when.

"We tracked just every little detail, all things, and we might follow a particular car of interest. There was a road that skirted the outside of the village into this flat area and continued up into the mountains. If the car moved past our position, we could pass it off to the other teams, and everybody picked up and had eyes on. If it eventually disappeared, we could pass it off to an air asset," Sgt. First Class Joey said.

The operation to catch the Taliban leader had been postponed a few times before the teams were mobilized, so there was a lot of hurry up and wait in the days before they infiltrated their mountain positions. Postponement of an operation is a classic war zone occurrence caused by a lot of factors, like the availability or condition of people and equipment, the weather, or a change in the intelligence landscape.

After the operation began and everyone was in place, several days passed with no evidence of the man's presence, like a sighting of his usual entourage.

But on their fourth day in the hide sites, the teams did witness what became one of the earliest controversies for the American military in Afghanistan, when the AC-130 circling overhead in support of the ground operation fired upon the village in what became known as "the wedding party bombing," though there was no wedding and the attack was provoked, the Special Forces snipers said, by militants on the ground foolishly eager to shoot down a mighty American gunship.

During the Vietnam era counterinsurgency doctrine took shape as leaders realized that the way to beat an insurgency was to dry up its source of support by winning over the people. The focus shifted from dominating terrain and the enemy to controlling the "human terrain."

Tactical operations, however, must be directed at strategic goals, and although the tactical focus on the human terrain did feed the strategic goal of counterinsurgency, America was defeated by the shift in public opinion against the effort. The North Vietnamese commanding general, Vo Nguyen Giap, said in a 1989 interview with Morley Safer as excerpted in *The Vietnam War: An Encyclopedia of Quotations*, written by Howard Langer and published by Greenwood Press in 2005, "The war was fought on many fronts. At that time the most important one was American public opinion."

In the current wars, America's enemies had realized early on that they could capitalize on any collateral damage that might be inflicted by U.S. forces by feeding images to the Western media. It was a short jump from there to planning operations to produce images that would garner the desired media effect. American military leaders lagged behind in realizing the shift in the center of gravity, which gave the enemy the opportunity to exploit what happened that night.

"There was an air strike because there were antiaircraft in that village trying to shoot down American aircraft," Sgt. First Class Ricky said.

After the AC-130 fired upon the village to take out the antiaircraft positions the snipers had seen, the first reports that reached the media claimed that the Americans had bombed a wedding party and killed three hundred people who were simply firing their rifles in the air to celebrate the marriage. The Taliban seized on the possibility of exploiting the media and turned a tactical defeat into a strategic victory.

"As far as I'm concerned," Ricky said, "it was just a ruse for them, a scapegoat to say the reason they were shooting was celebratory fire, which is bullcrap."

A senior Army spokesman and Afghan officials who went to the village within forty-eight hours of the attack in the summer of 2002 reported that the attack more accurately had killed around thirty and injured sixty and that a bomb was never dropped. "The B-52 never engaged," the Army spokesman said eight years after the event, citing what he could of classified reports on the event. "If it had engaged, there would have been a giant crater.

But that's almost irrelevant. People were killed, that's all they knew. It just wasn't nearly as many as they had said, and there was no wedding."

The military never disputed the shooting by the AC-130. A joint American and Afghan investigation later reported that something akin to a bridal shower had been going on in one of the buildings and when the shooting started, a lot of people, including the women, ran outside and became mingled with the antiaircraft shooters, who were also running for cover.

But the report of a bombed wedding party persisted, mostly because there were no independent observers on the objective, a pattern that repeated itself as the war in Afghanistan continued through the decade.

American and coalition troops learned that their ruthless enemy had no regard for the Law of War, which is after all essentially a gentlemen's agreement between nation states that it has no stake in. The enemy regularly used its own people as human shields, launching attacks from "protected" targets such as schools, mosques, or even a group of innocent civilians, knowing that not only would civilians be killed when the uniformed forces responded, but also that the images they produced would be broadcast around the world.

Immediately following those provoked attacks, the enemy issued its own news releases showing images of dead civilians, including children. Too salacious for the international media to ignore, images of the carnage, such as the alleged wedding party, were quickly posted, and the Taliban's version of events was reported without all the surrounding facts.

The Taliban in Afghanistan, with its own official spokesman and Web site, gained superiority on the stage of public opinion as the U.S. military slowly worked to change the way it disseminated its own information, sometimes by embedding journalists with units undertaking large operations. But with aviation resources in Afghanistan stretched thin, it was not always possible to get the media to remote outposts, nor was the media always there in large enough numbers.

Sgt. First Class Ricky and Sgt. First Class Joey said that in four days of watching the village of Deh Rawood, they saw no activity that would have indicated a wedding, including celebratory fire. What they did see that night was, instead, a barrage of fire and tracers coming from 14.5 mm antiaircraft guns, aimed at the American aircraft circling overhead.

"It's the tactic of the enemy. They know our weakness is political correctness," Sgt. First Class Ricky said.

The role of the ridgeline teams, he said, was primarily one of observing and reporting, so when the American pilots asked for confirmation that they were being shot at, the teams not only confirmed it but indicated which courtyards the shooting was coming from.

"We on the ground did not clear weapons hot for pilots or anything. They said, 'Hey, we're being shot at,' and the rules of engagement back then were a lot more lax," Sgt. First Class Ricky recalled. "When you have a Spectre gunship flying around up there, they know they're being shot at and they know where it's coming from. They just double-tapped with our information."

As it turns out, the Taliban leader they were seeking was not caught that night, even though the teams had what they considered to be reliable intelligence that he would be there to attend a big meeting.

"We saw plenty of antiaircraft guns, plenty from my vantage point. And there were tons of guys carrying AK-47s around. Obviously if there is antiaircraft shooting, there are bad people there," Sgt. First Class Joey said.

Making matters stickier for the Americans was the relationship between the leaders of the conventional and the unconventional sides of the Army, which back in 2002 didn't share information as readily or even work together as partners as they did later on. The details of what soldiers like Sgt. First Class Ricky and Sgt. First Class Joey knew they had seen that night were not relayed to regular Army investigators trying to set the record straight.

The tragedy of the civilian casualties lingered, but the attack had effectively cleared the village, if not the man they were seeking.

"We definitely killed a lot of bad guys, just not the bad guy we were after. When the cleanup crew rolled in there, they rolled into that guy's home and stayed there and wound up keeping a presence there. When I went back the next year, that was the house I stayed in for six months," Sgt. First Class Joey said.

The military's operational methods and the rules of engagement shifted as each new four-star general came in to manage the war in Afghanistan, but the sting of the wedding party faded only a little as time passed.

"Those civilian casualties were a black eye on us and what we were trying to do over there," said Sgt. First Class Ricky.

# CHAPTER TEN

# SNEAKING AROUND
# IN SALMAN PAK

For the better part of a year, Sgt. Mike and his team of snipers saw their corner of Iraq from the point of view of a bug, crawling around in the dirt, lurking among soggy saw blade grass, and sneaking through tropical fruit groves at the speed of slugs.

It was exciting, dangerous, and uncomfortable, a sniper's dream.

They were patient and worked hard to blend in by altering the clothing they wore, what they ate, and how they bathed.

By taking the low route, they learned more than they wanted to about the bugs, but they also learned a lot about the men they sought—where they hid their weapons, what footpaths they preferred, whom they kept company with, when they would show up, and even how they smelled.

"They had a strong body odor, like old, dumped-out french fries. It's the weirdest damn smell," Mike said, remarking that they became so good at their role of concealment and detection that "we could even smell our own guys. They smelled like Irish Spring or Pert, all the PX specials."

They never got caught crawling around in the grasses, though they had to shoot a lot of dogs. Apparently dogs are smarter than humans when it comes to perceiving anomalies in the landscape, and their snarling, growling, or barking could have given the snipers away.

There were flies, lots of black flies. At night it was mosquitoes, during the day it was flies, but the snipers didn't wear repellent because it's fragrant or slap a pest off the back of a neck because it's a jerky movement that makes a sound.

The snipers painted their faces in greens, blacks, and browns and wore ghillie suits or combinations of uniforms with different patterns, like the Marine Corps digital pattern, straight green cammies, or Multicam. They never, ever wore the Army's new universal camouflage pattern, Sgt. Mike said, because "they glow in the dark. In the daylight you look like a Smurf walking through all this green stuff."

The snipers would even melt the soles of their footwear or use tennis shoes so as not to leave the print of a U.S. boot, and they were careful not to leave a sound print either, using hand and arm signals to communicate. When it was something more complicated, the team of six, broken down into smaller teams of two or three men in a mutually supporting formation, would get "as tight as we could and whisper into each other's ears," Sgt. Mike said.

They carried one radio to communicate with the rear and tried to use predetermined communications windows. "What that means is, okay, every four hours I'm going to come up on the radio for fifteen minutes. If you don't have me in fifteen minutes, I'm going back off the radio because I'm not going to compromise my team sitting there trying to key a handset and passing you grids because you want to know where I'm at and what I'm doing," he said. "That's none of his business."

To be sure, the stalking and the wearing of ghillie suits by Sgt. Mike and the other team members were truly unusual for a war zone like Iraq. It is not completely unheard of, but the extent to which they worked in that capacity is rare.

Their field operations were intended to help clear a large area to create a buffer zone around a site for a planned combat outpost, and the snipers found plenty of opportunities to kill or capture suspicious characters.

Until Sgt. Mike's Third Infantry Division unit arrived there in 2007 and began looking for places to set up shop, the area was a pocket about fifteen miles southeast of Baghdad that had seen only sporadic U.S. presence. Many of the men who were trading in weapons and bomb-making material and training others in the tactics of insurgency had moved freely through the area for years during the war.

Many believed the lush, green area to have been a vacation resort and hunting preserve, but others say it had more likely been a bedroom community for Ba'ath Party officials and high-ranking officers in Saddam Hussein's elite Republican Guard.

Some of the richest vegetation in Iraq lined the banks of the Tigris River there, and large houses and boat docks dotted this enclave. It was a subtropical paradise for humans and birds and an oasis of arable land at the rough edges of broad, dry plains, perfect for growing pomegranates and maintaining shady date palm groves with trees towering to sixty feet and fruit tree orchards with limes and oranges.

The snipers helped themselves to some of the fruit and professed to enjoying a particular variety of sour orange that Sgt. Mike said "would probably be very good with vodka."

Plenty of foot trails and infiltration routes went down to the river landing sites, and the scattered villages were compounds with four or five houses tightly packed together. "You'd be walking around in this jungle and can't see nothing but maybe thirty meters in front of you; all of a sudden you walk into a group of houses," Sgt. Mike said.

The river flows around turns and curves, and as it approaches the area where the Third Infantry Division snipers were working, it makes a deep bend south around a peninsula with a small-size city of about twenty thousand called Salman Pak. The city, in archived reports before the U.S. invasion of Iraq, was said to be home to a terrorist training center.

The hull of a Boeing 707 was parked there, making others believe that it was more along the lines of "the Iraqi version of Delta to-do stuff like plane take-downs if a hijacked plane happened to land in Baghdad some day," said an Army officer familiar with the area, who asked to be described as "a military intelligence geek" because he refused to have any part of his name in print.

"During the whole buildup to the war, the site was labeled an AQ training camp, but I really don't think we had a good handle on it," he said.

At least part of the site was used for a demolition-explosives training course, and it is believed that many of the bomb makers who operated in Baghdad and its outlying cities and towns had been students or instructors there.

"I could never find any real links, but it was so hard to cross-reference anything to Iraqi records. We didn't have access to the right records, and I didn't have a group of dedicated translators to go through the documentation," said the military intelligence officer, who worked on the staff of a brigade that had responsibility for the area before the Third Infantry Division unit arrived. "I'm pretty sure a couple of the guys we captured had been there in some capacity. It doesn't take long into an interrogation cycle to find out if a guy has had some formal resistance training. We had some that surely had formal counter-interrogation training."

Against this backdrop, Sgt. Mike and his team were allowed by their commanders to venture out on foot or get dropped off for an overnight stalk to keep the pressure on what had been a haven for trafficking in bomb-making material with lots of places to hide safely and plan.

During Sgt. Mike's deployment, Gen. David Petraeus was the top commander in Iraq, and he requested and received thirty thousand extra troops for the surge. The aim was to smash violence wracking the country, especially in the big cities. He made it work by placing soldiers in small combat outposts on city blocks, and he began to pay the minority Sunni insurgents to work with U.S. troops. Those individuals became known as Sons of Iraq, or SOI, and it made for an awkward relationship, according to a lot of ground pounders, who only days or weeks earlier had been trading gunfire with them. Some who were listed as high-value targets were suddenly given trusted ally status.

But the bulk of what Sgt. Mike and his team did in the fruit tree orchards, irrigation canals, and farmlands of the Salman Pak peninsula took place before the SOI plan, and many of the men the team killed could potentially have become SOIs if they had lived long enough to enroll in the program. The snipers continued to work their area to make sure the SOI were doing their jobs and keeping insurgents from moving supplies and weapons through the area.

Sgt. Mike and his team canvassed an area he estimated was about thirty square miles.

During the day, as the SOI manned checkpoints near their stalking area, Mike and the other snipers wore full ghillie suits and stalked much more slowly because, even though they were theoretically working together, the snipers had no intention of treating the SOI as if they were trusted allies. But most of their concealed work was done at night on what they called the "zombie schedule."

It was slow going. Very slow. At about one hundred meters an hour, a five-hundred-meter movement could take all night, and the range of visibility was as short as what they could see through the grass.

"It was hard to track who was running supplies, because the vegetation didn't really allow for precision fire so it got to the point where we stopped taking the bolt guns out and the only precision assets we had were the [squad designated marksman] 5.56 rifles. The engagement was so small that that's all you needed," Mike said. "We would try to follow them to where they would take the supplies because we were undermanned. That small of a team operating by itself, it would take twenty-five to thirty minutes to get QRF here if we got into a gun battle."

When word started to spread that snipers were hiding in the orchards and canals, he said, people would try to figure out their pattern, and it became a constant chase for someone to make a mistake first.

"We'd be crawling, walking, hands and knees. We always moved one technique lower than the vegetation; it was the only safe way to move. There were times when people literally crossed ten meters in front of us, and they never knew we were there," he said. "It was extremely tiring to be out there for hours," Mike added, describing "scope eye," the fatigue that comes with looking through a high-magnification scope with one eye for a long time.

As they progressed, the activity died down and their profiles went up, said Sgt. Mike, who at one time had a bounty on his head of about $3,000, more than three years' pay for the average Iraqi. Becuase of that, he didn't want to use his full name in print.

The heaviest activity for the snipers was between March and October.

One night, early in the days of the zombie schedule when they were just learning the area, they saw a pair of headlights coming down one of the smaller routes near the river. It was after curfew—no one was supposed to be out.

Instead of taking a shot, they decided to wait and see where the truck went. The team had gotten turned around a little that night; through their night optical devices, they saw what looked like a lake but turned out to be the river. "We stop and do a map check and every guy on that team thought it was a lake. So we're trying as best we can to find a lake on this map because we thought we were way off target," he said. "We were just disoriented because we'd been walking so long. We'd been on the ground four hours, and we'd covered maybe eight hundred meters because of the different security halts. Like a dog would come up and we'd have to wait because we didn't want to spook it, or we'd hear something moving in the bushes so we'd sit there and scan."

Back on track and focused on the truck, the snipers listened for the engine to go off and headed toward where they thought they'd last heard it. As the narrow roadway turned, they saw a huge, three-story house before them. A truck was sitting in the driveway, and the snipers could tell through their AN/PAS-13 thermal weapon sights that the engine was still hot. They'd found their truck.

The team bedded down in the brush while Sgt. Mike called in a situation report and made a plan to develop it further, but activity started happening right away.

A man popped onto the roof of the house and, though a floodlight on the roof faced outward, the man couldn't see beyond the cone of the light's beam. He couldn't see the other team leader, another sergeant named Mike, standing in the middle of the road pointing the barrel of his gun at him.

It was three o'clock in the morning, and the team was assessing its options for action and extraction as events continued to unfold.

In the next heartbeat, a kid came around the corner on a bicycle and stopped dead in his tracks when he saw Mike's dark form on the road. Before he had a chance to say or do anything, Sgt. Mike, who was less than ten meters away in the brush, dove out and grabbed the kid, who was about fifteen, pulling him and his bike off the road and into the embankment.

"I straight out tackled him. I lay this guy out, and Mike decides not to engage the guy on the roof," Sgt. Mike said. "I drag this kid back up to the team. They tie him down and gag him." At this point the team decided that it was compromised and that its options were quickly dwindling. The snipers were already off their original course, they now had a detainee, and the clock was ticking. All they had in their favor was the knowledge that backup was on the way.

So, leaving his spotter and security guy behind with the radio and the detainee, Sgt. Mike and the three remaining snipers set out to hit/assault this three-story house, a multilevel, multiroom mansion that was easily 4,200 square feet.

"We didn't know how many people were in there, but we had to get it done. We needed some place to go because where we were at was not working," he said, conceding that the odds of a big fight were completely unknown and could have been overwhelmingly against them.

Sgt. Mike, the point man, had a radio headset on and a twelve-gauge shotgun in his hands; the other Mike had his squad designated marksman rifle slung over his back and an M4; his spotter had an M24 and an M4, and their security guy had an M4 with a 203. They were all wearing camouflage paint on their faces.

"We decided to hit it and just go with everything we had and scared the crap out of the people because as soon as we kicked in the door, we were in all different uniforms, had no helmets on, basically just got our plate carriers."

The event itself ended up being almost anti-climactic. They took no fire. There was no resistance. It was over quickly.

Six people were in the house—a six-year-old girl, two women, and three men.

But the people were nothing compared to the pay dirt they found in a search of the house. In what looked like a supply room, the American snipers found British, Australian, and American camouflage uniforms; various calibers of ammunition, from 8 mm Mauser to 7.62 x 54 mm rimmed, which is a sniper cartridge for a Soviet weapon; .22-caliber ammo; a couple of types of pistol ammunition; and six ten-gallon propane tanks, the size of a tank you see on the back of a forklift.

"We see all this stuff and we figure something's up. Then we start finding training manuals in this room, including a poorly translated copy of FM 23-10, which is the Army version of the Sniper Manual," Sgt. Mike said.

They thought they had probably come upon some type of school or training operation. The house may not even have belonged to the oldest man there, who they believed was about sixty, because militias were known to have planted regular-looking people in the neighborhood to keep up appearances.

"In our mind from the information we gathered, he was running a school and probably catching a little more money by storing IED-making materials," Sgt. Mike said. "But we didn't know who they were. It was more of an educated guess because the people who we were shooting and engaging with in Salman Pak were wearing similar camouflage and shooting similar caliber weapons. So it was about developing the situation and putting it all together."

The unit ended up detaining all the men, but without enough evidence to prove they were doing anything wrong, they all ended up walking.

Sgt. Mike was a Marine before he was a soldier.

He deployed with Third Battalion, Second Marines from Camp Lejeune, North Carolina, in March 2003 and was only a few miles away in Nasiriyah when the Army's 507th Maintenance Company was ambushed and most of its members were brutally killed.

In the five months he spent in Iraq that year, his only deployment to the war zone with the Marine Corps, he worked long hours and saw such heavy contact, he said, that the teams were expanded from three- to nine-man teams that each carried three bolt-action rifles.

The rules of engagement were basically all for free fire zones, he said, "to where if there was somebody in a certain cardinal direction that looked suspicious or was out after curfew or had a weapon or a cell phone or binos or a video camera, we had orders to reduce the target, so that's what we did."

Most of the guys they took down—he couldn't even begin to count them, he said—had weapons or were making attempts to gain intelligence on the Marines' defensive positions. At that time there were no established bases or combat outposts so the Marines lived where they stopped at night.

Sgt. Mike was a graduate of the Marine Corps' Scout Sniper School at Stone Bay, Camp Lejeune, North Carolina. He had had deployments to Okinawa, Iraq, and Djibouti before, at the age of twenty-two with one marriage behind him, he decided to quit the Marine Corps and go home to Michigan, where he stamped dyes and did metal fabrication in the prototype division at a company that supplied the big three auto manufacturers.

Working a lot and raking in good wages weren't enough to push the memories of sniping and running around in the woods out of his mind, and after only eighteen months, with a newborn daughter, a tanking economy, and a dearth of work in Michigan, Sgt. Mike visited a recruiter.

But the Marine Corps only hired prior-service Marines in March and November. It was May. "I made a brash decision and walked down the hall to the Army recruiter, asked if they were still hiring. They said yes. I said, 'Send me on the next thing smokin','" he said.

Ten months after putting on an Army uniform, Sgt. Mike deployed to Iraq, where in fifteen months he and his team supported company operations, stalked the peninsular vegetation, and conducted countersniper operations.

In Salman Pak, he said, the professionalism of the enemy snipers varied with each guy. A lot of them repeated their operational patterns, which made it easy for him and his team to find them. The Joes on the line also helped find sniper positions during their daylight patrols.

"The platoons were psyched to help because we started taking losses to snipers so the countersniper mission became a priority real quick. We lost a few guys to snipers, mostly Bradley commanders," he said.

Even the Iraqi police were taking hits, and it was on one of Sgt. Mike's missions to help the Iraqis with the same threat the Americans faced that he took a sniper out of business.

He did it from a joint security station in the middle of town, a police-military base with concrete T-wall barriers around the perimeter, guards posted at the entry and exit points and points of dominance, and guard towers.

"This particular sniper had been shooting at the same guard tower at the same time for five days in a row," he said. The Iraqi police dealt with it by climbing down from the tower around four o'clock when the potshots started, waiting for a couple of hours until daylight waned, and then climbing back up after dark.

Sgt. Mike and the other team leader, who had sent the rest of their team members to another base up north to get sandwiches, each grabbed a rifle and a set of binos, and hopped a convoy going downtown in time to get an hour jump on the enemy sniper.

Up in the tower, they began their sketch of the area. The Iraqi police were taking fire from the east in the direction of an Iraqi army compound directly across the street. Sgt. Mike wondered where he might shoot from if he were going to harass the Iraqi police.

"I narrowed it down to this one building that was about three blocks away, and there was a very limited window. I could see about fifteen feet of the rooftop and how I would make an escape from that position. Once I backtracked all the routes I might take if I was going to take a shot at that tower, I kinda had an idea where he was going to come up at," he said.

The cement tower was about thirty feet high with a ladder going up to it, a single five-by-five room with sandbagged two-by-three windows on each of the four sides, a seven-foot ceiling, and camo netting. "It was your basic Army issue, mass-produced concrete tower, reinforced by the Americans," Sgt. Mike said.

He put a blanket over the back window and blacked out the rest of the tower to conceal his position inside. All he could see was what was in front of him in the known area.

"It doesn't seem like you can throw somebody off by moving a couple of feet, but if you look at a bullet that's three-tenths of an inch big versus a three-foot window, there's a lot of room to hide," he said.

Using the existing loopholes in the stack of sandbags the Iraqis had put up for protection, he developed his area sketch and chiseled out a four-inch loophole in the concrete below the window with a hammer and chisel he borrowed from the kit in the Bradley that had dropped him off.

The time was approaching four o'clock, Sgt. Mike was watching, and the anticipation was building.

"It was kind of like when you're sitting up in a tree stand deer hunting. You're hoping something comes out, but you don't really know where it's coming from or what you're after," he said.

But it didn't take long before he saw a man wearing clothing with a coyote tan desert tiger stripe similar to the uniform worn by British soldiers going into the building he'd picked out. He wasn't carrying a rifle, but he had something on his back, a detail of which Sgt. Mike made special note.

"He's carrying a little schoolgirl's pink Barbie backpack, one of the plastic ones, and I can clearly see Barbie through the binos that I was using. So it was funny," he said.

About thirty minutes later a shot rang out and Sgt. Mike saw a flash from a third-floor window. The shot hit the tower, but instead of leaving the building, the man went up to the roof, "and that was the last mistake he made because the last thing I saw he was coming across from right to left, hunched over, carrying an 8 mm Mauser on his right side."

Tracking the hunched man with his own bolt-action rifle along the edge of the building, Sgt. Mike picked him off just before the building would have blocked his view. The shot was 378 yards, putting the man straight down.

"I don't like taking head shots because you can't guarantee hits so I aimed for his shoulder and the bullet ended up catching him just in the front of the chest, but there was enough friction on the bullet that it turned, and it got both lungs, his heart, and went out the other side of his body," Sgt. Mike surmised, concluding that it "was one more sniper out of the way."

The sniper was working with a very rudimentary weapon system, Sgt. Mike said. He didn't have a scope on it, but he was a good enough shot that he had hit two or three of the Iraqi police, wounding them and scaring them from returning to the tower.

As it turns out, the team went after three more the same month, though not in the same building. The team started working across the street and found out that more snipers were in that area.

Unfortunately, Sgt. Mike said, he was never able to confirm much about the sniper he had killed other than what he saw through his scope. When he asked for a squad to take him to check out the area and the rooftop, his request was denied. In an operation a month later, bloodstains were found on the roof, though the body was long gone.

Thinking back to the day he saw the man entering the building, it wasn't the Barbie backpack that stood out as significant. "It was a British uniform. That kind of lent itself to the theory of the camouflage we found in the house by the river," Sgt. Mike said.

# CHAPTER ELEVEN
# IN THE GLINT OF A SCOPE

Sgt. Ryan Coffield's pale blue eyes look tired. He's not tired, though. It's the pain pills that make him seem that way.

He says his friends like to invite him to go out because he's a cheap date. He reaches his alcohol limit at two, maybe three beers. They give him a hard time about what happened to him, but he likes it. He laughs with them about it, says it keeps him from feeling sorry for himself.

When they do go out to a bar and someone asks him about the ten-inch scar on the right side of his neck, he downplays it with the typical gallows humor of an infantryman, saying it happened in a freak lawn-mower accident.

But lawn-mower accidents don't usually produce an exit wound, and the bar patrons Coffield amuses with his tall tale can't see the little, coffee-colored dent on the left side of the back of his neck or the scar on his spine that disappears down the back of his T-shirt. None of it is that obvious anymore, not even his weakened left side.

In Iraq, where he was wounded in 2005, it wasn't unusual for a soldier to be shot during combat and almost not make it to his twenty-second birthday. For Coffield, though, it was unusual in that the person responsible for his gunshot wound was a rival sniper who got him first.

"I wish I had paid a little more attention," Coffield said through his raspy, wounded voice. "There's always something I could have done differently, but it's one of those situations that I could 'what if?' to death forever and it probably would all end up with me getting shot anyway."

When he was wounded on October 2, his unit had already been in Iraq for almost ten months. The Third Infantry Division battalion was headquartered at Forward Operating Base McKenzie on Samarra Airfield East, about sixty miles north of Baghdad in the Sunni Triangle.

But the place where he spent most of his time on patrols and over-watch missions was Ad Duluiyah, a town of about fifty thousand with a brand of insurgent who found success in disrupting supply convoys traveling through the area with roadside bombs that were detonated remotely or by a pressure plate activated by the weight of a passing vehicle. The bombs were a big problem for everyone in Iraq and ended up causing most of the U.S. troops' deaths there, but they weren't the only way the insurgents attacked.

Just two weeks before Coffield was shot, a convoy of supply trucks driven by unarmed civilians working for the contractor KBR followed its security element, a squad of soldiers from the Virginia National Guard, as it made a wrong turn into an area that Coffield's unit didn't even like entering.

After arriving at an unexpected dead end, the guardsmen and civilians turned back to return on the only route out and were trapped in a narrow kill zone that became a chaotic and deadly ambush for the outnumbered security escort and its convoy. Three KBR civilians were killed, and several others were wounded in a barrage of gunfire, rocket-propelled grenades, hand grenades, and roadside bombs from what some reports said were more than one hundred insurgents.

Coffield didn't see that much action.

Ninety percent of the time, he said, he and his team would go out to the north side of town and keep an eye on what they called "IED alley" because any truck going through on its way to Samarra about thirty miles northeast would get hit by an improvised explosive device.

For their missions, the snipers would go into an area with a platoon, dismount and do a patrol with them, and drop off in some dark, secluded area. Then the platoon would branch off and keep going, leaving the snipers behind. About twenty or thirty minutes later, the sniper team would get up and move.

At the time, the Army still hadn't issued every soldier the new combat uniform with its unpopular universal camouflage pattern.

Most soldiers still wore the tan and brown desert combat uniform. Coffield and his team wore the old green, black, and brown woodland-patterned battle drill uniform for their night missions because it was darker than the desert uniform.

They never wore their ghillie suits, and the few times they were compromised, it was by some harmless local who just forced them to move or exfil. More often, he said, they were denied an opportunity to take a shot at the insurgents because of a jittery chain of command.

"Our over-watch was hard because they insisted on checking on us with helicopters, and when they did that, they scared off the guys digging in the road," Coffield said.

There was one memorable shot, though, and it would end up being the only one he took during his one and only deployment to the war zone.

It happened during the summer of 2005 in a little village just north of Ad Duluiyah with a name Coffield couldn't remember how to spell.

All he knew was that no American foot patrols had been there in a while, leaving the supply route open to attack. In the days before the U.S. patrol went there, an Iraqi police station was blown up by a truck bomb and the unit received intelligence of activity in a shop where men would sit and watch for patrols coming through and relay the information to forward insurgent observers.

When the patrol arrived there one morning, Coffield dismounted the rear of their Bradley fighting vehicle with Staff Sgt. Brian Bryant, Staff Sgt. Logan Sibert, and Staff Sgt. Fritz Autenrieth, "and everybody in the town scrambled."

Unoffended by the local cold shoulder, they began a slow, tense walk along the unfriendly main street, and after a short while, Coffield said, "I see this guy with a big white sack walking down the road staring at us. As we start walking towards him, he takes off running. We yell, and he doesn't stop. He cuts into this driveway."

The four soldiers took off after him, running into an area of heavy vegetation and trees where they eventually saw a house. Autenrieth and Sibert peeled off toward the house, while Coffield and Bryant went around and followed a trail through an orchard to the back of the house.

Their eyes went to the figure of a man crouched near a tree. The sight slowed them to a cautious pace while they watched him and tried to figure out what he was doing. "He was just sitting there, and he kept raising his hand up. The vegetation was too thick for me to use my rifle. I had it slung over my back, so I had my handgun out," Coffield said. "We come to find out the guy was chained to the tree because he was, I'm not sure how to say this, but he was mentally handicapped. He kept bringing his hand up, and I thought he had a gun at first. It was a real close call. But he was just trying to get loose."

As far as he knew, members of his unit came through after them and released the desperate man, but at that moment, with a suspect still on the run, the chained man was history for Coffield and Bryant, who continued in pursuit of the fleeing man with the white sack.

"We saw him about a few yards up the trail. He was ducked down digging in the bag," he said. As Coffield and Bryant approached, they saw the man take an AK-47 assault rifle out of the bag and start to load it with a magazine. He was oblivious to how close the U.S. soldiers had gotten, probably assuming they wouldn't give chase with all the poundage of kit they were wearing. But he was wrong about the determined infantrymen, and by this time the four sergeants were on line together and had the man in view.

"We start yelling at him, and he kind of looks up with that 'oh shit' look and takes off running down the trail again," Coffield said. They all gave chase, and Coffield, responding to an order from an NCO to fire a warning shot, took a knee in the dust and fired with his M24 sniper rifle.

"I put a round off his left boot heel. But he didn't stop," he said. The trail went deeper into an overgrown field, and the man was approaching a sizable bush in the middle of the trail when Coffield took his warning shot.

"The guy went around it after I fired and kept going down the trail, but I could still see him through the bush. I got the command to fire and I shot him. I got him right in the back, in his spine. He was fifty or sixty yards away," Coffield said.

When they reached the man, his legs were immobile; he was barely alive and crawling with his arms. He died a few feet from where he fell.

"Supposedly there was a second guy who ducked off, but we never found him," Coffield said.

At some point after that day, Coffield doesn't know when, his battalion intelligence section learned that a sniper was lurking around their area of operations. Reports that a soldier in another company had been shot in the chest and saved by his body armor didn't trickle down to the other companies.

And the sniper section didn't have any discussions about a countersniper plan because in ten months of patrolling, over-watching and observing, enemy snipers hadn't been a threat and as far as the team knew, still weren't.

What Coffield learned after he recovered from near-death was that the day he was shot, his fellow soldiers ended up catching the sniper's spotter, someone presumed to be a local insurgent who basically hosted the sniper's visit, driving him around and showing him the area, the routes the Americans liked to patrol and where some good hide sites might be.

On October 2, the battalion's scout platoon, about ten cavalry scouts with two Bradleys and one Humvee, set up a traffic-control point near a main intersection on a north-south road called Route Milton that came to a T with an east-west road called Route Dover. The platoon's mission was to check cars for explosives or other contraband.

Coffield and his partner, Staff Sgt. Jason Staszewski, dis-mounted with them, and each took a position on one of the roads. Coffield walked south down Route Milton and set up with his M24 sniper rifle behind some random barrier on the west side of the road almost directly across from the checkpoint. His partner, whom everyone called "Ski," was on Route Dover above Coffield's position.

"Sgt. Brandon LaBar was driving the Humvee, and when he got out, that's when the first shot came. It barely missed his head. We had only been there about ten minutes," Coffield said.

The shot came from somewhere to the east on Route Dover. "When the first shot was fired, I had my attention focused down south looking for any cars that might be trouble," he said.

The terrain around the intersection was flat and dominated by one-story, flat-topped buildings with an occasional two-story building. It was around 2 p.m., and traffic was moderate, the streets empty of pedestrians because the soldiers had the area cordoned off.

Shouts of "Sniper!" from the scouts immediately followed the crack of the bullet, and everyone ran for cover toward the vehicles lined up near the intersection, leaving the area at the checkpoint on Route Milton exposed.

Coffield ran toward the vehicles, too, and climbed an interior staircase to the roof of the two-story building nearest the intersection. LaBar, who had been to Sniper School but wasn't in the sniper section, went with him to the roof.

The two took a knee and hunkered behind a nearly four-foot wall around the edge of the roof. They scanned east down Route Dover and spotted a building they thought might be a likely hide site for their unwelcome shooter.

But, by the time they got up to the roof, about ten minutes after the first shot, Coffield said, "I didn't know it, but this guy had moved to a position on the road right where I was at near the traffic control point. That's when he got me."

Looking at a map years later, Coffield identified a hidden footpath behind the shooter's presumed building and other structures that led to an opening to Route Milton. He thinks the man slipped out of his hide, and, taking advantage of the distraction of the first shot, smoothly made it to the other road, where he may even have had a rifle pre-positioned.

"He was in plain clothes. He could have walked right past us," Coffield said.

In his online scrapbook, Coffield has a photo of himself on that rooftop that shows his head and shoulders in profile. It was a shutter release on a digital camera by a soldier on the ground that captured the very image the sniper may have seen before he pulled his trigger.

Coffield scanned the east route with his scope, then turned his gaze to the southbound road to look with his bare eyes. In that split second, as his head turned, he saw the gleam of a scope and the man holding the rifle.

"When I looked at it, that's when I was like, 'Shit.'

"It felt like somebody had slapped the back of my neck. All my muscles relaxed, and my entire body started going limp. I fell backwards, and I started seeing blood gushing out everywhere," he said.

The bullet had zipped straight through his neck on the bias, clipping the internal carotid artery just above the junction where the common carotid splits in two, before exiting the back left side of his lower neck. His external carotid was still supplying blood to his brain, but the bleeding was horrific. Coffield was dying, and he knew it.

"The blood that wasn't going to my brain caused me to have a little bit of an issue." He was conscious, though in a dreamy, odd state with voices coming through in echoes.

"Sgt. LaBar started yelling for a medic, but for some reason we didn't have a medic with us that day. He did what he could do to control the bleeding," he said.

Other soldiers ran to the roof, and everybody worked in a calm panic to get Coffield's body armor off, loosen his bloody clothing, and get him into position to carry him down to the street, but they had no litter and the stairway was narrow, about three feet wide. The men were big and bulky with gear. Time was slipping away, and Coffield thought he was slipping away with it.

"I heard the words 'just breathe, just breathe,' but everybody else who was talking was just muffled, it was the echo. My neck had swelled, and I was having a hard time breathing. I was taking really short, shallow breaths. It was like sucking through a straw," Coffield said.

He was scared.

"I just remember everybody yelling at me to keep my eyes open, and I just kept going in and out," he said.

Before the platoon got to the intersection, Coffield and LaBar had been discussing their families back home. Coffield told his buddy that he didn't think he'd be home from the deployment in time to see his son born. Lying in a pool of his own blood on a dusty rooftop in the Sunni Triangle, his hopes of ever seeing his son were in the front of his fading mind.

"I did think I was dying. As soon as he shot me, I was like, 'Ah, that's not right,' and once I saw all the blood coming out, your mind starts going through so many thoughts that you can't focus on one thing and then it just stops," he said. "Like it's completely clear and you're like, 'Shit, this is it.'"

But it wasn't the end for the young sniper. His buddies shimmied him down the stairs and loaded him into a waiting Bradley, where he passed out and came to a couple of times. He snapped back as he was being loaded into the Black Hawk medical evacuation helicopter and snapped back again as the bird landed at the combat support hospital at Balad Air Base a few miles south.

"I woke up in Balad as they were trying to figure out what my Social Security number was, and I didn't have my dog tags either. It was not a very good day," he said. "I barely managed, but I told the guy who was about to operate on me where my ID card was."

Everything after that was a blur of nightmares, surgery, and feed tubes. He was discharged from Walter Reed Army Medical Center in Washington, D.C., three months later and fifty pounds lighter.

His C-3 and C-4 vertebrae had been fractured, causing some nerve damage that may account for the weakness on the left side of his body. Or he may have had a stroke. The doctors didn't know.

Coffield's career in the Army was over, but he got away with his life and a vivid memory of that day.

The man was about 150 yards away. He wore jeans and a brown shirt and took the shot from a standing position. The outline of his weapon was clear—black with a brown handle on either a Russian Dragunov rifle or a Romanian PSL rifle.

"I saw the glint of his optic," Coffield said, speculating that if he had been wearing his Kevlar neck protector that the Army issued with its body armor, he would have surely been killed because it would have slowed the speed of the bullet and caused it to lodge in his neck instead of going clean through.

Soldiers, especially snipers, often choose to leave their neck protectors behind because they chafe the neck and restrict head movement.

What he thinks saved him, though, "was the fact that I was turning into the shot, because if I hadn't even noticed the guy, it probably would have come in right behind my ear."

Coffield believes the sniper was after him because he carried a long rifle, and he believes that the sniper predicted that the American soldiers would race up to the roof as soon as the first shot was fired, one of the only two-story buildings around.

There was evidence that soldiers from another unit had been on the rooftop before. When he and LaBar got up there, they saw a bunch of telltale brown pouches, wrappers, and other trash that came from MREs, or the "meals ready to eat" that U.S. troops carry on the road.

The sniper probably knew it had been a previous hide, and when Coffield saw the picture of himself up there years later, he figured it out, too. In the picture, a loophole for a scope and barrel is clearly visible in the brick wall at the edge of the roof.

Coffield doesn't know what became of the sniper, but he learned that after he was medically evacuated, the sniper's data book was found with information that dated back to 1986.

"Afterward, piecing everything together, the battalion said he might have been Syrian. At that point we were seeing a lot of guys from Chechnya, and the jihad over there was like a Super Bowl for them. They were coming from all corners of the earth to get Americans," he said. "I think what happened is, after he took the shot and hit me, he took off and never came back around. He was probably going to link up with his spotter later, but we got to him first."

Coffield regained his weight, crediting "grandma's cooking in Alabama" for the calories, and he started the process of earning a degree in business management after he got out of the Army.

"I'd love to be a sniper again, but not for revenge. I just miss the job," he said. "To me it was the greatest thing ever. That's the hardest part, not being able to do it anymore."

He still goes to the range and shoots every chance he gets, but it's not the same.

"It's just a little more expensive now. I didn't realize how expensive those match-grade round bullets were."

# CHAPTER TWELVE

# FREAKY BULL'S-EYE SHOT

Rolling out of a U.S. compound anywhere southwest of Baghdad meant being ready for anything. The area was known as the Triangle of Death and had lived up to its name formidably.

In both directions along the banks of the Euphrates River and along the main supply routes used by the U.S. military coalition, a maze of ditches, berms, irrigation canals and farmland, tall grasses, and narrow footpaths became a place for U.S. soldiers and Marines to die.

The endless string of roadside bombs that killed most of them were supplied and resupplied by innumerable weapons caches buried throughout the valleys and plains west of the Euphrates River, an infinite desert that extends to the borders of Saudi Arabia, Jordan, and Syria.

Troops assigned there were bedeviled by unmapped trails on the fringe of the desert that provided a way for Al Qaeda fighters to commute between Fallujah in Al Anbar province and the Shiite holy city of Karbala to the south, with stops in cities and villages like Yusufiyah, Mahmudiyah, Musayyib, Iskandariyah, and Latifiyah along the way.

The first car bomb to take the lives of dismounted soldiers happened in the region. The only two ambushes and abductions of soldiers in static positions that occurred during U.S. operations in Iraq took place in the Triangle of Death. None of them were found alive. The area even drove the soldiers crazy, leading to heinous crimes against the locals and, at least once, against one another.

The Iraqis who lived there were a mix of Sunni and Shia, and when they weren't attacking and killing each other, they were attacking U.S. troops and anyone who worked with them.

Saddam Hussein's elite, and later disbanded, Republican Guard trained there. A closed bomb factory yielded hundreds of unemployed and disgruntled bomb makers. And the narrow, raised roadways that coursed through the farmland were only big enough for vehicles the width of a small pickup truck, not wide-bodied Humvees, allowing the insurgency to fester and safely harbor car-bomb makers and their suicide drivers.

When the sniper teams with First Battalion, Sixty-seventh Armor of the Fourth Infantry Division's Second Brigade Combat Team rolled out on their missions from the corroded Soviet-era power plant they called home, they never left without their high-value target list. The list, a computer printout of names and corresponding faces produced by the battalion's intelligence section, identified the bomb makers, their leaders, and other henchmen in the movement to disrupt peace building and progress.

Plenty of rats were scurrying around at night and digging up the roads to plant 155 mm artillery shells. They could be picked off if the snipers had a good over-watch mission. And a lot of them were. But every now and then, and sometimes quite deliberately, the snipers would also see one of the weasels on their target list and get the opportunity to take him out.

The mission that sticks out most in Sgt. Ben Redus's mind is the one in May 2006 when he and his team "eliminated Abu Omar." It was supposed to be a surveillance mission, and it was, but the team had clearance to kill, or get permission to kill, anyone they saw on the list.

The team's infiltration route, concealment, and tactics were flawless, and it arrived at the house it planned to watch at the time it planned to get there. The team members walked in darkness over coarse farmland a distance of nearly ten kilometers.

"We had every aspect of the mission covered," Redus said, explaining that Staff Sgt. Timothy L. Kellner, the sniper section leader, "had contingency plans for his contingency plans. We had primary and alternate escape and evade plans. It was sick how much planning came out of two hours of war gaming."

What they hadn't expected was to see two of their wanted men at the very house they were going to watch for a few hours. Charlie Company was planning to target the house within thirty-six hours, and the sniper team was there to get a set of eyes on the place and see what kind of activity the infantrymen might encounter.

"The guy we were looking for was Rasool Bandre Aass Fayhen Al Janabi. We didn't have a good picture of Rasool, but we had a good one of Omar," Redus said. "When we shot him, we had his picture propped up right under our rifle. We made sure it was him."

The evening of their daring cross-country infiltration, the four-man team staged at a place called Carnivore Island, a patch of land in the river that had been cleared and secured for use by the American soldiers, with a vacant house they took as an outpost.

The shooters started out on foot from the house just after dark, walked around the island, and crossed over to the mainland on a bridge made from a date palm log.

Redus was the point man, Pfc. Christopher Lochner walked behind him, Kellner took third position, and Sgt. John Nebzydoski, who was tapped to provide extra security, brought up the rear. They wore ghillie suits, but the terrain was crisscrossed with elevated roads that would have silhouetted the men if they'd walked on them. So, once they crossed the log bridge, they skirted the lower edge of one of the elevated roads until they reached a crop of date palm trees where they could move a little more freely.

Their route through the date palms ended at a main road, one they knew to be saturated with improvised explosive devices. "Needless to say, crossing an IED-infested road is not fun, especially when the area is known for pressure-plate-activated ones," said Redus. As point man, Redus took the lead on the crossing, gingerly stepping on the asphalt and scanning intensely to avoid anything that looked like a trigger device. The other men followed squarely in his footsteps, pulling security for each other on each side of the road according to the meticulous plan.

The next crop of date palm trees led the team unexpectedly through the front yard of a house. They slowed to a snail's pace and got as quiet as dead men just in time for the next surprise.

"We made it halfway through the yard when we realized that a man was in front of his home enjoying a cigarette, unaware that we were there," Redus said. "I froze in place, and so did the rest of the team. The standard is to take a knee, and if there's still a threat, you go prone on the ground. I went to a knee and dropped my rucksack so I could attack if needed. Tim gave me the go-ahead to draw my knife just in case."

Redus carried a twelve-inch bowie knife that, he said, "is meant for damage." But he didn't have to use it. After five long minutes the man finished his cigarette and went back into his house. Giving it just a few more minutes, the team resumed its movement, feeling confident that, without the advantage of night vision optics, the man hadn't seen them.

They circumnavigated other homes in the area using the canals and irrigation ditches, but the landscape sometimes had a life of its own.

"I ran into a few new obstacles such as little crossing bridges that had been there a few days ago had been moved or removed altogether. I plotted a new route that skirted a canal," Redus said.

And so it went. During the overnight movement, the team methodically made its way toward its objective, slogging through canals or hugging the side of an embankment, working to keep the tags and threads of the ghillie suits from getting caught up on anything.

The discomfort of wearing a cumbersome ghillie suit was out-weighed by the team's heightened sense of awareness and adoption of a battle mind-set, said Redus. He described the weight of the disguise as feeling "like a heavy, thick leather jacket. It's hot, it's warm, you sweat continuously. They get snagged on every-thing. But the itchiness and stuff in your face is nothing com-pared to having someone come around the corner to shoot you. You get into battle mode, and you don't feel as much fatigue, you just go."

In one backyard they traversed, the foursome had to cross a water pipe to get over a canal—a four-inch, rusty pipe. Kellner doesn't like crossing pipes.

"Tim came up to me and whispered, 'Fuck you, I hate going across these damn things.' Of course, he knew that we had to cross it, and indeed we did in good fashion trying to look like gymnasts, except we were humping forty pounds of personal gear and sixty-pound rucksacks."

At the next house, Kellner wiped out on the slippery downward slope of a ditch, an unintended clownish sight gag that set off the church giggles in the other three men. The stifled laughter was a much needed tension breaker for the team, which had moved eight painstaking kilometers and still had 1,500 meters to go.

"We saw him go down. I ran over and checked on him. He was kind of sitting there, and he asked me if it had been loud. When you're moving at night, noise is your biggest enemy. It was funny. But then everybody calms down, can re-cock and continue," Redus said.

After walking all night, following the footpaths, walking where the locals walk, crossing where they cross, the snipers arrived at the outer edge of the targeted property and found what Redus called "a great spot."

At the edge of the property, a fifteen-foot drop led to a small drainage ditch. Behind that was a larger drainage ditch with intermittent reeds rising as high as ten feet. The team set in on the far side of the larger ditch, nestled into a nice little saddle that allowed them to stay underneath the edge while still using the reeds for concealment. The barrel of their suppressed M24 sniper rifle was aimed at the house but concealed by the reeds.

Redus and Lochner were at the front of the position, watching the house about four hundred meters in front of them, while Kellner, who maintained radio communication with the commander, and Nebzydoski set in behind them.

Between them they had the M24 with a 10-power scope and three M14 rifles. Redus had a 40-power spotting scope, the kind that looks like a fat, mini-telescope, and Lochner was on the M24.

The weather was mild for that time of year in Iraq, about ninety-five degrees, and a breeze blew gently at between three and five miles per hour. The men had not eaten on the overnight walk.

They were fatigued, but on mission. The sun began to rise about an hour after they set in and no sooner had the area been washed in fresh light than they saw a man come out of the house.

They suspected and even felt certain it was Rasool, but the grainy computer printout of his face left room for doubt. They watched him walk over to a neighbor's home, then return to his own house a few minutes later. He walked over to the neighbor's again a short while later, but this time he brought a small box that he placed on the doorstep before returning to his house.

At the neighbor's house, the sniper team saw a curtain move in a window. The door opened a crack, and a man stepped out, scooped up the box, and quickly went back in and shut the door.

About three hours had passed since the first man had walked over to his neighbor's house, when the neighbor came out and walked over to the first man's house. Using his 40-power scope, Redus easily identified the neighbor as Abu Omar, "a terror cell leader with Syrian connections. He controlled and funded IED emplacement teams all across western Iraq."

The two men met and walked directly and unknowingly closer to the snipers' position, to a field where the team could see women working and children playing. The neighbors sat on low benches, the man who looked like Rasool to the side, facing Omar's left side. Omar sat and rested his elbows on his knees. The neighbors were 336 meters away from the barrel of Lochner's M24.

Redus and Kellner confirmed to each other that they had positively identified Omar, and each had a strong feeling about Rasool, but a strong feeling wasn't enough to shoot him. Redus said, "We couldn't 100 percent ID Rasool, not nearly with the certainty we had on Omar."

What Kellner saw definitively were the blasting caps and detonation cord in Omar's hands. Kellner had already given Redus the okay to set up the shot, so Lochner was ready.

"I reached over and squeezed Chris's arm to let him know to get ready to take the shot. I got set behind my spotting scope and talked Chris on target. He had already dialed his scope for the distance, we reconfirmed wind, and started the fire commands," Redus said.

He recalled Kellner saying to them, "Spotter up, shooter up. Send it."

In what seemed like an eternity waiting for the shot, the team was rewarded with a "crack" and saw a bit of trace as the bullet struck Omar squarely in the spine between the shoulder blades. It was a satisfying bull's-eye shot. But it got weird.

"Omar did not move. I could see the blood pooling up on his shirt. I knew he was hit. Chris knew he was hit, but they just sat there and nothing happened," Redus said. "It was not what I expected. You see in the movies when someone gets shot, they go flying and all hell breaks loose. That was the exact opposite."

The team was stunned, and the scene was made all the more macabre because Rasool kept talking with Omar, who still had his elbows planted on his knees. He sat there motionless while the children still played and the women still worked.

About a minute later, the team saw one of the children come over to say something to Omar, who didn't respond. When the child touched his arm to get his attention, his body slumped over dead. Rasool stood in shock, and the children and women burst into screams of hysteria.

Lochner was ready to take another shot but didn't have to. The terror had had its effect and launched a series of events that enabled them to capture the man they thought to be Rasool.

With the quick reaction force on the way to pull the snipers out, they continued to watch the yard as a Toyota pickup truck with about five men inside pulled onto the scene and loaded Omar's body into the back. As they began to pull away, Nebzydoski fired a shot from his M14 rifle into the vehicle, and every man, including Rasool, got out with his hands up, looking around in fear, trying to figure out where the next shot was going to come from.

What happened next did sort of happen the way it does on TV. The quick reaction force screeched onto the scene and a bunch of infantrymen dismounted and began to remove the stunned men from the property, including Rasool, who was positively identified once they had him in custody.

Meanwhile, the snipers followed the same ditch they were in out to the road where the infantrymen were and loaded up into a tracked M113 armored personnel carrier. They were dirty, tired, and still wearing parts of their ghillie suits. After their concealed movement all through the night, they weren't too worried about being seen, even with all the people around.

"At that point there was so much chaos going on over there, we could have walked out in Hawaiian shirts and no one would have seen us," Redus said.

Kellner, who caught up to his waiting team in the vehicle after briefing the company commander about the details of the mission, returned to find them "laughing and joking and just rolling. We couldn't stop telling the story over and over again how he wouldn't go down. That's the kind of shit you see in a movie," Kellner said. "We were like, 'What the fuck happened?' We watched the guy's shirt wave from the impact. It was weird."

Weird, yes, but not a weird act to shoot one of the enemy, said Kellner, particularly one who, according to a variety of sources that track sniper activity, racked up the highest number of kills in Iraq.

His feelings about killing Omar and men like him, if he had any feelings, are always tempered by the care and precision that go into the missions of finding them and by the discomfort and trouble the snipers endure for a chance to kill someone before he kills Americans.

"I've expended days' worth of energy to get to a position. I'm soaked in two-day-old sweat, covered in mud, or worse. I haven't eaten a real meal in days, have to hold a piss for hours sometimes," he said.

Sleep, even a few minutes, doesn't feel like sleep at all and lying in the same position in the same spot for three days makes a person cramped and sore.

"You can't talk out loud. Your only entertainment is what the idiots you're watching are doing; then remember that he is a threat and wants you and others dead. What do we feel when we shoot? For me it's, 'Fuck him, I'm going back to my cot and writing my kid a letter.' But that's just me," Kellner said.

The team went back to Carnivore Island to regroup a little before heading back to Forward Operating Base Iskan. Swirling around in their heads was the freaky shot, the perfect freaky shot and the effect it had on the insurgents.

"Chris and I were still in awe," Redus said. "We got to see the effect of what we were doing."

And part of that perfect shot, he said, was their perfect hide site, which, because of the shape of it, dampened every noise, including the suppressor.

"I want to think it's the acoustics of the drop, the sound was dissipated down the ditch rather than on the other side of the ditch," Redus said.

They were lucky that day. They chalked it up to training.

"You have to look at where you are and what's going to happen after you shoot. It's part of training. We just had a great spot," he said.

# CHAPTER THIRTEEN
# SHOTS NOT TAKEN

Most U.S. troops who deployed to Iraq and Afghanistan never fired their weapons. That is the conventional wisdom among snipers and a great many seasoned combat arms troops who were down-range several times.

In these wars, where there is no front line, even the average infantryman might never have fired his rifle. Add to that the squeeze of the ever-tightening rules of engagement and you end up with only a few thousand who have fired their weapons and purposely killed people many times in direct action, over-watch operations, sniper-initiated ambushes, or self-defense.

Consider the numbers. At the height of the 2007 surge in Iraq when close to 150,000 U.S. troops were in country, more than half of those were combat support or combat service support people whose exposure to life outside the wire was limited to a terrifying ride from point A to point B.

On the mean streets of Iraq, everyone had to be ready to shoot, but not everyone did.

Unfortunately the majority of casualties in these wars, including deaths among those who did fire their weapons on many occasions, can be chalked up to the ubiquitous improvised explosive devices that continued to indiscriminately kill and maim anyone wearing a military uniform.

Even in Afghanistan, where it was decidedly more of a shooting war, the human toll from giant roadside bombs remained, so much so that the military set out to design ground vehicles that recognize the IED threat far into the distance.

Being a trained sniper at war doesn't always mean a shot is taken—even during a yearlong deployment. But the instances when snipers have wanted to take a shot and couldn't or didn't, even when they had a strong gut feeling that the guy in his cross-hairs was rotten to the core, have been frustrating for a few, even haunting.

## Sgt. First Class Pete Peterson
### *"To this day I know I should have shot those guys."*

Sgt. First Class Pete Peterson remembers the first time he regretted being unable to take a shot from a sniper hide. The second time happened nine years later in Iraq—but not for the same reason.

The place was Port-au-Prince, Haiti, and the time was September 1994, when twenty thousand U.S. troops deployed to the island nation as part of a U.S.-led multinational force for Operation Uphold Democracy.

A month after they arrived, Lt. Gen. Raoul Cédras of the Haitian army was ushered out of the country by the United States government so that Jean-Bertrand Aristide, whom Cédras had ousted in a bloody coup in 1991, could be reinstalled as president.

What was to be a forced invasion and an expected fight evolved into a peaceful authorized landing and the eventual United Nations mission in Haiti.

From Peterson's point of view aboard the U.S.S. *Eisenhower*, the ship that brought him and his fellow Tenth Mountain Division infantrymen to Haiti, "the rules of engagement changed several times while we were on the ship," and by the time they arrived, the actions they were authorized to carry out were few, if any.

Flying to shore with seventeen guys on the floor of a Black Hawk helicopter, they arrived at a landing zone in the port and Peterson and his men took up a position on the roof of the port's headquarters building.

The Army had trained him to be a sniper about a year earlier, but this wasn't exactly war. It became a long over-watch mission as diplomatic angles were brokered. There was a lot of waiting, day and night. Just waiting and watching. Things were calm. They were in the tropics. No one was shooting at them.

But that balmy Caribbean air was pierced one night by the bloodcurdling screams of a woman near the port's main gate. The

American troops watched in horror as a man savagely bludgeoned the woman, and there was nothing they could do about it. The snipers were forbidden from taking a shot, even a warning shot.

"My guys wanted to take a shot so bad, but the ROE at the time didn't allow us. He killed her right in front of us; he beat her to death," Peterson said, recalling the team's frustration so vividly that it seemed as if the murder had taken place the day before.

"We even asked if we could go down there and do something but we were told it was not a matter for us to handle," Peterson said. "We were told to stay where we were."

The snipers would never take a shot in Haiti. Then again, the opportunity never came as clearly as it had that night when they wanted to take the shot out of moral outrage more than anything else.

Peterson started shooting competitively when he was twelve in Washington, where he grew up playing in the woods in the high mountain desert town of Ellensburg.

"I was always the last kid off the school bus, the end of the road," he said of his rural home in the northwest of the country.

But then Peterson became one of those soldiers who was always in the right place at the right time for deployment, the Forrest Gump of the Army's late-twentieth century conflicts.

He spent an initial two-year enlistment at Fort Drum, New York, and was sent to Fort Carson, Colorado, after reenlisting. From there he went almost immediately to Operation Desert Storm as a door gunner on a Chinook helicopter with the 101st Airborne Division after he stepped forward during formation when someone asked for volunteers. He wasn't even assigned to the 101st, and when he returned to Fort Carson, he was a private first class, one of only a handful of soldiers of any rank who had gone anywhere.

Disenchanted with the Army's handling of some administrative issues after he redeployed, Peterson took advantage of the military drawdown in December 1991 and returned to Washington and a ten-month stint in the National Guard. There, he shot on the rifle team and was sent to Airborne School and the Infantry Leaders Course.

He decided to return to active duty in October 1992 and had only been at Fort Drum about a month when he shipped out to Somalia. In the summer of 1993, he was sent to Sniper School. After the rotation to Haiti in 1994, he moved to a unit in Vicenza, Italy, just in time for a deployment in Bosnia.

When Peterson landed at Fort Benning, Georgia, his morale plummeted as a trainer in a basic training brigade. It looked as if he had been all he could be. And then the United States was attacked.

"That's when I switched over and went to Kelley Hill," he said, referring to the section of Fort Benning where the headquarters for the Third Infantry Division's Third Brigade Combat Team is.

In the rush to Baghdad in March 2003, First Battalion, Fifteenth Infantry blazed a trail and took no prisoners, and most of what Peterson and his snipers did was scouting. But he got to take a long shot in one instance.

At the intersection of Highways 1 and 8 on the south side of the city, his platoon set up a blocking position to keep anyone from moving in or out of Baghdad from any direction. The platoon had a Bradley, two M1 Abrams tanks, and a scout truck with a long-range advance scout surveillance system, or LRAS, which is a $200,000 box with two GPS units and a range finder that goes out to about ten thousand meters. They could see people coming down the road way before the people could see them.

If the sound of .50-caliber bullets zipping past their cars, layers of concertina wire, overturned vehicles, and warning signs in Arabic didn't dissuade Iraqis from continuing forward, the bodies of the combatants the U.S. soldiers had already killed should have, and most people did turn around.

Except this one guy who kept coming despite the dire warnings.

"The guy gets mad, gets out of his car, looks around, sees a dead body there and an AK, and he picks up the AK and I'm like, 'TA-DA!' You just met our ROE! If you have a weapon in your hand, you've now met the magic requirement. It's time for you to go away. As soon as he picked up the weapon, he became a combatant," Peterson said.

The man, who was about five hundred meters away, futilely aimed the weapon at the Americans. Peterson trained his M24 sniper rifle on the man but couldn't get a clear shot from his position on the side of a tank. He ran to the other side, tracked the man as he moved, and watched him fall after taking a shot at him. The penalty for stupidity in a war zone is death.

"The Joes in the Bradley are like, 'Hey, good shot, good job man,'" said Peterson, confident that the man he shot and killed, like all the other guys on that road who had been killed before him, had been taken care of well within the rules of engagement.

Fast-forward about three weeks to a rooftop in northern Baghdad, and the same rules would spark outrage in Peterson by preventing him from taking a shot. And unlike that night in Haiti, his desire to kill the two men he knew were the enemy had nothing to do with morality.

In the early weeks after the March 20 invasion of Iraq, when Saddam Hussein's statue had been smashed and the hunt was on for the men whose faces were printed on a deck of playing cards, U.S. troops were all over Baghdad doing what they could to keep order and stop widespread looting.

Peterson and a couple of other snipers set up a position atop a building that was a high-rise version of an American military post exchange and was known to be frequented by Saddam's elite Republican Guard soldiers. It was a potential treasure trove for looters.

"This building was seven stories of nothing but durable goods," Peterson said, describing thousands of square feet packed with men's and women's clothing, miles of fabric, stacks of rugs, and rows of household goods and fixtures on the upper floors, and heavier-gauge items on the lower floors, like compressors for air conditioners, washing machines, and tires.

"You got to understand, in Iraq this was a lot of merchandise, this was good stuff," he said, lamenting the fact that even with all that merchandise "they didn't have any damn socks. And let me tell you, we looked." After weeks of mobilizing toward Baghdad, Peterson and his soldiers just wanted some clean socks, he said.

The scout platoon and some infantrymen from one of First Battalion, Fifteenth Infantry's line companies conducted security at the base of the giant fenced-in shopping building, but the area was a large one to patrol so the snipers tried to cover what they could for the guys below.

From his perch high above the street, Peterson watched over the neighborhood and began to identify the rhythm of quotidian life among its residents.

He saw a truck and two cars packed with men pull up in front of the building, presumably preparing to take whatever goods they could fit into their vehicles. These men were very obviously not from the block.

"They got out of the vehicles, and they're like high-fiving each other like 'Woohoo, yeah, we made it here, this is gonna be magical.' Then they come in the gate, and I yell at them to get out. I'm yelling, '*Qif, qif,*' which means stop, but they don't stop. I put a couple of rounds by the guy's foot, and after that they looked like clowns trying to get in the car. One guy's running down the street chasing the car; he's the last one in, the door's open, and he dives into the car," Peterson said.

But the Keystone Kops–style humor of the would-be looters faded quickly when Peterson's eye caught a shady looking twosome walking calmly past the building, one of a number of key objectives a few blocks apart that the battalion was responsible for holding in northern Baghdad.

One building in their area was what Peterson called a "terrorist training camp," where the soldiers found pictures of F-15s being shot down and one of Saddam smoking a cigar in front of the burning World Trade Center towers in New York City. The camp also had a stockpile of weapons and ammunition and an indoor rifle range, and Saddam reportedly used it as a showcase for out-of-towners from neighboring Arab countries like Syria and Lebanon.

"We shot one guy one time, and when we checked the body, he had Lebanese money on him and he was fair-complected," Peterson said.

Peterson imagined that the two men had come into the neighborhood to see what was left of the training camp and were leaving after finding it had been taken over by the Americans.

As Peterson was watching these two guys walk down the road, their outsider status glaring, he was focused on the gym bags they were each carrying. One guy was exceptionally tall and looked to Peterson like an Afghan, like a member of the Taliban.

"He had a big ol' Afghani beard; he was not a local. The locals wore close-cut beards, and his beard was thick. And he was wearing a dark man-dress. All the locals were wearing white man-dresses," he said.

"The other guy was clean shaven and looked like a guy you could pull off a street corner in the USA. He was white with short dark hair and wore western-style clothing. They looked like they had good meals, and they were walking out of town with their gym bags," he said.

Besides their appearance, another tip-off was their lack of interest in the U.S. troops, who were used to being surrounded or at least approached by curious Iraqis.

Peterson's rage mounted as the men sauntered past, and an internal debate waged as he looked at them through his scope.

"I wanted to shoot these guys so bad, but the ROE had changed at that point and you had to see a weapon or have a positive identification. They had to present a hostile force. I knew these guys were bad, but I couldn't prove it," he said.

He called the soldiers who were pulling security below and asked them to go after the men, but it was too late. By the time they gave chase, the sinister duo had slipped away.

"I had to let them go. It was the worst feeling. I have that guy's face in my head, both those guys. To this day I know I should have shot those guys," he said.

## SGT. FIRST CLASS JASON
### *"They killed the wrong American that day."*
The visit at dawn by a team of Special Forces soldiers was not part of a hospitality call for tea. The bad guys knew it meant the jig was up.

In the few moments before the Special Forces ground mobility vehicles arrived packed with Green Berets and their Afghan counterparts, the villagers who had something to fear were able to grab their weapons and come out fighting. Some died. Others took off running and fled for the hills.

One of those who scattered was an older man with a distinctive, bushy, white beard. Sgt. First Class Jason had him in his sights, but he didn't shoot to kill because the man was unarmed, even though his gut told him the guy was shady and needed to be stopped.

"I fired some warning shots at him, and now, I'm like, you idiot," he said.

The rules of engagement would not have allowed him to take the shot anyway, but following the six years of war he experienced there and in Iraq after that day, he said, he looks back and realizes that part of his hesitation was a lack of clarity on what was allowed, what wasn't, and why.

"I didn't know how I should deal with that situation, and if faced with that exact situation again, I'd probably make the same decision because I wouldn't have a clue that this dude would be part of something later," he said.

The incident happened on his second trip to Afghanistan, and he was one of the new guys on his team in the Third Special Forces Group.

Jason chalks it up partly to his own low level of experience at the time, but he places at least as much responsibility on his leaders who, he says, should have made the rules of engagement absolutely clear and imbued him with the assurance that if he did take a shot within those rules, he would be backed by the command.

"This was in 2004, but the leadership was new and I was new, so I didn't really get an ROE brief. I should have been told what was expected of me. So I let this guy go," said Jason, who invoked the almost universal request of Special Forces soldiers that his last name not be used.

The night before, Jason and five other men had walked seven kilometers under the cover of darkness to the far end of the village, split up into smaller teams of three about eighty meters apart, and taken up a position in the low saddle area between two mountains.

They waited there and maintained radio communication with the other half of their team, which was to come into the village from the opposite end in their GMVs. When the other half of the team began to roll through the valley at first light, it kicked off an ancient early-warning system. "The warning network there is amazing," Jason said. "I could hear them yelling, they had smoke signals, and they just knew. I didn't even know our guys were coming until I saw the Afghans running to the hills."

A gunfight began, and four bad guys were killed as several others ran.

"To my left I see this older guy with a huge white beard, a big turban on his head. He's probably only like fifty; they don't age real well, no dental plan," Jason said wryly, "but I can't detain him because there's a small gunfight going on in front of me, and the other guy on my team is like, 'What do we do?'"

After Jason fired his warning shots, they both watched as the man got away.

Jason still remembers his impression of the old bearded guy and his assumption that, since he wasn't doing anything bad at the time, there was no justification to shoot him. But since then, Jason, a meticulous note taker and chronicler of the most minute detail of every combat engagement he's ever been in, has thought a lot about what it takes to squeeze the trigger. His conclusions are now being taught at the Special Forces Advanced Reconnaissance Target Analysis and Exploitation Techniques Course at Fort Bragg, North Carolina.

In the course, he uses as an example the story of Sgt. Leigh Ann Hester, a military police officer in the Kentucky National Guard, who in March 2005 killed three insurgents during an ambush by more than fifty enemy fighters on the convoy for which she and her fellow guardsmen were providing security.

After the attack, she became the first woman since World War II to earn a Silver Star Medal and was celebrated for her bold actions as were her male counterparts. But her willingness to shoot to kill, Jason said, had nothing to do with training.

"If you really think about it, is she trained that well, at the same comparative level that I am? No. But something got her fired up, and she did this and earned that Silver Star. I've seen guys in the Special Operations community that don't do that well," Jason said, pointing out that he thinks a soldier needs more than training to be able to kill.

A strong belief in the mission coupled with a clear understanding of the rules of engagement are critical, he said, but a soldier also needs to know that he won't be hung out to dry by his command for taking a shot he felt was justified.

The rules of engagement play a big role, and Jason acknowledged that shooting someone is not a natural thing to do whether you're a Green Beret, a Navy SEAL, or a Georgia National Guardsman.

"But if you feel justified in what you're doing, by killing him we're better off. I truly believe wholeheartedly that every guy I ever shot . . . had it coming," he said.

Jason joined the Marines in 1993 assigned to First Battalion, Fourth Marines at Camp Pendleton, California, and five years later he enlisted in the Army so he would have the option of going into the Special Forces.

After two years with the Third Armored Cavalry Regiment at Fort Carson, Colorado, he made it through Special Forces selection, then the Qualification Course, and landed in the Third Special Forces Group in May 2003.

During his training to be a Green Beret, he befriended a young officer named Danny Eggers. The two men later ended up on the same team in the Third Special Forces Group and became close friends. "He was pretty much as green as I was, so to speak. The only difference was, he loved the Afghan culture, I mean he loved it," Jason said.

Eggers spoke Pashto fluently enough to be able to conduct meetings with the village elders without an interpreter, and his sensibilities as a soldier, Jason said, were very much in the spirit of the classic Special Forces mission to help foreign nationals develop their own forces and the skills needed to provide for their people.

"He was very involved in it. He was just a great guy overall. He loved the SF, and he loved the locals," Jason said.

About three weeks after the early morning gunfight in southern Afghanistan, Eggers, Jason, and the rest of the team were clearing another village, one that was too big for the group of men they had with them.

"We tried to contain it, but we couldn't. There were a few guys shooting at us here and there, but we couldn't locate them, we couldn't find them and didn't know where they were at," he said.

During the course of the morning, they received some intelligence that the shooters were moving away from the village toward the team's base, so the team headed back home to engage them in place.

It is the norm in Afghanistan for there to be only one road to get anywhere and it's even more common for that road to lead into a narrow pass. Turning that combination into a lethal snare is the remoteness of vast areas, which gives the enemy ample opportunity to plant big bombs under those lone roads. All that needs to be done to activate one of those bombs is a battery hookup.

Jason and his team drove their loaded ground mobility vehicles, which were specially equipped Humvees, toward a narrow pass, and as soon as the lead vehicle rounded the corner, there was a monstrous *Kaboom!* The blast destroyed the first vehicle, put the second vehicle into a ditch, and rocked the third vehicle off the road.

Before the dust had even settled, it was clear to everyone that the lead truck had been decimated, ripped apart by an enormous explosion caused by four IEDs daisy-chained and buried under the roadway.

Eggers; Navy SEAL Boatswain's Mate First Class Brian Ouellette; Army Staff Sgt. Robert Mogensen; and Army Pfc. Joseph Jeffries of the 329th Psychological Operations Company were killed in the explosion.

Through the devastation, a gunfight ensued, and the enemies they had been looking for started moving out. Another Special Forces team that was headed to a separate mission found out they were in trouble and diverted their helicopter to help out.

"They were able to box these guys off a couple of terrain features away about a mile away and were able to kill about nine dudes," Jason said. When he got back to Kandahar and saw the after-action (site exploitation) pictures of the dead assailants, one thing was clear. "One of the dudes we killed was the old man. Was he in charge of this? I don't know. But he was one of the dudes," Jason said.

In hindsight, and after more than a half-dozen trips to the war zone, Jason said he still wrestles with the decision-making process he went through at the time he had the chance to kill the man, though he stopped short of saying whether he would have shot him outside the rules-of-engagement parameters.

"To this day, after so many trips to the war zone, what was the right answer? I think I knew what the right answer was. He was part of this. He was partially responsible for these guys being killed. Those are those gray decisions," Jason said.

About Eggers, Jason remembers a dedicated soldier who might have made a difference to a great many people in Afghanistan.

"They killed the wrong American that day because he gave a shit about them; he really truly cared," Jason said.

### Sgt. Ray
**_"Sir, we don't do warning shots."_**
The men pulling the razor wire off the wall at the combat outpost on the edge of Sadr City in Baghdad were already dead men as far as Sgt. Ray was concerned.

It was 2 a.m. He had them in his sights. They were messing around with the outpost's perimeter security wires the same way they had done a few nights earlier when they planted a homemade bomb in one of the walls. These guys just had to go, and Sgt. Ray, who asked that his full name not be used, was ready to take care of them.

He and his team chose a high building next to Bravo Company's outpost to set up their hide. They were there at the request of the company and battalion commanders who asked them if they could "fix the problem."

The team expected it to be a quick, easy job if the guys showed up. But when the guys did, the company commander, who was the only one authorized to give the team the go-ahead, balked.

"We called in and said, 'Hey, we got three guys pulling on the wire. Do you want us to take care of the problem, to go ahead and shoot?'" Sgt. Ray said. "No, we have to wait until they do something hostile," Ray recalled as the commander's response.

Sgt. Ray and his team from Second Battalion, Sixteenth Infantry of the First Infantry Division, had already racked up numerous kills during night operations to over-watch the main supply routes in eastern Baghdad, and for those operations the team used an established shooting parameter, a set of guidelines in which they could shoot individuals who were out after curfew and those doing suspicious things, like digging in the dirt along the roadway or threatening to harm coalition supply convoys from their vehicles.

But on other occasions, such as this targeted mission for Bravo Company, the call was at the commander's discretion, and Sgt. Ray and his boys ended up having to obey an order.

Sgt. Ray said he told the captain that they could see the men pulling down the razor wire.

"We can shoot them right now," Sgt. Ray offered.

"Do you have positive identification?" the captain replied.

They didn't; they couldn't see the bad guys' faces over the six-foot wall that shielded them. The snipers had seen the men clearly as they entered through a narrow walkway behind the walls, and their plan was to fire a round from their .50-cal into the wall and engage them as they hauled ass back out.

Instead, the commander told them to hold while he sent a foot patrol over to scare the guys off.

It worked.

For a while.

But as the snipers were getting ready to close up shop and go in for the night, they saw a young boy coming from the opposite direction. When the boy started pulling down the same strip of wire, the snipers asked again for permission to shoot.

"Sir, you've got a ten-year-old over here pulling on the wire. Do you want us to shoot?"

"No," Ray recalled the captain say over the radio.

"Sir, he's pulling off your wire, request permission to shoot," he said, and was dismayed to hear the captain reply that he wanted the snipers to fire a warning shot.

"Sir, we don't do warning shots. We don't want to give away our location. We either shoot or we don't," the sniper responded. Following a few minutes of battling one another on the radio, Sgt. Ray acquiesced.

"I put a tracer in my M4, pulled the trigger, and put a warning shot about four inches in front of his nose. I saw the red tracer come in. It blew a hole in the concrete around him, and he took off running."

Sgt. Ray said he considered the company commander "soft" in his leadership style, and the battalion commander, about three weeks later, told Sgt. Ray he could have, and should have, shot to kill.

"It was your call; it was always your call," Sgt. Ray recalled being told by the battalion commander at the time, but the battalion commander Lt. Col. Ralph Kauzlarich, asked about the event three years later, responded by e-mail from Iraq, where he was on his third deployment.

He defended the captain's decision, taking a longer view of situation that, in hindsight, may have been the right call for everyone.

"The good captain was on the ground and made the call. I always told my guys that they were the ones that would have to deal with their conscience when all was said and done."

Kauzlarich concluded by writing, "Our war doesn't stop after getting home as we'll live with our actions and decisions for the rest of our lives. With that being said, I've slept well every night, and I hope my men can too."

## SGT. RON FELICIANO
### *"I'm like, is that the guy?"*

A split-second decision kept Sgt. Ron Feliciano from squeezing his trigger, sparing the life of a man whose face only resembled that of the target he was after. Today, he says, he's better off for having played it safe that morning in Baghdad in 2006.

"I was disappointed, but I was actually really happy I didn't shoot the wrong guy. It's something I would have to live with," he said.

Military snipers spend 90 percent of their time doing reconnaissance and reporting and building battlefield intelligence that can lead to a shot taken on the spot, an air strike, or a larger ground operation with a quick reaction force.

Over the course of two twelve-month deployments in Iraq, the jobs of watching other people and sneaking around in the dark were Feliciano's favorite things to do as a sniper, though it might have been harder for him than for most.

"It's kind of weird because I'm actually terrified of the dark when I'm alone," Feliciano said, admitting that even when he sleeps, he needs to have the TV on. "If I'm with someone, I'm fine, but I would start screwing myself over and I would just freeze if I were alone."

Luckily for everyone, he never went out alone. His was almost always a night mission, and the thought of getting caught was the only thing that made him nervous. In fact, he said he preferred the relaxing aspect of doing an infiltration to sit and observe over the rush of a harried raid on a compound to snatch a high-value target, which he considered "not necessarily as exciting."

"I wanted to get out there, get in position, get set up, and get eyes on the objective. It's probably the greatest feeling to me to be sneaking around a city at night. Everybody wants to be the cool, secret-spy guy crawling around in the dark, but it's about staying concealed, being quiet, being disciplined," he said.

Feliciano did his two rotations in Iraq with First Battalion, Twenty-fourth Infantry in the Twenty-fifth Infantry Division and ended up working with a lot of different platoons because he and his team knew every detail of the urban landscape. More important, he learned the art of developing enough intelligence to convince higher-level commanders that a particular mission was worth doing.

On his second deployment he used some of what he'd learned and in late 2006 told his company commander that he'd gotten information on a man who was kidnapping people to raise money for insurgent operations and beheading those who were uncooperative.

Feliciano said his team learned that the man's wife had left him and gone back to her family, and her relatives were his source of information. So he worked with the family and his platoon to coordinate a plan for the man's return to the house under the guise that his wife would let him take their son.

"They gave me a picture of the guy. I gave it to my team and said, 'Study this picture, get it into your head,'" Feliciano said.

The target house was in a Baghdad neighborhood on a street that had houses on both sides. The team chose an abandoned house diagonally across from the target so that if the man pulled up and got out of his car, Feliciano said, "I would have plenty of time to engage him."

After a short dismounted patrol with the platoon around dusk, the team and several members of the platoon stayed behind when the platoon left.

Feliciano was in the house with three others, and a rifle team was one floor down with the platoon leader, who kept radio communications with the command outpost, though Feliciano wasn't accustomed to setting up a hide site with an officer one floor below.

"This was a mission where we were actually going to kill this guy so I guess they wanted to maintain comms," he said.

After everyone was in place and some time had gone by, a family member who was with the company commander was getting vibes from phone conversations with others that the man they wanted to take out seemed to be getting suspicious and wasn't going to show. Throughout the night, the situation went back and forth, and it didn't look as if the mission was going to occur as first thought.

Around 2 a.m., Feliciano said, "I see this guy. I thought it was the guy. I was excited because I didn't think he was going to show up."

He watched a car pull up to the house that fit the description of the car they were on the lookout for, and through his 10X optic, he saw the man's face. Doubt crept in quickly.

"I'm like, is that the guy? This is my decision to say yes or no. I could not give it 100 percent that this was the guy. I had the picture. You can't get a great picture; it was probably printed off a color printer," he said.

Time was running out. The man had no idea that snipers were there or that a whole fire team was in the house with them, and everything stood still for a moment.

The man got back into the car and left. No shot was taken, and no one was ever compromised. Feliciano had made the decision to hold off because he was unsure.

The man was stopped at an American traffic checkpoint at the end of the street. It turned out he was the wanted man's brother. They only looked alike.

"I don't want to do this job so I can shoot people in the face. No. I do this job because it's an honor and prestige and you're a combat multiplier," Feliciano said. "I'm not God, that's not my job. But ultimately, that's what we do."

## STAFF SGT. JOHN BRADY
### *"My most infamous miss ever."*

Staff Sgt. John Brady's problem was not that he didn't take the shot. He took plenty of shots while he was in Iraq for fifteen months.

His unit, First Battalion, Twenty-third Infantry Regiment, was part of the Third Stryker Brigade Combat Team, which brought the first Stryker vehicles ever into combat in November 2003. The Stryker vehicle, which gives the brigade its distinctive designation, is an eight-wheeled tactical troop carrier armed with a .50-caliber machine gun and a computer networking system that makes it a superior command and control platform. More important, the vehicles are transportable by air and can carry nine infantrymen, four more than the twenty-five-year-old tracked Bradley fighting vehicle.

The unit's first month there, it did what most units did: push north from Kuwait to a final destination, with multiple stops.

One of those was in Samarra, just days before the December 13 capture of Saddam Hussein in Tikrit, the town next door, and after several more stops, the unit ended its journey to Mosul at a base near the airfield where they would stay for six months.

"The snipers' mission at that point was pretty overt," Brady said. "The enemy feared snipers. We would do a lot of rooftop presence, like, 'Here we are, look at us,' and there wasn't a lot of countersniper threat at all so that kept control of the area. They knew there were guys on the roof watching them, and they weren't going to do a lot of stuff. It was pretty slow at first."

But two days in 2004 stand out in Brady's memory. One was April 8.

"It was the day my son was born, which was April 9 for us. We were sitting up in an observation post similar to this," he said, while sitting in the shade five years later at Burroughs Range on Fort Benning, pointing to a three-story building that the Sniper School uses for practice, not unlike the flat-roofed buildings in Iraq.

It was a quiet day in Mosul, and Brady and his men were keeping it fresh, saving their energy for a planned night mission. The quiet would soon be broken.

In fact, the day Brady's son was born was marked by mass chaos all over Iraq.

Ten days earlier, on March 31, four private security guards who worked for Blackwater USA were ambushed and killed while running a mission through the city of Fallujah, west of Baghdad. Their burned and mutilated bodies were strung up on a bridge over the Euphrates River. In response to the attack, and the deaths of five U.S. soldiers in a roadside bomb attack near Habbaniyah, an unsuccessful offensive by Marines and Iraqi security forces to take control of Fallujah was launched on April 3.

By April 9, the insurgency had organized its own form of synchronized attacks, including a savage ambush on a twenty-six-vehicle supply and fuel convoy near Baghdad International Airport, that left two soldiers and eight civilian drivers working for the private contractor KBR dead. Sgt. Keith "Matt" Maupin was abducted and remained missing until his skeletal remains were found four years later. One civilian, Timothy Bell, remains unaccounted for.

In Mosul on the same day, Brady was in a building with his sniper team, when, wafting through the mid-afternoon air like a siren with bad news, "we heard some weird chanting coming out of the mosque. It just wasn't normal. When you're in theater that long, you don't know what they're saying, but this sounds a whole lot different," Brady said.

While he was downstairs getting their interpreter so they could find out what the weird chanting was, Brady got word of his son's birth. No sooner had he and the interpreter started climbing the stairs, gunfire erupted and rocket-propelled grenades were launched at their forward operating base from a mosque about five hundred meters away.

The eerie chant turned out to be some sort of call to battle for about 150 armed and unarmed people who burst onto the streets from the mosque and headed toward the base gate that Brady and his snipers had covered. Within the first minute of the commotion, Brady's teammate, Sgt. Andrew Furman, alone dropped three people, and the crowd began to disperse but not disappear.

"They fell on the road, and the whole crowd stopped, turned around, and ran away from our compound. After that happened, people started flanking our whole compound, taking potshots. We stayed in position there while they were ramping up other squads to push out and clear out these other insurgents," he said.

It was a complex engagement that lasted a few hours, and all the snipers took several shots. April 2004 would become one of the deadliest months on record during the entire U.S. operation in Iraq.

But of all the shots taken that day and in the months before and after April 9, one particularly annoying shot that stands out for Brady is the one he loudly proclaims as "my most infamous miss ever on the fuckin' planet."

He and his partner were in a hide site that summer, and they saw, in broad daylight, a man standing on top of a roof about 1,375 meters away—a little outside the range for his M14 and his buddy's M24 sniper rifle.

"We saw him up there so we were like, 'Hey, let's try,' This jack is standing up on top of a frickin' roof with a rocket-propelled grenade trying to shoot at Kiowa helicopters," Brady said.

He and his partner did frame shooting, where simultaneous shots are fired to make it sound like one rifle and it doubles the chance of hitting the target. "It reduces the signature of the shooters because it sounds like one shot. The Marine Corps does it a lot," Brady said. They figured they'd miss, but they fired on the "T" of two after counting down five, four, three, two. The shot went off without a hitch, sort of.

"I'm like, crank the scope up, hold four high, you take left side, I take right side and engage. We both shot and both broke, and we saw both rounds hit this little wall," he said. "I was like hold just a little bit higher and we'll reengage."

So they did. They reacquired their target and on five, four, three, two—*gsshhh!*

"It was boom! Right over his right shoulder, and the dude's like, "Huuhh?" and he jumps off the roof, and I'm like, 'Holy fuck, that would have been the fuckin' coolest shot ever. Most infamous miss ever," Brady said in an uproarious laugh. "It went right over his shoulder, which amazed the hell out of us! He probably didn't hear it because of helicopters."

At 1,325 meters, he said, "That motherfucker's way subsonic by that point. The bullet's going like, 'Are we there yet?' Like, okay, find me a wall," he said.

After that day, Brady's unit spent the next six months playing a sort of SWAT team role, speeding long distances to where it was needed, like only the Strykers can do. They crisscrossed the country and fought in places like Samarra, Tal Afar, Mosul, Al Kut, Al Hayy, Al Suwaria, and Yousufiah.

The infantrymen, including the snipers, rolled into every hot spot and engaged in a lot of gunfights, but Brady and his colleagues also engaged as snipers.

"The sniper mission has its role in Iraq, but I think a lot of people get into sniper situations by chance or luck. You really got to have a good section leader to plan the missions and create missions, and even if you have that, you have to have your higher echelons to approve it," he said.

# CHAPTER FOURTEEN
# SNIPERS, BROTHERS

The day Cpl. Neal Brace killed a man became a personal turning point for him and a source of amusement for the rest of his team, Marine scout snipers who didn't think he had it in him.

It happened on a blazing hot morning in May 2008 in Afghanistan's Helmand province a few days into the first major U.S. offensive in the seven years since the Marines were first there. But it would be a fleeting moment of levity for the team of scout snipers because no one knew that only thirteen days later a tragedy would unfold against an enemy unlike any they'd seen in Iraq.

Brace and the Marines from First Battalion, Sixth Marines, the battalion landing team for the Twenty-fourth Marine Expeditionary Unit, were part of a force of more than three thousand Marines who streamed into the Taliban stronghold to help NATO and Afghan forces take control of the lawless area.

The 1-6 Marines had deployed from their home at Camp Lejeune, North Carolina, almost two months earlier and were deep inside Taliban country with practically no training relevant to the Afghanistan mission.

In fact, they weren't even expecting to go to Afghanistan. They were preparing for, perhaps dreaming of, a standard six-month Mediterranean float, just as Marine units had done before the war, with glamorous ports of call in places like Spain, Portugal, and Italy. The Marine Corps has Marine expeditionary units around the world at any time in order to be prepared wherever there is trouble. While they were at sea doing general training, they got word that they'd be going to Afghanistan.

"We were all looking forward to it," said Brace, who had one deployment to Iraq under his belt when, in January 2008, Defense Secretary Robert Gates announced the March deployment of the

Marines to Afghanistan for the first time since their 2001 trip there. "We were totally pumped up about going to Europe, but we realized it was absolutely insane to hope for that."

The region they went to in Afghanistan was dangerous and largely unchecked by coalition troops who were already stretched thin. Blanketed with poppy fields and crawling with fighters who were ready to take on the Americans and their coalition counterparts, the province belonged to the Taliban, which had had plenty of time to build up the battle space to its own advantage.

The Marines, many of whom were on their first deployment to Afghanistan, stumbled upon fighting positions that appeared to be old Russian outposts and random giant mounds of dirt in the middle of villages that had fighting holes on all sides. There were steel-reinforced bunkers, slits in the hillsides that ballooned into giant hiding spaces behind the outer earthen walls, and land mines. There were irrigation trenches with hollowed-out passages that led to underground bunkers in the middle of a field. When flooded with water, the trenches gave no clue of the bunkers' presence.

"The thing with Afghanistan was, they knew we were coming, they were fortified. Everything you can think of is made for warfare," said Cpl. Joel Alvarenga, a fellow sniper in the Weapons Company's surveillance and target acquisition, or STA (pronounced "stay"), platoon. Alvarenga had been to Iraq twice and wasn't sure he was ready or prepared for the rigors of the Afghan fight. "It's hot, you gotta hump everywhere. I'm pretty fit, but they told us we were going into mountains, too, so I thought it was going to be a lot of hiking. I lost thirty pounds in a month."

Their team, led by Sgt. Justin Cooper, was supporting A Company and was paired with another team for one of their first missions that the sniper team leaders developed to catch Taliban reinforcements traveling in from the west for the fight.

The twelve snipers and their Navy corpsman moved out from A Company's patrol base in the southernmost corner of Garmsir in a grueling overnight trek. They were loaded down with more than 150 pounds of equipment each, fighting heat and dehydration as they tried to find the quickest route to their destination west toward the Helmand River.

The route they took didn't end up being that quick, and at least one person fell out from exhaustion as they navigated through a swamp. They circled it twice and came across wadis and other rugged terrain that was infinitely more challenging on the ground than it looked on the map.

Their journey ended at a farming area, a cluster of individual walled compounds laid out in traditional Afghan style, an outgrowth of a war-torn land where every home is a fortress complete with fortified walls and gates. Each had several abandoned buildings that had a good number of windows and doors from which to get eyes on all approaches and shoot if they saw anything. The location was dangerously remote for the two teams, and a quick reaction force would have taken some time to arrive if the snipers were compromised. Still, they were imbued with the confidence and spirit of young men going out to prove themselves in combat— and they were heavily armed.

Each team had two M40A3 bolt-action sniper rifles—one of the best combat weapons ever devised and battle-proven in Iraq and Afghanistan—two Mk11 semiautomatic sniper rifles, and a Barrett SASR .50-caliber rifle, plus two M249 squad automatic weapons, M4s, M16s, and M203 grenade launchers.

They settled into one of the mud brick compounds, splitting the two teams into separate buildings that each had five or six good shooting ports.

The landscape was a combination of fertile soil, tree orchards, and acres of poppy fields that fed the bulk of Afghanistan's lucrative opium trade and fueled the Taliban. The village was abandoned because its residents had moved out in anticipation of the arrival of the Marines, warned that there would surely be gun battles or worse.

It didn't seem possible to the teams that the area had truly been vacated, but emptiness was exactly what they found. "We were in this one-hundred-yard by one-hundred-yard compound in the middle of nowhere, and the closest compound to ours was four hundred yards away," Brace said. "There was no way anyone was going to see us or hear us."

It was desolate and quiet at 6 a.m. on May 6, and the temperature in the sunbaked Helmand Valley was creeping up toward one hundred degrees.

The unusually large group of snipers got as comfortable as they could in their spacious hide sites and tried to stay cool. The shooters sat on chairs or blocks with their weapons resting on the windowsills, scanning the vast open farmland for activity that never surfaced in the other empty compounds.

They placed canvas tarps overhead in the courtyards and doorways, but the tarps didn't do much to keep the heat at bay.

The first two guys on security in one building were Alvarenga, a battle-hardened sniper with a list of daring capers and kills he had racked up in Iraq, and Brace, an inexperienced sniper with one deployment to Iraq who was on the team more for his skills as a radio operator than as a reliable shooter.

After three years in the Marine Corps, Brace had only fired the .50-caliber rifle in training, and his reputation for having fired a warning shot at a pair of young, armed kids in Iraq instead of shooting to kill didn't help. He didn't fit the classic mold of a Marine, much less a killer, among his young and gritty enlisted teammates.

He didn't drink, spit, smoke, party, or curse, had no exploits with women to brag about, was careful with his money, reflective in thought, and while the other Marines were lifting weights at the gym in Afghanistan, Brace was off to the side doing calisthenics exercises.

Some Marines called him the church kid.

Physically, he was slender and fair-skinned, with smart blue eyes and a neat, steady way of carrying himself that screamed bookworm more than leatherneck. He could be unctuous, and he asked people questions that made them suspicious. "I honestly think they thought I was gay, and people actually asked me if I was in the criminal investigation division because of the way I interact with people," he said. "I just rubbed people the wrong way, and they didn't think I was a killer."

But Brace, who had joined the Marines with the intention of becoming an officer and later changed his mind for a host of reasons, held his own in his own way.

He regularly scored the maximum three hundred points on his physical fitness tests, led other Marines in physical training, and he knew his job exceptionally well, which put him beyond reproach as an asset for the team. Plus, he was better than anyone on the radio, and at least one Marine, a visionary platoon sergeant, saw Brace's value and potential, which would be revealed as he took on an important role in the days after the mission at the abandoned village.

Still, on that mission, in the middle of nowhere with eleven other snipers, Brace said, "nobody was expecting me to shoot."

From one vantage point in the house, the snipers could see about one hundred yards of what looked like a main path that intersected with a couple of other trails, and they began to spot men walking down those trails to the main path as well as those trying to be sneakier, who were crossing through a grove of trees before taking the main path. The men were dressed in robes and sometimes in uniform. They were all armed, and they had no idea that the Americans were watching them.

The first one came into view about an hour after the snipers set up in the house. Scanning the blindingly bright landscape with his 40-power scope, Cooper saw a lone man armed with an AK-47 assault rifle.

"Coop's like, 'I'd say that's a positive ID for enemy combatant,' and he shoots the guy with one shot, and the guy's dead," Brace said, recalling Cooper's words and his own reaction to the swift kill. "I was like, okay, this is our first mission. We've only been here an hour, and we've already killed a guy. This is interesting."

Another ninety minutes went by, and another armed man walked into the line of sight coming down the same trail in the opposite direction. He was bloodied and dazed for some reason, but his weapon made him a legitimate target so another Marine shot and killed him, too.

And on it went.

Less than an hour after the second armed man showed up on the trail, three men carrying AK-47s and RPK light machine guns came walking down the same trail. "Two rounds, two guys dead. One more round, one more guy's dead. So we've got five guys dead, and forty-five minutes later, Al and Coop kill another guy walking down the same trail," Brace said, referring to Alvarenga and Cooper by their nicknames.

"It was the total opposite of what we expected. There were just all these guys walking with guns. Every single one was a bona fide target, and they had no idea we were there," said Brace, who after five hours on the farm was now taking his turn on the .50-cal. It was dialed in for 760 yards when he and Cooper saw a man walking with a bicycle loaded down with weapons.

Coop fired, Brace fired, and the ball of dust from the .50 cal obscured Brace's view. Alvarenga saw the shot. "He looked right at me, and he's like 'Holy shit, Brace you just killed a guy!'" It was the first man he'd killed, and his reaction came from the gut.

"I started laughing, kind of like, I couldn't believe how easy it was, it was stupid. They told me to shut the hell up, but then they started laughing too," he recalled. "They're like, 'Brace, you're the guy we've been making fun of for two years now, and you just killed a guy with a .50-cal sniper rifle and you're laughing about it.' Then ten minutes later I killed another guy, and I guess it was just kind of overwhelming."

Over ten long hours in the heat of Afghanistan's southern plains, the team would kill twelve armed men who walked down that trail. Because of its isolation, the snipers' hide site, which they had now named the "reaper farm," would have been a haul for reinforcements to show up if things went south, but things had gone exceptionally well, and they were satisfied with the success of their dangerous mission. It proved to their commander that they could operate effectively for the company, and they got to plan more missions after that.

But the reaper farm mission would pale in comparison to a short, tragic battle some of them would witness on May 19.

## BONDS FORGED OF STEEL

Cooper was an influential man, a six-foot-tall people magnet from a small town in Mississippi with a natural way of bringing others along. His searching eyes, sensual good looks, and confidence were at once loathed and admired, and he inspired loyalty by being fair and keeping promises.

Nobody thought he was perfect, but he was perfect for them. He was capable and bold. His superb technical skills and personal instincts as a sniper were emulated and occasionally equaled by others on the team. He helped others get better by spending the time to share his knowledge, sitting and talking one-on-one. In the way he carried himself and showed faith in others, he taught simple, intangible things, like how to survive as a team in a life-and-death setting most Americans never see.

His acceptance of an unusual Marine like Brace was an example to everyone, though Brace never imagined himself hanging out with a guy like Cooper, whom Brace described as an "alpha dog" who did every rowdy, raunchy, rugged thing young men did to embody the image of a rock-hard Marine, pushing the limits and getting away with behavior that other Marines got in trouble for.

"He was a rascal, and I would call him somewhat of a pirate. He probably didn't like me as a person, but I couldn't tell because he would task me with things and I'd get them done and he was happy with that," said Brace, who also recalled Cooper's ability at the young age of twenty-two to understand and manage a group dynamic.

"He would not side with one group against another and say, 'You guys are all wrong, shut up, I'm the leader, you're done.' It was like the best possible form of mini-democracy I've ever had. Coop would listen to me. He'd listen to other people. He was just a good leader."

On May 19 Cooper was killed while deviating from his sniper mission to help a platoon that was pinned down in a fight. It was a dark day for the team.

His Marines hung their heads in sorrow, grief, and anger and forced themselves to move on without him for the five months they had left in their deployment. The faces of the Marines pictured around a shrine to him at his memorial service in the war zone show defiance, sadness, and regret, a hard resolve to accept the unacceptable.

Cooper's death was an especially heavy loss for Alvarenga, who saw their friendship as something beyond what he'd ever known. "He was like a brother. My brothers are my brothers," Alvarenga said, "but I've never been that close to anybody."

At boot camp on Parris Island in January 2005, Cooper and Alvarenga were in separate platoons, but they became fast friends during Infantry School at Camp Lejeune and deployed together almost immediately because their names began with letters at the top of the alphabet and that was how the Marine Corps chose the first thirty-seven in the class.

"They stopped at G," said Alvarenga, the son of Salvadoran immigrants who put three years of college aside and enlisted after learning of the death of a high school friend, a Marine he'd seen only weeks earlier whose descriptions of the war stirred something inside.

The friend, Cpl. Binh Le, was Vietnamese. He had been raised by an aunt and uncle in Virginia since the age of six and received his U.S. citizenship posthumously. A suicidal jihadist driving a car packed with explosives killed Le and another Marine, Cpl. Matthew Wyatt, on December 3, 2004. Three weeks later, Alvarenga drove to a Marine Corps recruiting station and signed up to honor his friend's sacrifice.

By August 2005, he and his new friend Cooper were on the streets of Ramadi, going on patrols and getting their feet wet on what would be the first of two deployments there. They became a pair to reckon with.

At home, the two were inseparable, protecting and defending one another, looking out for each other's girlfriends and forging such a trustful bond that they even anticipated one another's thoughts, decisions, and next moves.

"Coop was a badass, very confident. I'm the same way, but I know my limits. I don't think he knew his limits at times, and that's why he had me around. That's why we were on the same team because nobody could ever talk to him like I could talk to him," Alvarenga said. "I felt like if anybody messed with him, I was going to beat 'em up."

Cooper felt the same way about Alvarenga and actually did beat someone up outside a bar one time, another Marine who went to the bar management with a complaint about Alvarenga.

In the war zone, they honed their knowledge and got smart about sniping together.

Neither Marine was trained in the coveted courses at the prestigious Marine Corps Scout Sniper School, which is not uncommon for Marine snipers who often are chosen for abilities that look good on paper and then are trained by the team.

Alvarenga and Cooper learned their jobs on the go from their platoon sergeant, a Marine they considered a guru in the art of sniping.

"He's the best sniper I've ever met. He's a master, he's a teacher, and he taught us well. He passed on a lot of knowledge to Coop and me," Alvarenga said of his mentor, a staff sergeant who did not wish to be identified in print. The sergeant would also bring Brace into the fold of the team when Brace arrived for the team's second Iraq deployment in 2006.

The platoon sergeant, a thoughtful, measured man with a soft-spoken demeanor and a healthy suspicion of outsiders, taught his young Marines what to look for, how to spot the small things a sniper needs to detect the enemy, like a reflection on a little piece of glass, things that seem out of place, and shapes or materials that don't belong in the environment. He taught them how to conceal their outlines in a hide site, how to move at night, how to choose the right equipment for a mission, how to lighten their loads by learning to leave behind what they could live without.

They learned how to watch what the enemy was doing, and if it was something good, how to adopt it and enhance it. By the same token, they saw their own tactics used against them.

On a mission in northern Ramadi, Alvarenga saw such a tactic and couldn't really believe what he was seeing at first. It happened while his team and another sniper observer team were hiding out in the administration building of a medical college—a building they wrongly assumed was empty—to watch a highway for insurgent activity.

The snipers infiltrated at night, their faces streaked with black over a chalky white base, and settled into observation positions before dawn, taking for granted that the nice furniture and neat offices were normal for an abandoned building. Then the faculty who worked there started to arrive.

"We had no idea that the college was still running," Alvarenga said. "By 0600 we had detained like twenty people, and there were more people coming. We were running out of room to put these people in."

It wasn't the first time something like this had happened to a sniper team in Iraq. But it was the first time it had happened to them. They tried to deal with the wave of arriving workers like a batter dispatching flying baseballs in a batting cage. One by one.

They searched the men, left the women alone, and herded everyone into different rooms, soon concluding that the ratio of detainees to Marines was growing disproportionate.

"We ended up detaining like forty people, and there were only like eleven guys and more people were coming," Alvarenga said. "They would try to run when they saw our guys with their faces painted."

Everyone knew it was time to let the detainees go and suffer whatever consequences might arise from their release. But the snipers were surprised when, only thirty minutes after releasing the workers, their signal intelligence cell informed them that an attack was being planned on the building.

"The workers had contacted bad guys and told them there were a bunch of Americans in the building," Alvarenga said.

Trapped without an immediate escape plan, and told by their commanders to stay put in the two-story building for a while longer, the snipers blocked and covered all the windows, moved tables and chairs to the doors, fortified the entrances as best they could, and set up in additional areas where they could observe the building's perimeter.

Alvarenga slid his tactical periscope up into a window over-looking a building across the street. Almost immediately he saw a small flock of squawking birds surrounding one window and some kind of activity that looked unnatural.

"I see all these seeds flying, coming out of the window where the birds were. I was looking and zooming in closer, and I see this one bird sitting there with a little box right in the middle of his chest. So I was like, that can't be a bird, what the hell is that?" he said.

The bird seemed stiff, as if it moved mechanically. In one hair-raising moment, Alvarenga—and the sniper with the bird peri-scope across the street—realized they were staring at one another.

"He popped down, then slowly came back up to look at me, then popped down again, and I would do the same thing. Basically we're communicating that 'I see you and you see me,' but I also saw something in the periphery that's moving," he said.

Next to the window with the bird was a door with a hole the size of a small melon, and he could see the distinct outline of a machine gun barrel of some sort through the hole. No sooner had he seen it than it sent a burst of rounds, and so did the man from the window with the fake bird.

Alvarenga had wanted to call for a two-thousand-pound bomb to be dropped on the building because it was clear to everyone that, even though it was a school, which was off limits to shoot at according to the rules of engagement, insurgents were using it so it was fair game. Instead, he said, "When they popped their machine gun out and started shooting at us, I let them get their thirty rounds out, and then I popped up and started shooting back into that win-dow, I shot two right through the window."

Alvarenga disintegrated the building's wooden frame with his M249 SAW machine gun, blowing away whatever sanctuary the bird shooter and doorway machine gunner thought they had.

During the three-hour gunfight, a car zoomed past the building and placed a stop-and-drop bomb in front of the only door, so the snipers breached a wall in the rear of the building that night and got away with no casualties.

Alvarenga never saw the bird again, but he was struck that the enemy was using the Americans' own tactics against them and then learned that other Marines had seen periscopes from time to time, homemade devices made with PVC pipe.

"The tactic with the bird periscope was the smartest thing I've seen over there. They learn from how we do things, and they get a lot off the Internet. People think these fighters aren't smart, but they are," he said.

Cooper and Alvarenga would go on hundreds of missions together and earn a reputation for being the kind of smash-and-bash Marines who weren't afraid to get the job done.

On their second deployment to Iraq, they were introduced to new team members, including Brace, who they thought was a joke.

"Al and Coop hated me. They had already been on one deployment, and they were really, really tough guys, like meat-and-potatoes, snake-eater types," Brace said. "They were pretty much the opposite of anybody I'd ever want to talk to or hang out with. And it wasn't just Al and Coop hating me, but everybody else hating me too, and I was like, this is bad."

During the seven-month deployment, the platoon sergeant was the one who took the time to get to know Brace, and he thrived as a Marine because of it.

More than an instructor, the platoon sergeant became a mentor with the credibility of someone who'd walked the walk and taken some bold action in battle that was never talked about outside the barracks. Approachable and easy to talk to, he was a sort of spiritual guide in terms of all things sniper related. He assigned Brace to a team in Iraq with an older, more mature leader who allowed him to become a radio operator, and he became a damn good one.

The platoon sergeant's relationship with Brace evolved into a different kind of mentorship, one that was based on their shared faith as Christians as well as a higher standard he demanded that Brace achieve.

"I didn't fit the mold as a Marine at all, and he realized that early on," Brace said. "He treated me a little bit differently. He was a little tougher on me than he was on the other guys, which was good because that finally got Cooper and Al to recognize that I was a pretty good radio operator."

After the deployment, back at Camp Lejeune, Brace stuck around and eventually Al and Coop asked him to be on their team, which stunned and pleased him because other guys were actively trying to kick him out.

"Coop had some grace and asked me, 'Will you follow me and my team and do the best you possibly can and will you protect me and the rest of the team if we get in trouble?' I said yes and remember thinking, Wow! Not what I expected from the beer-swilling, woman-hiding, rough and tumble, scream-in-everybody's-face kind of guy. I'd heard they were ruthless killing Marines, and if you wanted to survive, you would be on their team. I found out that was very true in Afghanistan, and I was very glad I was on their team," Brace said.

## THE AMBUSH

After the reaper farm mission in Afghanistan, the sniper team, led by Cooper, worked like dogs on back-to-back missions in the Helmand River valley against well-entrenched Taliban fighters who defended their territory with a vengeance and strong combat tactics. As intelligence about Taliban activity trickled in, the Marines responded by closing the distance with violence of action, and the snipers were an important part of that move.

In a village near A Company's patrol base on the southernmost reaches of Garmsir, it was learned that Taliban meetings were being held in a two-story building surrounded by dozens of other buildings occupied only by other Taliban, a perfect mission for the snipers.

On May 19, 2008, Cooper and another sniper team leader led their combined team of twelve snipers from the A Company patrol base on foot at 2 a.m. and headed toward the village to set up and watch the building.

The dark, early morning air was thick and hot, and each guy carried more than one hundred pounds of gear, enough essential equipment to stay mobile for at least four days: items like radios, batteries, C4 explosive, ammunition, food, water, and optics, plus their sniper rifles. The Barrett .50-cal rifle alone weighs about thirty pounds, and all the weight was in addition to the Marines' personal protective gear like body armor and helmets.

The walking infiltration as weighted down as pack mules was familiar to everyone; each man had done it repeatedly. And on this occasion a platoon of infantrymen was sent ahead to clear the village so the snipers could walk through to their predetermined hide site, passing the infantrymen after they had made it safe to move in.

As infantrymen themselves, the snipers were always ready to jump in and help if something happened, but it was understood that their mission was to reach their destination safely and begin eliminating targets of opportunity.

The sniper team's movement was about five kilometers and took more than an hour. Violence was expected, because the only people left in the village were fighters.

"We'd done this so many times I can't even count them all. We knew what we were doing. As soon as we walked out, we took fire outside the headquarters. We went right back in and planned another route," Alvarenga said.

The Taliban, they assumed, had night vision capability because they'd recently killed an entire squad of British soldiers and taken their equipment.

When the snipers got close to the infantry squads, Cooper found their commander and said they'd help clear the rest of the route, which the commander welcomed. But Alvarenga started to wonder why Cooper would bust out and offer help when they'd already had one setback and needed to get where they were going.

The idea became even more ominous as they walked up a pathway to the village, felt a rocket-propelled grenade fly over their heads, and saw the entire squad of infantrymen lying on their bellies on either side of the path, quietly aiming their rifles toward a three-foot wall leading into the village.

"I tell Coop, 'Hey, man, we are weighed down here, we have so much stuff. We don't do this, we're not here to do infantry work.

It's not our job, and there's only a small amount of us who can do what we do,'" Alvarenga recalled telling his friend.

But Coop insisted, telling Al, "I know, man, but we gotta help these guys."

Not wanting to challenge his buddy, Alvarenga went along, following Cooper up to the low wall past the eerily quiet Marines on the ground, wishing later that one of them had spoken up.

"This is what really pissed me off. None of these guys along the path said anything to us, and we continued to walk along this path to the three-foot wall. There was a bunker they were taking fire from they could have told us about," Alvarenga said.

The infantrymen, in fact, had already fired on one bunker and possibly killed everyone inside. It was quiet, but as the snipers put their heavy loads on the ground and approached the wall, a tree behind a building just off to the right at about the two o'clock position burst into flames—a tactic by the enemy, they assumed, that was aimed at drowning out the Marines' night vision goggles.

Cooper found the lieutenant he'd spoken to earlier and told him to cover him and a four-man team that would go in and clear a small area to the left of the fire so the snipers could proceed.

They took a shot at the cleared bunker for good measure. The five of them—including the two sniper team leaders, Alvarenga, and two other snipers—lined up along the low wall, and then events happened quickly and went wrong even more quickly.

"Before I could tell the rest of the team, the other team leader had already jumped the wall, and I saw Coop jump the wall with them and two others jumped. I was like, 'He's not going by himself, forget that,'" Alvarenga said.

The five-man stack, with Cooper in the second position and Alvarenga in the fifth, and last, position, came under a sudden burst of fire from a bunker that was hidden between the burning tree and a building that was partially obscuring it. The only two Marines cut down by the fire were Cooper, who was mortally wounded, and Alvarenga, whose vest caught a bullet that exploded the attached M203 rounds and knocked him into an old bomb crater behind them.

No one else was shot.

As the rest of the stack scattered and began returning fire, some from back on the other side of the wall, Alvarenga came to at the bottom of the crater and heard someone shout that Coop was down. "I jumped up with nothing. I didn't have my gun and ran to Cooper and grabbed him and his gun. I was shooting with one hand and dragging him with the other, and the other team leader is firing and everybody's firing," Alvarenga said.

In the crater, Alvarenga desperately tried to wake Cooper while the Navy corpsman who jumped in after them desperately tried to figure out what was wrong with him. Cooper was unconscious. They started to undress him, and the whole time, Alvarenga said, "I was shooting back and freaking out. I told the guys to get him out of the hole and over the wall so they could get him out of there."

Alvarenga's world was spinning around the sight of his best friend, who was unresponsive, bleeding to death, slipping away right in front of him. With the casualty evacuation helicopter on its way, the infantry guys came with a stretcher to load Cooper up and get him to the landing zone back down the path.

Alvarenga was in charge of the team now so he couldn't go to the LZ. Ever protective of Cooper, "I told one of the infantry guys, 'Hey, take my friend to the LZ,' while I gathered the whole team. We continued to fire. The guys ran out of the bunker; we killed one, but by then a Predator was on station watching. All the guys were killed by a bomb that was dropped on the bunker."

As soon as he could, Alvarenga dragged both teams to a safer rear area to reorganize and then ran as fast as he could back around to the LZ, carrying Cooper's guns and one hundred-pound pack. His inner panic made him run faster, and the speed felt as if it might help Cooper overcome the terrible thing that had just happened to him.

On the ground, hunched over his patient on the stretcher, the Navy corpsman applied a tourniquet, did a tracheotomy, and started CPR, none of which would save Cooper, who had been shot by a bullet that went through the tricep on his right arm, pierced his armpit, and ripped into his torso.

The corpsman saw the blood coming from Cooper's nose, but he couldn't figure out the source of the bleeding. Alvarenga watched with a tension he'd never known. Here was a problem for which he had no solution, a circumstance that was wildly out of his control.

"It was so in the moment," he said. "We were trying to do everything we could. We took all his crap off, but there was so much going on, he didn't see the bullet wound in his armpit. It wouldn't have mattered—the bullet went right through his chest and every vital organ. Even the doctors said even if it had been near a hospital in America, he wouldn't have made it."

Cooper hadn't uttered a word. He took his last breath before the helicopter arrived, as Alvarenga remembers it, and as the bird descended for a landing, Alvarenga told Cooper for the last time that he loved him.

Standing alone in the windy wake of the chopper, a sickening wave of guttural anguish possessed Alvarenga, a sucking grief so deep and overpowering that it nearly blinded him. He dropped his gun and stood there, weak-kneed, his hands covered with Cooper's blood, heaving heavy, dry sobs that took his breath away. His eyes watered and he cried, and cried, and cried. He was unable to stop crying.

He'd never had a cigarette in his life, but he smoked one that night and smoked the rest of a pack over the next two hours. Then he smoked a pack a day for the next two months. It was as if he couldn't get enough air, and the tobacco that filled his lungs let him know that he was at least breathing something.

And he thought about Cooper a lot. It was all he could think about. Of all the sniper missions they'd been on, it was hard to believe he would get cut down in a traditional small unit movement in an ambush they never saw coming. He and Coop had been invincible.

"I felt weird about this deployment, and I told him. I said, 'We've done a lot of crazy stuff already.' Our Ramadi deployment was pretty bad, and there were times we were scared a lot because bad guys were right next door. We put our life in danger all the time, but I told him there's something about this deployment. I didn't know why," said Alvarenga, who pondered another out-of-the-ordinary thing that happened that night.

"I have a hard time sometimes believing in God, but there's one thing I remember about that night," he said.

Before they went on the 2 a.m. mission, everyone was sleeping. That is, except Cooper and Alvarenga, who were talking quietly about home, their girlfriends, and what they were going to do with their lives. They considered trying out together for the Army Special Forces or going to school. They laughed about being neighbors when they got older.

Alvarenga saw Cooper reading his Bible, something he'd never seen him do.

"I said, 'You know, you gotta let me read that,' and he was like, 'Yeah, I'm working on it, too, on all this stuff.' There's something that happened that has to do with that moment we shared right there that night because I carried his Bible after that and I would read passages," Alvarenga said.

Cooper's death sent shock waves through the sniper platoon, and back at battalion headquarters, where Brace, the platoon sergeant, and their platoon leader, First Lt. Jason Mann, had gone the night before to resupply, his body was prepared for transport to Kandahar and then home to Mississippi.

Brace was sleeping when the news came in, and Mann went straight to his bunk and jostled him until he stirred.

"All I remember is that it was one of the most jarring moments of my life. It was shoving. Wide eyes open. 'Brace! Brace! You awake? Coop's dead, man.' I thought it was a nightmare," Brace said.

Mann, who was in shock himself, continued with his blunt bulletin of bad news, gruffly telling Brace: "Your team just got into an ambush and if you want to come see Coop before they take him back to Kandahar, you can come and see him."

In what Brace considers more than a coincidence to this day, Cooper had ordered him to go to battalion headquarters on the resupply with Mann and the platoon sergeant the night before the mission, even though they hadn't been given the mission before the threesome departed.

"He just said, 'You're the only one who's married so you're going back.' I probably would have been one of the guys in the stack, and as radio man I would have been next to Cooper," Brace speculated.

After the incident of May 19, Brace was tasked with interviewing everyone who was there and to write up a report. He, too, was baffled by the lack of action on the part of the infantrymen on the path to the ambush to stop the snipers from walking toward danger.

"What I heard is that this platoon couldn't operate. They had lost complete effectiveness; you could call them shell-shocked. They were lying down in a ditch, and the squad leader wasn't talking to anybody or doing anything, and our team walked past them," he said.

With Cooper gone, Alvarenga did his best to rally the team he was now in charge of. The team was benched for about five days before being tasked with another mission, and Alvarenga quietly pulled Brace close to him, even though the job of assistant team leader fell to another sniper.

The two men, once at odds and in opposite corners of their own idealistic worlds, now worked together, wrote stuff together, and attended meetings together. They handled Cooper's death differently.

"Al did the best he could to kill as many Taliban as he could possibly kill, and he killed dozens through a variety of means. I was more measured. I guess I realized that in a war you're expected to die. I didn't take it personally. I took it personally on the level that it was my team leader. But Al, it was his brother, they were as close as brothers," Brace said. "We didn't talk about Coop. I was just glad to be pulled face-to-face and being told, 'You're going to be my right-hand man now."

The pace of operations continued to be demanding, but dropped off during June, and on July 17, Mann, who was exceedingly well liked by the men, was killed when the building he was sleeping in collapsed in a non-hostile incident, crushing the team again and putting the platoon sergeant in charge of everyone.

In October, the Twenty-fourth Marine Expeditionary Unit packed up and left Afghanistan. Some of the snipers of 1-6 Marines stayed in and deployed again, but others, like Brace and Alvarenga, moved back into the civilian world.

Alvarenga got a job in Washington, D.C., working for a Vietnam veteran who counseled him on his grief for Cooper, telling him to use everything he'd done and seen to improve his own life and make himself stronger.

"He told me people like me are in a different category because of what we've seen and done. Not a lot of people have done what we've done," Alvarenga said, still lamenting the plans he and Cooper had for their Mediterranean float, pointing out that it's what young men join the Marine Corps to do.

"We were supposed to be in Spain," Alvarenga said, reflecting also on his acceptance of Brace.

"Neal was like a little brother. He proved himself on our first mission in Afghanistan. I think I helped him more than he helped me. After Coop died I put my feelings aside and stored it away until these guys were home and safe and then after that I fell apart," he said.

Alvarenga eventually returned Cooper's Bible to his family and has remained friends with Brace, who said he never thought he'd get to know, much less grow fond of, a man like Cooper.

"I trusted him," Brace said. "If he were around today, I'd follow him to the end of the world."

# NOTES AND ACKNOWLEDGMENTS

When we were first approached about writing this book, we jumped at the chance. We recognized it as an opportunity to contribute to the pages of history through the stories of American snipers in this war.

It seemed like a manageable concept for us because of our individual connections and experiences with the military and we found a few snipers right away who were eager to tell their stories.

But others had to be cajoled into coming out of the shadows because, by its very nature, the profession of sniping is a secretive and very personal one. It's quite different to look through a scope at a person you identified on a city block than it is to react to fire on patrol.

We learned a lot from the snipers who talked with us about the changes this war has brought to bear on their profession and we thank them, more than anyone, for telling us their stories.

This book belongs to them and the hundreds of other snipers out there whose voices didn't make it into these pages, for their willingness to put their lives on the line for their brothers and their country.

My first thanks belongs to my dear, longtime friend, Maryann Karinch. I can't believe we've graduated from splitting the charges on a phone bill to collaborating on a book. I always knew your college degrees would come in handy. Thank you for your love and support.

Thanks also to the editors at Lyons Press: Gene Brissie for taking on the project in the first place, Steven Talbot, Kristen Mellitt, and to Keith Wallman for his tireless support and interest in this subject and for taking it from being a project to being a book. A big thanks to a true friend, Michelle Tan, the "Little One," and the crew at *Army Times,* our publisher Elaine Howard, my editors Tobias Naegele, Alex Neill, and Richard Sandza, for allowing me to disappear from the newsroom and work on this book. A special thanks to Chuck Vinch who helped me sort out the human toll of the war and who feels for the loss of every U.S. troop. To my colleagues Matthew Cox and Rob Curtis for your technical support, to Sheila Vemmer for making me look good, and to the rest of the *Army Times* staff for picking up the slack during my absence.

The time I spent at the U.S. Army Sniper School at Fort Benning, Georgia, was richly rewarded by the generosity and friendship of people like Robert Roof and Ken Noack and all the boys there who made time to talk to me and show me how it's done. Thank you for your professionalism and courage.

Thanks also to Capt. Matthew O'Brien at the Weapons Training Battalion at Marine Corps Base Quantico for introducing me to the world of Marine scout snipers, and special thanks goes to a gunnery sergeant in California who decided to trust me.

My appreciation and thanks to Tarrol Peterson, Tim Kellner, Walter Gaya, Sean Kirkwood, Pete Kranenburg, Bill Gunter, Ben Abel, Tracy Bailey, Brenda Donnell, Ali Bettencourt, and Commander Cody; the Army Sniper Association; the Columbus Public Library; and my friends at the Coffee Beanery in Columbus, Georgia, who kept me watered and fed while I hashed out my prose.

With my deepest love and gratitude to my cousins and brothers and sisters, especially my sister Francesca, one of the funniest, smartest, most capable people I know, who gave me the room I needed when she needed me most. My thanks to you Bill, Kyle, and Evan.

Thanks also to my good friends Katy Campbell, Monica Bresnahan, Jennifer Bentley, Corinne McManemin, Keith and Maria McCabe, and the Pierce family—Claire, Charlie, Chuck, and Lynn.

And to Matt. You kept me together, educated me, and loved me. I would be a basket case without you.

—*Gina Cavallaro*

To my family, my parents who gave me a sense of adventure and to my children who put it in perspective and put up with a father called away by it. My deepest gratitude to my father George Larsen who taught me what it means to be a man; and to my grandfather Bob Fischer, who was a champion bench rest shooter in his day and taught me what a rifle is capable of in the right hands long before I showed up at Marine boot camp.

To my first sniper partner who taught me what he had learned as a sniper in Beirut, Command Sergeant Major Mike Hall, who is the finest soldier I know and who with Jeff Marlow taught me most of what I know about leading men.

And to the soldiers and Marines that I served with for twenty-two years and continue to serve to the best of my ability—I can think of no finer companions to have shared misery with around the world.

Others who deserve mention for supporting me and for their friendship are Ben Durham, Brian Duff, Mike Rach, Ted and Eric Runci who are truly my brothers, and "Crazy" Larry Allen, the hardest man I know, who "set the standard for others to follow."

And to Gina, who knows more about soldiers and the war than anyone, who has shared their fears and experiences and truly cares about them. There is no one more qualified to tell their stories, and I love her.

—*Matt Larsen*

# GLOSSARY

**19 Delta** A U.S. Army job code for a soldier who is a member of a tank crew.

**Alpha teams** A Special Forces Operational Detachments Alpha (ODA), or "A-Team," is the primary operational element of the Special Forces. An ODA consists of twelve men, each of whom has a specific function on the team, though all members of an alpha team conduct cross-training. The ODA is led by a detachment commander, usually a captain, and an assistant detachment commander, usually a warrant officer. The team also includes the following enlisted men: one team sergeant, usually a master sergeant; one assistant operations and intelligence sergeant, usually a sergeant first class; and two weapons sergeants, engineer sergeants, medical sergeants, and communications sergeants, usually sergeants first class, staff sergeants, or sergeants, any one of whom could have the additional duty of being a sniper.

**Bongo** A small utility truck usually found in countries outside the United States, including Asia, Europe, and the Middle East.

**Brad** A shortened term for the Bradley fighting vehicle, a tracked, armored vehicle armed with a 25 mm gun and a crew of three— a commander, gunner, and driver—and a troop-carrying area that can transport six infantrymen to battle.

**Chalk** A specific grouping of a load of soldiers assigned to a helicopter or other aircraft flying toward a mission.

**Chest rig** A load-bearing vest with pouches or heavy nylon webbing that allows a soldier or Marine to attach or carry his ammunition, grenades, and other items he needs close at hand.

**Close with the enemy** A term that describes the deliberate and aggressive movement toward an enemy to get close enough to engage in combat.

**Commo** A shortened version of the word "communications."

**Contact** Engagement with the enemy. For example, being "in contact" means being fired upon and shooting back during an engagement with an enemy force.

**DCU** Desert camouflage uniform, the tan and brown uniforms that most troops deployed with at the beginning of the wars in Iraq and Afghanistan.

**Dip** A shortened version of the term "dipping tobacco," a moist, smokeless tobacco product that commonly comes packaged in a small tin and is used by troops as a stimulant.

**Drag bag** A custom weapons case used by snipers for carrying rifles and other gear over long distances.

**E-7** The military numerical and pay grade code for the rank of sergeant first class in the Army, gunnery sergeant in the Marine Corps, chief petty officer in the Navy, and master sergeant in the Air Force.

**EOD** Explosive ordnance disposal.

**Exfil** A shortened version of the word "exfiltrate," the removal of military equipment and personnel from an area of the battlefield.

**Frag, fragged** The word "frag" is shorthand for fragmentary order, which is a change to original orders issued by a commander, usually based on updated information to a battlefield situation; it can also stand for being attacked or attacking with a fragmentation grenade.

**Ghillie suit** A type of camouflage apparel that is designed and worn by snipers to look like a natural or urban environment with the attachment of cloth or fiber strips to a net or piece of fabric. The name was derived from *gille,* the Gaelic word for "servant," which was used in the nineteenth century for local men who assisted in deer hunting expeditions in the Scottish Highlands. The ghillie suit was developed as an easily transportable hunting blind.

**GMV** Ground mobility vehicle, a customized version of the Humvee used by Special Operations units.

**Hardball** A word used by U.S. troops to distinguish a road that is paved with asphalt or concrete from a dirt road.

**Helo** A helicopter.

**Hold** The point of aim a sniper uses while engaging a target. Based upon range or conditions, this may or may not be directly on the target.

**Hot** A term used to denote an area of a battlefield, such as a main ground travel route or air space, that is dangerous because of enemy presence or enemy live fire.

**Hover** A helicopter maneuver that allows it to remain stationary in the air over one position.

**Hump, humping** This term describes the act of carrying something heavy, usually in a rucksack, on one's back on foot over a long distance.

**IED** Improvised explosive device.

**Infil** A shortened version of the word "infiltrate," which is the movement of military personnel and equipment into a battle area.

**In the rear** A military term that denotes an area behind the lines of the battle. In the war on terrorism, where there is no traditional "front line" with the enemy as there was in World War II, the term "in the rear" has meant back home in the United States.

**IR** Infrared.

**KIA** killed in action; also common is the term "EKIA" for enemy killed in action.

**Kims** A memory exercise used at military or law enforcement sniper schools. The student is given a short time to look at a group of objects or people's faces and then asked to recall and describe them after some time has elapsed. The name Kims is short for Kim's Game, a reference to an episode in Rudyard Kipling's novel *Kim*.

**K-pot** A term troops use to refer to their helmets. The letter "K" is a reference to Kevlar, the bullet-resistant material with which the helmet is made.

**Loophole** A small hole or holes made in a wall or other blocking device through which a sniper can shoot a bullet from a position deep inside a room or enclosure.

**LZ** Landing zone or cleared area for a helicopter landing.

**Mil dots** A mil is a measurement of angle representing one yard at a thousand yards. On some military sniper optics there are dots along the vertical and horizontal lines of the reticle placed at one mil increments. These "mil dots" are used by snipers both to estimate range by comparing the size of known objects such as a man's torso and in selecting an alternate point of aim when using the scope hold-off method of adjusting for windage and elevation.

**Mini binos** Small or "mini" binoculars.

**NCO** An enlisted service member who is a noncommissioned officer such as a sergeant.

**NOD** Night optical device.

**PEQ** The AN/PEQ-2 is an infrared laser sight for use on rifles. It has two infrared laser emitters: one narrow beam used for aiming the rifle, and one wide beam used for illuminating targets, like a flashlight. The beams can only be seen through night vision goggles.

**PTSD** Post-traumatic stress disorder.

**Pucker factor** A term used by troops in combat in reference to a biological reaction to fear that causes the anal sphincter to contract.

**Quick reaction force** A squad or platoon of troops in an "on call" emergency response status for another squad or platoon that is outside the base on a combat mission.

**Reticle** A grid of fine lines in the focus of an optical instrument such as a rifle scope, used for determining the scale or position of what is being looked at and providing an aiming point.

**ROE** Rules of engagement.

**RPG** Rocket propelled grenade.

**Rucksack flop** The action of flopping backward onto a heavy rucksack for a rest, without first taking the rucksack off.

**Saddle** A topographical feature on a map that depicts a dip between two areas of higher ground with lower areas of ground on each of the other two sides.

**SASR** Special application scoped rifle.

**SDM** Squad designated marksman.

**Snivel** Warm clothing, also referred to as cold weather gear.

**SOTIC** Special Operations Target Interdiction Course.

**STA** Surveillance and target acquisition.

**Stryker** The short term used for the Army's Stryker armored vehicle, a wheeled, armored troop carrier that can transport nine infantrymen to battle. The Stryker first made its appearance on the battlefield in Iraq in 2003. The Stryker was named in honor of Medal of Honor recipients Spc. 4 Robert F. Stryker, for his actions in Vietnam, and Pfc. Stuart S. Stryker, for his actions in World War II. The soldiers were both killed and are not related.

**TOC** Tactical operations center.

**Violence of action** The execution of actions with surprisingly over-whelming speed and force.

**Windage** The effect of wind on the flight of a bullet over range, one of several environmental factors a sniper takes into account when preparing to take a long shot.

# INDEX

on sighting of wanted men, 154
on team's infiltration, 153
Triangle of Death and, 152–53
on weight of disguise, 155
Roof, Robert, 49

**S**
Salman Pak
  as home of terrorist training
    center, 132–33
  sniper experiences in, 134–37
  stalking enemy snipers, 139–41
Scates, William, 18–19
Screaming Eagles, 2
Second Battalion, 2
Sibert, Logan, 144
snipers
  adjusting for wind and
    elevation, 14–15
  attitude of team members, 4
  avoiding leaving traces, 131
  blending in, 130
  choosing hide sites, 40–41
  dogs and bugs, 130
  enemy threats to, 83–84
  face painting and clothing, 131
  getting compromised, 98
  organization within units, 45–46
  rapid engagement, 76
  recognition of value of, 62–63
  Salman Pak and, 131–32
  struggle for command
    understanding of duties, 45
  training prior to Afghanistan
    and Iraq, 44–45
  U.S. military development of, 44
Solano, Justin, 4
Sons of Iraq, 133–34
Special Forces
  advantages of sniper instruction
    positions, 74–75
  art of the hide, 80–83

  assignment to sniper
    teaching, 74
  development of sniper role, 75
  Khost crash landing and, 6
  lightweight gear and, 100
  sniper training, 3–4
  training formulas, 75–76
Special Operations Target
  Interdiction Course
  (SOTIC), 3
Staszewski, Jason, 146
Stout, Craig
  on Adam Peeples, 29
  first sniper mission in Ramadi,
    32–33
  on urban battle in Askan, 23, 24
supply routes, 110–17
Swanson, Christopher, 33

**T**
Taliban
  accuracy of fire, 10–11
  clothing of, 10
  description of fighters, 8
  dominance of territory, 12
  fighting strategies, 9, 10
  use of DShKs, 11–12
Thompson, Matt, 31
Tinsley, Coy
  on action in Ramadi, 27
  on enemy fighters, 26–27
  on evolution of enemy
    fighters, 27
Triangle of Death, 152–53

**U**
Uthman, Mohamed, 19–20
Uzbekistan, 6

**W**
World Trade Center, 2, 166

# ABOUT THE AUTHORS

**Gina Cavallaro** is one of America's most experienced war correspondents. She has traveled to every corner of the war zone and walked the dangerous streets with the troops to tell their real stories of life on the ground in America's most protracted conflict since the Vietnam War. She is a writer for *Army Times* and *Marine Corps Times* and lives in Alexandria, Virginia. This is her first book.

**Matt Larsen,** a longtime trainer in hand-to-hand combat and survival techniques, served as a sniper in the U.S. Marine Corps and the Army Rangers during the course of a twenty-two-year career in the military. He recently revised and updated the *U.S. Army Survival Handbook* (Lyons). He is the director of the Modern Army Combatives Program, which he created, and the commandant of the U.S. Army Combatives School, which he founded at Fort Benning, Georgia. He lives in Columbus, Georgia.